# AWAKENING A CHILD
# FROM WITHIN

D0933206

# AWAKENING
## A CHILD FROM WITHIN

## TARA SINGH

LIFE ACTION PRESS
LOS ANGELES

10 9 8 7 6 5 4 3 2 1                5/92

Library of Congress Cataloging in Publication Data
Singh, Tara, 1919-
Awakening a child from within.
p. cm.
1. Parenting - United States. 2. Parenting - Religious aspects.
3. Child rearing - United States. I. Title.
HQ755.8.S54  1991  649'.1--dc20  90-19698
ISBN 1-55531-254-3 Hardbound
ISBN 1-55531-253-5 Softcover

Quotations from *A Course In Miracles* and *The Gifts Of God* are reprinted by permission of the copyright owner, the Foundation for Inner Peace, P.O. Box 1104, Glen Ellen, California 95442. Quotations from *Commentaries On Living: Series III*, from *Krishnamurti To Himself*, and *The Beginnings Of Learning* by J. Krishnamurti are reprinted by permission of the Krishnamurti Foundation of America, P.O. Box 1560, Ojai, California 93024. Quotations from *Saint John of the Cross* by Willis Barnstone are reprinted by permission of New Directions Publishing Corporation, 80 Eighth Avenue, New York, New York 10011.

We would like to express our appreciation to the Metropolitan Museum of Art, New York, New York, for permission to reproduce the painting of St. Joan of Arc by Bastien-Lepage on the cover.

Cover design by David Wise, Wise Creative Services, Montpelier, Vermont.

# ACKNOWLEDGMENTS

I would like to express my appreciation to Charles Johnson, Lucille Frappier, and Aliana Scurlock for their long hours of devoted work in the preparation of this book.

In addition, I would like to thank the following friends for their help with tape production, transcribing, editing, proofing, graphic design, and layout: Susan Berry, Johanna Macdonald, Jim Cheatham, Barbara Dunlap, Frank Nader, Jim Walters, Norah Ryan, Karin Lewis, Kris Heagh, Melanie Coulter, Joann Nieto, Selina Scheer, LeAnn Lundberg, Howard and Bette Schneider, Cynthia Baehr, Rachel Logel, and David Wise.

For her support in making this book possible, I would like to extend my gratefulness to Victoria Berry.

# DEDICATION

*"What is God's belongs to everyone,*
*and* is *his due."* [1]

*"As forgiveness allows love to return to my awareness,*
*I will see a world of peace and safety and joy."* [2]

The truth of these two Eternal Laws,
governing relationship with creation
and relationship with one's fellowman,
will endow parents with a spontaneous awakening
that can be extended to their children.

This book is dedicated to parents
who aspire to live by Eternal Laws.

# CONTENTS

## THE SILENT WAY

Choose once again. For it is given you
To trail the peace of God across the world
Without exception. Every child receives
The gifts you bring, and men and women turn
To you in thankfulness. With joy are you
Accepted everywhere. For you have come
Only to bring Infinity's appeal
To those who are as infinite as He.
You come with memory of God in you,
To waken this same memory in those
In whom it seems to sleep. The world would die
Without its saviors. Do not, then, deny
Your proper place. For Christ has called to you
To follow Him, and choose the silent way
That brings you to eternity today.*

* This poem is from *The Gifts Of God* by Helen Schucman, the Scribe of *A Course In Miracles* (Foundation for Inner Peace, 1982), page 29. It is an incomparable book of poetry containing some of the most important words ever spoken.

# INTRODUCTION

Relationship within the Sonship intensifies the love that one gives and receives simultaneously.

Due to lack of interest, we often do not question. But by formulating the right question and demanding intense self-honesty, we call upon a subtle energy. This energy is the discovery of one's own potentials. It asks questions that are objective and profound. No verbal answer satisfies it.

In the writing of this book many of my colleagues have contributed. But the process of discovery and the sharing of holy instants took place with Charles Johnson and Aliana Scurlock. This communication enriched each one of us because what is Given is shared also.

The reader, having the capacity to receive, can make contact with this etheric, creative energy. The intensity of your interest will introduce you to the purity of attention which in turn becomes aware of that which is Impersonal.

What one receives is what one extends – the glory of the given state of everlasting gratefulness.

There is another way of teaching, another way of awakening. Although it remains unknown to this age, it must be explored for the sake of our children and future generations. The truths that the sages of ancient times knew are still here. Whenever any human being brings the Eternal Laws to this level, the light of those Laws is accessible and remains the treasure of all humanity.

How would one educate a child? How would one awaken that child? How would one go about making the child aware that he is so much more than a body? Each of us must place that challenge before us.

# CHAPTER ONE

# 1

## RESPONSIBILITY FOR THE ENERGY ENTRUSTED TO US

W hat is the purpose of the entry of the human being upon the planet? What is the purpose of the physical energy of the earth, the physical energy of thought, and the energy of the divine spirit? What is the true function of man – the bearer of the energy of the light of the spirit – on the material plane as he sojourns in time through childhood, youth, maturity, and old age?

The energy which is entrusted to the human being by Divine Forces is to be aligned and connected with the energy of creation. As a child of flesh we are subject to the laws of time and of society, as well as of the spirit. We die, like all things on earth, and yet we are deathless. That potential which takes birth is not of the earth but is entrusted to man, who is the altar of God on earth. The use we make of this energy determines the destiny of the planet. Industrialization has brought humanity to crisis because it has violated what man was meant to do. When man is awakened from within, he makes right use of this human energy.

Whenever a child is born, that child brings with him certain abilities which he aspires to extend at this physical level. Each one has a different vibration and different potentials. In discovering his potentials, there is also the possibility of making the corrections he has to make. In extending his potentials, he can be helpful to others while also undoing the cycle of cause and effect within himself.

The stark reality of what happens, however, is that from the moment we are born very few of us have a minute to realize what our potentials are or what the unique abilities are that we brought. We are totally beguiled by the world's values.

The child is indoctrinated to want to be something other than who he is. He goes to school and gets a job. Everything becomes false. It is as if he is born to serve the corporation and the state. And because he is not at peace within, he goes for outlets – food, cigarettes, stimulation – in the mistaken idea that these indulgences might make him happy. In a false atmosphere, love and self-honesty become impossible. It is difficult for us to be responsible until we have found our own potential.

Mr. J. Krishnamurti* said to me, "Don't spend a penny on anything unessential. I don't buy shoelaces unless I need them." I was so glad to hear that. For me it was a commandment. For years and years I never bought a thing that was not absolutely essential.

How many million beer cans and soft drink bottles are thrown away each day? One has to be very crude to be wasteful – very dull and insensitive. What do you think the effect of waste is on our consciousness? Where there is wisdom, waste is not possible and one loves correction. Millions of dollars worth of stored butter was never given to a starving humanity. It became rancid and was thrown away.[1] Where is our conscience? Where will our irresponsibility lead us? All because we have not discovered the potentials we brought with us at birth to extend.

Our children are stimulated into wanting to buy things. Toys have become a poison. And as parents, we have become

---

* Jiddu Krishnamurti (1895-1986) was a world-renowned teacher and philosopher. (Editor)

indifferent and helpless. Schools do not awaken, they merely teach skills and information. They deny everything vertical and lofty. We have lost the capacity to think for ourselves, and in the process, have lost a sense of discrimination and value. People become weak through imitation.

Do you have anything of everlasting value to give to your children? They have overwhelming problems to face in the years ahead. What would you give them to meet these challenges? They will need the ability to undo their own limitations, just to keep pace. But we have not undone anything. The younger generation sees the contradiction in us and doesn't want to hear our "good advice," and for good reason.

In nature, the wildebeest gives birth to her young one while the herd is grazing. Only twenty minutes are available for the newborn calf to stand on its feet and walk. If he delays for an extra five minutes, the calf is somebody's breakfast. Likewise, the child is surrounded with dangers. There is another pace.

We listen to this and can even agree, but we have lost the strength that would give us the energy to change or bring anything into application. The sensitivity of direct knowing has all but disappeared. More and more, we rely on someone outside ourselves to tell us what to do and what to think. And in future years the computer is going to rule our lives. The technology of the computer is only interested in the point of view of business, enhancing accumulation. Business and government will use this technology so people will conform without resistance and be more receptive to influence.

This is the world we are faced with. And there is your child. We can't become indifferent. The parents' responsibility is to awaken the child's internal faculties so that he is aware and has the capacity to undo his own thought. The trend toward irresponsibility is so powerful today. The moral conviction within us that can say, "This I will not do," is getting weaker and weaker. Awareness alone can undo the deceptions of thought and hardly anywhere is awareness awakened.

What introduces one to the present – a state outside of time – is one's own God-created, true Self, which has been kept impeccable, protected from ever being contaminated. *A Course In Miracles* introduces one to that true Self. It comes as a blessing from God to his eternal Son. It offers the involuntary action of miracles, insights, and holy instants. Miracles make the correction; insight and the holy instant provide the space for the creative Action of Life to extend its compassion. No longer do we need to feel lost or helpless.

All scriptures of the world are sacred. The difficulty lies in the fact that very few of us know how to read, or have the "ears to hear." [2] Everything passes us by like a breeze. The true words of Lord Buddha, Jesus, Mohammed, Moses, or Lao Tzu are rarely applied in our lives. "LOVE YE ONE ANOTHER" [3] remains an idea at the level of thought, not actuality. *A Course In Miracles* offers a step-by-step curriculum to bring one to awakening. There is a lesson for each day of the year. And it is in English, free of translation and interpretations. [4]

What happens when we read is that we interpret; therefore, the brain instantly makes it into an idea and nullifies the truth. Attention, on the other hand, bypasses the brain and its tendency to accumulate information. There is a different way to read. The attention you give would provide the space to discover the new, the unknown. In this stillness of awareness, transformation takes place. Your values change and you can no longer settle for beliefs, opinions, or assumptions – the world of thought. Facts, and the insights they offer, become part of your own inner awakening. Because your words are true and are not mere ideas, they will have an impact on the child. He will have conviction, and will grow in the beauty of his own purity.

One of the lessons from *A Course In Miracles* states:

*Father, I give You all my thoughts today....*
*Be You the Guide...*
*Today we have one Guide to lead us on....* [5]

We have so many guides that we can't afford to have the one Guide. There is sanity only in the wholeness of the One. We must bring our children to the awareness of the one Guide.

The Indian culture is filled with wonderful, strength-giving stories. One story concerns Lord Shiva, the destroyer of illusions, and his consort Parvati, whose energy created the universe. One day they were both sitting on a particular peak in the Himalayas, Mount Kalash. All of a sudden Lord Shiva vanished. And almost as suddenly he returned. Parvati asked him, "Where did you go?" Lord Shiva answered, "One of my devotees was being robbed and beaten. Because he prayed for my help, I went." "But Lord, why did you come back so soon?" Lord Shiva said, "He found a stone. There was no longer the need for me."

Can we begin to see that what we do matters in the whole of creation? Generally, we don't think that way. Our lives are personal.

And now the period of childhood is becoming shorter and shorter. This is alarming. First came the crib and the baby no longer slept with the parents. Then came the bottle, the babysitter, the television, the school. Now he is like an orphan and we want to know what to do.

How can the mother correct the child? She would have to correct herself first in order to correct her own patterns which are within the child. The father as well. Since that doesn't take place, the child is confused – especially in a situation where there is a divorce.

If there was harmony in the family, at least it would not be so contradictory. It would be easier for him to find more of himself. Now divorce is the norm. What is the lot of these children? It is similar to the time when Moses returned from the mountain with the Commandments and the people had already built the golden calf. They had to wander nearly forty years. Today most children will have to wander forty years in the wilderness to undo the vibrations that the parents have passed on to them. The children grow up, get married, have children of their own and get divorced. For forty years they wander around.

Figuratively speaking, the child is born to suffer. The issues are overwhelming. It is as if there is an allotted time for certain things to get corrected and balanced. If the correction doesn't take place then, it may not be all that easy. In every birth, however, there must be the potential to come to *I am as God created me.* [6] One's own purity of intent is the critical factor in bringing this about. Life is a precious opportunity.

What will relate us to our own inborn potentials is interest. The scriptures say you can only learn about yourself. Start by observing how greedy, how fearful, how selfish, how pretentious you are. No book is needed for one to become self-honest. Get interested in that. You may learn something extraordinary. You may discover, "Life is provided for me to find out about my insecurity, my attachments, my pretenses, my fears. Unless these traits are corrected in me, I can't help my child!" This is the only sanity. When the parents start with rightness in their own lives, that rightness will have its own extension in the child.

Once you have worked on correcting your traits, you will know the difficulties involved, how the ego wants to evade, what order you have to bring into your life, what urgency, what responsibility. You would be a wise person and bring that wisdom to all children in the world, not just your own child.

When you are the father of one child, you are the father of every child. Your little boundary breaks away and you become unified. You include. You love the child because he or she is an extension of you. And you don't want to give that child selfishness, or fear, or ideas, but trust.

We make things difficult when we don't want correction. We choose to wander in the wilderness for forty years. But there may be no such thing as the wilderness or the forty years. The promised land is just a stone's throw away. It only becomes difficult when one holds on to one's own conclusions. Our responsibility in life is to be true to who we are as God created us. Then we bring the Kingdom of God to earth and the whole planet vibrates differently.

During the Civil War, Abraham Lincoln felt there must be some other wisdom or insight available to him than what his generals were saying. The generals were reporting that they needed ammunition, supplies, different strategies. But Lincoln said, "No, we need something else." He didn't know what this "something" was, but for three years he never let go of this question until he broke past his own ideas.

Lincoln discovered that divine forces were accessible to him since he was the head of a nation. To a king, a president, or even the head of a family these divine forces are accessible. But one must be just. When there is someone for whom you are responsible, other potentials are given to you.

There is a story in the First Book of Samuel in the Bible about an extraordinary woman who knew trust. Her name was Hannah. She had no children. In the latter part of her life she cried bitter tears, went to the temple, and prayed, "Lord, I am barren. Bless me with a child and I will give him back to You to serve You."

> "AND SHE [HANNAH] WAS DEEPLY DISTRESSED AND PRAYED TO THE LORD, AND WEPT BITTERLY. AND SHE VOWED A VOW, AND SAID, O LORD OF HOSTS, IF THOU WILT INDEED LOOK ON THE AFFLICTION OF THY HANDMAID, AND REMEMBER ME, AND...GIVE TO THY HANDMAID A SON, THEN I WILL GIVE HIM TO THE LORD FOR ALL THE DAYS OF HIS LIFE."

Hannah went to the temple where the Ark was kept. The priest who was responsible for the Ark was called Eli. He was the one who could speak with the Lord and get instructions. Hannah sat for a long time in the temple and prayed with all her mind and heart for a child. Eli came out, saw this strange woman muttering and sitting there for so long and thought, "This woman must be intoxicated." He questioned her.

> "HOW LONG WILL YOU BE DRUNKEN? PUT AWAY YOUR WINE FROM YOU. HANNAH ANSWERED, NO, MY LORD, I AM A WOMAN SORELY TROUBLED; I HAVE DRUNK NEITHER WINE NOR STRONG DRINK, BUT I HAVE BEEN POURING OUT MY SOUL BEFORE THE LORD. DO NOT REGARD YOUR MAIDSERVANT AS A BASE WOMAN, FOR ALL ALONG I HAVE BEEN SPEAKING OUT OF MY GREAT ANXIETY AND VEXATION. THEN ELI ANSWERED, GO IN PEACE, AND THE GOD OF ISRAEL GRANT YOUR PETITION WHICH YOU HAVE MADE TO HIM. AND SHE SAID, LET YOUR MAIDSERVANT FIND FAVOR IN YOUR EYES. THEN THE WOMAN WENT HER WAY AND ATE, AND HER COUNTENANCE WAS NO LONGER SAD."

God blessed Hannah through the priest who was in communication. Because God worked with the one who was in charge of the Ark, Hannah was certain that she would have a child. And from that moment on she was happiness itself. Thought, with its unfulfillment, no longer bothered her. Her countenance was no longer sad.

Hannah became pregnant and gave birth to a child whom she named Samuel. She and her husband enjoyed the child's company. When Samuel was weaned, Hannah took him to the temple.

> "AND WHEN SHE HAD WEANED HIM, SHE TOOK HIM UP WITH HER...AND SHE BROUGHT HIM TO THE HOUSE OF THE LORD AT SHILOH; AND THE CHILD WAS YOUNG... AND SHE SAID, OH, MY LORD! AS YOU LIVE, MY LORD, I AM THE WOMAN WHO WAS STANDING HERE IN YOUR PRESENCE, PRAYING TO THE LORD. FOR THIS CHILD I PRAYED; AND THE LORD HAS GRANTED ME MY PETI-TION WHICH I HAVE MADE TO HIM. THEREFORE I HAVE

LENT HIM TO THE LORD; AS LONG AS HE LIVES, HE IS
LENT TO THE LORD." [7]

Hannah took him and offered him to the priest and said,
in effect, "Teach him the way of the Lord. Awaken him to his
*everlasting holiness and peace.*" [8] Have you ever prayed that
your child be awakened to everlasting holiness and peace?
She kept her promise. Have you ever made a promise that no
external circumstance could affect? Your word has the power
to transform you.

Hannah kept her promise and her promise prevented her
from getting attached to the child. Unless we have that space,
thought goes on and on. If you longed for that newness, you
would make space in your life. You would have a different
order, a different rhythm.

How Samuel must have loved being with this wise man!
The true teacher brings the child into contact with the living
moment. He connects the child with his own God-created Self.
That is awakening. Do you know anyone wise? Is there
anyone wise in your schools?

Where is the woman who can give birth to a Samuel today?
Is it asking too much to pose this question? Is it utterly
unrelated to the fact of modern living? There was a time when
it was possible. Virtue was a person's strength and society
valued that. Integrity was respected. Now physicality has
become the norm. Our literature reflects it, as does our education. We are bombarded with artificiality and commonplace
pornography. There is hardly a film that shows a man who is
a law unto himself and will not compromise. This book,
however, is not just for this age. Compassion is unchanging,
unaffected by the external situation. Although sensation,
externalization, and outlets have become rampant, a Hannah
could still evolve.

*A Course In Miracles* makes it very clear that physicality is
of the earth. It came into being when separation occurred and

it is nourished by earth forces.* But physicality carries within it something of the spirit. Everything that is born of the earth functions by instinct. Only man, who is on the earth and yet not of the earth, has a relationship with the Will of God. The human being alone has the capacity to know something that is not of the earth. His body is the temple of God on earth and he can bring the Eternal Laws to this plane.

As long as we are limited to the senses of the body, the tendencies of the body, its appetites and desires, must be mastered. Love is not desire. But to expect that one should act from love and not desire in this culture is to limit it to the extremely exceptional being. It must still be possible, for compassion is possible. Other Forces would help, for earth forces are not the last word. The Source of life cannot be limited.

Hannah was related to this Source of life. She cried and said she would give her son back to God. The modern woman can also cry for that kind of child and therefore come to determination to be guided. As long as there is willingness and receptivity, it will work. We must call upon that strength within us and never feel helpless. If you feel that you want to give birth to a child of a certain purity and nobleness, prepare the atmosphere. Changing everything would become natural for you. It will not be a struggle. If your husband is in agreement and there is like-mindedness, it is more likely that you would attract an evolved entity.

In a strange way, it may be easier to do this today because we are much more disillusioned. Life must compensate for the drawbacks. In the past, a great deal of conformity was demanded. Now we are so much freer. There are certain advantages. To know Hannah's story, how she brought Samuel up and then took him to the temple, is very inspiring. That is its virtue. But the Hannah of today and the Samuel of today may do something very different.

---

* For further discussion of "earth forces," see *The Future Of Mankind – Affluence Without Wisdom Is Self-Destructive* by Tara Singh (Life Action Press, 1992). (Editor)

If *Awakening A Child From Within* awakens eternal values in you, it is of service. We are making the virtues of the past accessible to present times. The past need not be imitated, for the creative spirit always extends its own newness.

Our education does not directly relate us with the Eternal Laws of love, goodness, or gratefulness for these are given *to* the brain, they are not *of* the brain. This is why awakening the child from within is a necessity. Without this, parents would be stopping short.

Any education that is based on self-survival limits one to the brain. The animal knows only so much and he is content with the fact that his needs are met. But the human being is also part of the Mind of God. Inherent in his brain is the capacity to receive the light, a capacity the animal brain does not have. When we become preoccupied with thought, we lose our capacity to receive the light. It is a turning point. The brain is the deciding factor. Would it relate with the Mind, or would it relate with self-centeredness, its own isolated function of survival?

As long as the child is in the womb, he is subject to the involuntary Laws of Creation. He is going to grow ears and fingernails. This action is part of the perfection of the Eternal Laws. *You* are not doing anything. When he is born he is subject to the human being's world. That is why the parents have to be responsible. Are they going to train his brain with skills, with religious beliefs and survival instincts, or are they going to awaken him?

To awaken him they need no school; they need nothing external, for everything the child needs is within his wholeness. He need never know a want. In his awareness there is no lack.

Since we live at this level of good and bad, wrong and right – the level of degrees and opposites – consequences are inevitable and self-projected. But they are not part of Reality. To think that one person is less than another is the denial of the Sonship of God. We are all holy, all equal. At the worldly level, we say, one is a poet; one is a peasant; one is a king; one is a laborer. Yet, their livers are not different, their teeth do not grow differently, and their eyes wink exactly the same. There is only the One, the whole. Love is love.

To live on this physical plane where all things are provided for us is a blessing. The human being needs liquid, and water is provided; we need light, the sun is provided. Nothing that is provided for the sustenance of life is invented by man.

> *The teachers of God have trust in the world, because they have learned it is not governed by the laws the world made up. It is governed by a Power That is in them but not of them. It is this Power That keeps all things safe.* [9]

The scribe of *A Course In Miracles,* Dr. Helen Schucman, shared these truths with me:

> "What God has not created is not real.
> Fear is always related to unreality.
> Nothing has purpose or meaning without love."

Whatever your child does, make sure that he can give his attention to it in a natural way. His giving the attention is taking the greed and the selfishness away, making him aware. That would relate him to the intrinsic where motivations end. He would be doing it because it is what he loves. When attention is there, the brain receives the light. It does not receive the light, however, if greed is there.

Through jobs and the specialization they require, we are usually limited to the preoccupation of the brain. No wonder we need outlets – only one faculty is at work, the mental. What havoc routine is playing in man's life! Industrialization has brought disaster to humanity and the planet. For its survival, industry must keep on producing. And to maintain jobs, people have to buy what it produces. If you look at what economy is in truth, you would see it totally validates wrong-mindedness. It doesn't extend anything other than self-centeredness and fear.

When you give attention to what you are doing, you are not part of routine. In attention, the brain comes to energy and receives. The man who does his work with attention has divine leisure. He doesn't need outlets.

Find out what is natural for your child to express. He can do that for his bread and butter. But first introduce him to real order and rhythm in life. This would relate him to the rhythm of creation, the rhythm of universal forces. The potential is there. Relate him to primary needs, not just to a job or abstract ideas.

The abilities he was given at birth will provide for him. The real joy comes in extending this potential. Potential has its own interest when you allow it to extend. That is finding your own inner calling, what is natural for you to give your energy to. It would make a child happy and keep him free from desire and indulgence.

Consistency and attention liberate a human being. When you are consistent with your calling, then your potentials and your attention will solve every problem. It would purify and uplift you. Most people have but one function – to get a job and serve the corporation and the system. We have become slaves of economy, subject to abstract systems that have no reality.

Let us see if we can, by awakening the child from within, awaken ourselves also. All that is required is attention. Attention silences the world of thought. Not unless the brain is freed from conflict will it ever realize the glory and power of certainty, truth, love, or goodness. Intensified awareness is a gift given by the action of grace.

*By grace I live. By grace I am released.* [10]

Only in the simplicity of wisdom is there the glory of awareness in which there is no lack. Every single thing is part of the whole. You see the earth and the individual tree but what you really see is wholeness extending itself in the tree and laying below as the energy of the earth. You look at the sky and you see the same wholeness – that is from where the light and the rain come. You see differences but you see them as part of the wholeness. The parents have to realize that this is the only real education the child needs.

We are all part of the great Self. In it, there is no conflict, fear, or greed. These are the interferences. Our education, our science, our commerce, our economy, all serve the function of intensifying interference.

There is no interference in serenity, in unity, in honesty. There is no interference in perfection. The law is love. All is already perfect. The wise lives and extends perfection and his life is impersonal and holy. Freedom is a state of being. True awakening – the ending of the illusion of "becoming" – is an intrinsic discovery of one's own divinity.

The awakened child embraces the wholeness of humanity in his awareness. When he becomes aware, in that awareness he is whole. There is nothing for him to do. We forget the wholeness and teach him how to manage without it.

Life is wasted in self-indulgence and business is becoming the violent enemy of serenity. It thwarts man's greatness as an eternal being of the spirit.

Everything that the brain has created thwarts the greatness of man. Mankind has survived poverty. One questions whether it will survive prosperity. Mother Teresa has expressed this concern so beautifully in *Love: A Fruit Always In Season.*

> "In the countries of the West there is no material poverty in the sense in which we speak of poverty.... But in the West you have another kind of poverty, spiritual poverty. This is far worse. People do not believe in God, do not pray. People do not care for each other. You

have the poverty of people who are dissatisfied with what they have, who do not know how to suffer, who give in to despair. This poverty of heart is often more difficult to relieve and to defeat." [11]

The abilities with which we came are meant for something intrinsic and for that we need space. True abilities always extend love. The brain's abilities will always extend self-centeredness, or short-sighted aims. Now the only abilities we know are the ones we go to school to get. And once we have them, we have likely turned our backs on our inner calling. Then we are unable to listen to the voice of God. We are unable to listen to the voice of the Holy Spirit. We are unable to listen when Jesus says in *A Course In Miracles*:

*If it helps you, think of me holding your hand and leading you. And I assure you this will be no idle fantasy.* [12]

Well, we just can't. We neither have the eyes to see nor the ears to hear true words, so we live by a substitute. Within the substitute, we try to make our isolation comfortable. How can isolation be comfortable? It abuses nature; it abuses people.

Our responsibility is never to be dishonest to ourselves. Our work as parents is to help our children keep their wholeness intact. Such children – awakened from within – will be a blessing to mankind for generations to come.

# CHAPTER TWO

# 2

## AWAKENING AWARENESS IN THE CHILD AND THE PARENTS

The preparation for the awakening of the child begins at the time of conception, and with each phase of growth our responsibility as parents increases. Inner evolvement has its own rhythm and pace, extending beyond the resources of the body. It is not difficult to be whole, natural, and timeless; it is merely different. The world of the spirit is ever there but our alternatives prevent the vision of the sacredness of life. The parents are the child's first teachers and their responsibility is to awaken him to the spirit.

Unless the child is awakened from within, it will be difficult for him to know wholeness. It is likely he will only know the physical world and the physical light of the sun. If your child can come to know what is of God, he or she will be a light to all humanity. Wise parents want their children to be as God created them and do not claim them as their own. They give their children back to God.

In the animal world, the mother usually takes care of her newborn as part of an involuntary action which comes and then leaves. Thus the innocence of the little one is protected. In human beings, a change of vibration actually takes place in both parents when the child is born, drawing them to the innocence of the child. This innocence awakens in them a sense of protection and care for the child which never leaves.

Because the child does not interpret, his earliest years are the most impressionable. He is innocent of anything other than what he directly perceives and feels. As long as what he encounters has no name, his response is a pure response. When the senses of the child are beginning to awaken and develop, a parallel movement of awakening of the spirit must take place. If the parents do not *value what is valueless*,[1] then this is also what they will communicate.

It is the parents' responsibility to make sure that the child is welcomed, nurtured, and adored. The foundation of his early years will carry him through his whole life. If the child is treated in a gentle way he will not feel any sense of distance or separation, and he will not know loneliness.

If the mother reads inspiring lives of virtuous beings when she is pregnant – especially after the fifth month of pregnancy – she is learning for her child, as well as for herself.* It is good to continue this practice after the child is born as well.

Until the time of the child's walking, the parents should surround the child with prayers while he is awake and when he is sleeping. Your very thoughts about the child and your pure intent are the prayer. Your prayer for yourself should be never to be touched by anxiety or worry. Once you have prayed, rest in peace. The goodness with which you surround your child, independent of attachment, has a profound effect on his astral body and spiritual centers or *chakras*, as well as on his psyche. His true being recognizes and makes contact with this goodness. The "idea" of being good parents is not good. It is intellectual. It does not give life, for it is personal. It merely stimulates and, in the long run, subjects the child to sensation. Attachment is not goodness.

What will the parents communicate when the child does not interpret? How great the need now to overcome irresponsibility for what one says, what one does, how one makes a living! The parents must begin to do the inner work of undoing the conclusions and beliefs by which they live. This

---

* See Recommended Reading/Listening For Parents and Children, page 393.

inner work may keep the child from having to go through distractions, deceptions, or even temptations. The minute we move towards them, we do so at the expense of the laws of love. Are we going to affect the child's impressionable state by moving from the laws of fear or the laws of love?

Although the parents may be insecure, slowly they can begin to discover that insecurity is a state by which they have been conditioned. Insecurity is not of God; it is of society. Fear is not of God; it is one's own. While the child is growing, the parents must come to recognize the limitation of these psychological patterns and undo them.

Can the parents keep the child's mind empty of ideas, free of all that is abstract and projected? There are other cultures in which there is more natural wisdom to protect the child from these harmful intrusions, for they know his growth would be his own. Unfortunately, in this culture, we divert him – almost deliberately.

Inner awakening cannot be taught. *A Course In Miracles* begins with: *Nothing real can be threatened. Nothing unreal exists.* [2] What the child *is*, is real. Can the parents refrain from introducing him to the world of the unreal, the world of ideas, beliefs, opinions, fear, attachment, and dependence? They would also benefit from this correction. Perhaps God does not see the child as a child or the parents as parents. He may just see them all as His children.

When I was growing up in rural India, the people didn't even know that they were living in India. There was very little sense of nationalism. Their world revolved around their inner life and the scriptures. They sang songs of God no matter what they were doing, which brought an atmosphere of blessing to the home. The tone of the voice that sings the songs of God emanates peace, serenity, and fulfillment.

In the West today, at least one parent in the family works at a job where the external assumes great importance. Can parents who are working come to the child as if for a vacation?

Could they create a space where the world does not intrude? When the child is born, there should no longer be a need for television. The parents are naturally interested in what the child does and says – his discoveries. The child can be the center of attention and affection.

> *PARENT:* Often I feel tremendously isolated. It is not all rosy. When I go to the park, I see other mothers like me, focused on their child. But we are all lonely.

The pain of loneliness is one of the products of this fragmented society. There is more loneliness today than ever before. If you really saw this, I think you would try to end the loneliness in yourself and prevent your child from ever knowing it. As you make the correction in yourself, the correction will be made in him. You are inseparable. Something of yourself is mirrored in the child. If you knew he was your extension, you would give him what is true, wouldn't you? We have destroyed so much that is natural. Our food is not food anymore; our sleep is not sleep anymore; and we give the baby a bottle instead of nursing him at the breast.

The child is born of the mother's womb. The first sound that he hears is the mother's heartbeat. Who knows the glory of that sound – possibly the greatest of all music. It has a pause in it that introduces the child to stillness. And when the mother nurses her baby, the child again hears the familiar sound and feels at home. The pause actually becomes the holy instant upon which time and the body cannot intrude. Out of that pause, meditation is born.

The child introduces the parents to love. The brain does not want to love, nor does it know how to love. All it wants is pleasure and comfort. But now, for the first time, it makes contact with the protected innocence of the child. The innocence of the child awakens tenderness in the parents and they begin to care more for him than themselves. Now that the child is born, the woman is no longer a wife; she is a mother. Her horizon widens because she is learning to care.

The most selfish girl automatically begins to discover the goodness in herself through the birth of her child.

What it must be to the mother and the child the first time the child nurses from the mother's breast! While the child is nursing and being caressed, he is slowly being introduced to the fact that the external world is full of love. When he was in the womb, he didn't realize he was separate. Slowly it begins to dawn on him. Only in love does he not feel frightened, insecure, and helpless. Through the mother's tenderness there awakens in him a sense of safety and protection, a sense that God is ever there. The divine laws are perfect, always protecting. Because the child is your extension, your responsibility now is to allow your love to unfold naturally. The birth of a child is a very holy event for the whole family.

Initially, the child only knows the mother. Then when the father comes to hold the child and kiss him, he begins to recognize this other one. Something else is awakening in him – discrimination for outer things and discrimination for inner things. Because that discrimination is so direct and unspoiled, we must begin to introduce the child to different values, a different tenderness, a different kindness, a different thoughtfulness. Not to toys, nor clothes; not to a better rocking chair and a better crib. Things have no meaning for the child. Your atmosphere – who you *are* – is the child's world. A sense of responsibility and care would be the parents' ally in doing the right thing.

The more pleasure-oriented and dependent on the man-projected world the mother is, the less in touch will she be with the God-created world. If the mother wants her child to be sacred, she will become interested in what is sacred. The action starts with her. Before the child understands the meaning of words, he understands the tone of the voice. Then he recognizes that this is his mother's voice, this is his father's voice; this is a friendly voice, this is a harsh voice. First, crying is his only response; then comes a smile which melts your heart. The minute the child looks at you with his innocent eyes, he is purifying everything within you. He is your Christ.

When Jesus was crucified, He said, "FATHER, FORGIVE THEM FOR THEY KNOW NOT WHAT THEY DO."[3] Mary and Joseph's Child was never regulated by the externals. He was in pain but things of the body and of the world were external to His Reality. Can you fathom that Mary didn't introduce Him to anything external? Continually she imparted: *Nothing real can be threatened. Nothing unreal exists.* * Until your child is rooted in the Real, it is wise not to introduce him to anything of the unreal, of the world.

*PARENT:* How would you do that?

Surround him with your love. Provide everything he needs – the laughter, the joy, the company, the songs. Very good music, softly played. Ask yourself: "Are we preparing our child to fit into the world, or are we preparing him to bring a new light into it?"

As he begins to understand a few words, what words will you teach him? If you love your child, you will make contact with the attributes of love and, from that space, share with him without introducing anything abstract.

When you bathe your baby, be sensitive to the temperature of the water. Massage him gently every day with natural almond or peanut oil and introduce him to your peace. These things come naturally to the mother who cares. How many exceptional people had very little education. Look how many great men the American Indians produced. I wish we could see how detrimental our society is to anything authentic. If you saw it you would have the strength to protect your child in the early years.

How awkward it must feel for a baby to have shoes on his feet! You think you are doing him a favor but you are imprisoning his feet. Be careful not to dress the child in synthetic clothes. Select soft, natural fabrics. Give your child space and do not make him too dependent. As the child recognizes things in his world, he wants to go to whatever draws him.

---

* *A Course In Miracles, Text,* Introduction.

His eyes get fixed and off he goes. He has very little sense of distance. Let the child go around on his knees. Children must be able to branch out and you must feel secure in letting them do so without surrounding them with too many "no's." The house belongs to your children. The best protection is recognizing ahead of time what in your home could be dangerous and removing it. Prevention is better than the cure.

When the child begins to crawl and move around, begin to awaken his awareness. The majority of children today are limited to the conditioning of their brains. But awareness is not of the brain. It is an inner awakening. Awakening a child from within means that as the child starts to move around and explore, you will introduce him to something more than his brain. Keep away the abstract world of "good" and "bad," the world of opposites. Use awareness and awaken the child to that awareness within.

The brain is subordinate to inner awakening. In the formative years, the child must be awakened to another light. When inner awakening is not of value to us, we send the child to school or to day care at a very young age. Obviously, this makes it more difficult for that child to know wisdom. He will be given skills to go and work and it is likely he will turn out to be a mercenary. Mercenaries can write well, get good jobs, but they have no contact with wholeness. Only awareness makes contact with wholeness.

> PARENT: You say that parents who are
> aware would not introduce duality to the child.
> What actually is that awareness?

The brain does not know awareness. The brain only knows, "No. Don't do that. You're going to get hurt." There is fear behind it. Awareness does not see through the eyes of fear. In awareness, a totally different light within emanates from you. The child becomes aware of something gentle when you are caressing him. If he is going full-speed toward the water, your awareness can just pick him up gently and redirect him. Then the only thing he is becoming aware of is your love, your peace. That is the awakening of awareness – in you and in him. Your awareness keeps you ahead of the child. If you are not aware, you are just another child.

Awareness is something you receive. You are enriched because you have a child. In fact, you've got the universe behind you. Because you lack nothing you need never feel helpless. You just need to learn to receive. The Given is there, always accessible. The child demands that the parents have the capacity to receive. The fact that the child is there requires that kind of responsibility from you. Either you react and make problems, or you respond.

Three years of age is too young for a child to go to school. He needs his own divine leisure, his own rhythm. It is better to wait until he or she is at least five or even seven. While he is at home, what are you going to introduce him to? Are you going to introduce him to funny books, Bugs Bunny and Mickey Mouse? Or are you going to introduce him to life and nature, to squirrels and willow trees? Even in the city, young children can plant things which grow quickly in pots. Sunflower seeds sprout within two days.

There is no need to make problems. As mortals, we tend to want the situation to change; therefore we act from unfulfillment, anger, and deprivation. Even if you have nothing and live in a hut, the twilight is still there; the dawn is still there; the wind, the stars, and your love are still there. Why do we give so much importance to the externals?

Whatever your situation is, don't wish for it to be different. Accept that this is how things are. All the child needs is to be surrounded with your love. It is best not to introduce him to a sense of lack. If you do, you will bring in an atmosphere filled with desires. The young child is still related to the Changeless, to that which does not change. The parents must also become well-centered in the world that does not change.

Our heroes need to be those universal beings, like Jesus, Lord Buddha, Sri Ramakrishna, Sri Ramana Maharshi, Mr. J.

Krishnamurti, who lived according to Eternal Laws and represented the Kingdom of God. If you want your child to represent the Kingdom of God, you need to surround him with those values. You will be enriched by making contact with them also.

Hui Neng was an enlightened being who lived in the 7th century B.C. His story is told in the *Diamond Sutra and the Sutra of Hui Neng*. [4] When you read Hui Neng's story, you wonder how he got to be so wise and responsible. Who must his parents have been? He was burning inside for God and Truth when, by chance, he heard someone in the village reciting a *sutra*.* For the first time, he knew the power of true words and he was uplifted. He wondered to himself, "Are there words that can awaken?" He asked the man, "Where did you learn these words?"

When the man told Hui Neng that he had heard them at a monastery some distance away, he decided to go there. First, however, he had to take care of his responsibility to his mother since his father was no longer living. What must that mother have imparted to her son? He could hear true words and yet he had the strength to do the right thing. Rarely do we go beyond the world of appearances. This mother gave birth to a God-lit son. He had not been with swamis, with gurus, with lamas; his mother awakened something in him. Nothing moved him from the fact that he was responsible to care for her.

Someone once asked a man who was plowing his field what he would do if he were told that he would die that evening? He said that he would finish plowing the field. How sure, certain, and simple. Utterly unpressured. What rightness there must be in that life!

After fulfilling his responsibility to his mother, Hui Neng traveled to the monastery. When he arrived, the Abbot took one look at him and said, "You savage, what do you know about reading and writing?" Hui Neng asked if only educated

---

* A sutra is a precept or maxim that summarizes Vedic teaching.

people could gain the knowledge of God? There was a reason for that question and there was a reason that Hui Neng was illiterate.

Hui Neng was sent to the kitchen to pound rice and chop wood. Imagine how the world is going to treat someone who is relegated to the kitchen. They probably gave him a little gunny sack to lie on, not even a bed. They called him a lay person, a barbarian.

In the weeks that followed there was a growing atmosphere of expectation in the monastery. When Hui Neng inquired about the festivities, he was told that everyone was preparing for the day when the Abbot, an enlightened being, would hand over the mantle and bowl of the Buddha to one of the thousands of monks studying at the monastery who wrote the best sutra. "Best sutra" meant that those words would have the power of truth in them, like the words Hui Neng first heard in town.

Words have power. Are the parents going to give their child true words? If you were to give words that were at least real to you, what corrections would take place automatically in your life? Who is the teacher? The Bible says: "...AND A LITTLE CHILD SHALL LEAD THEM..."[5] I wonder if we would listen. Your child is trying to lead you to God.

The power of true words brought Hui Neng to the monastery. He didn't have a teacher. His parents were his only teachers. Hui Neng spent some time in quiet. Since he did not know how to write, he asked a student to write down the sutra he had composed. The fact that Hui Neng was illiterate demonstrates that education is not necessary. Hui Neng was actually far ahead of the others because his parents kept him innocent of all external learning, of all sense of lack and insecurity.

Hui Neng did not have paper on which to write so he asked the student if he could just write it on the wall of the hall. Hui Neng's sutra had the power of truth in it. It could have awakened the student who was writing it if he had had the "ears to hear." Which one of them is superior? The student is preoccupied with the external festivities. Hui Neng is not. He is awakened from within; the other one is mentally educated. When you are able to put the mental education aside, knowing that it doesn't awaken, you will have grown centuries.

What awakens the child is your putting away your preoccupation with the externals. It is not necessary to teach the child; it is necessary to protect him from being invaded upon by the externals. Don't teach him anything; just preserve the state of *I am as God created me*[6] within him.

You need not limit yourself. Everything needed will be provided. If you give your pure intent to parenting, the Lord will send you a teacher who will take it further. The brain limits; awareness does not. As you come to awareness, you will not limit yourself and your child will know no lack.

The student wrote Hui Neng's sutra on the wall and when the Abbot passed by and read the sutra, he asked which person had written this response. From this you can tell he was a real abbot. Only awareness would recognize the power of truth in Hui Neng's words. The student, terrified that he might have done the wrong thing, stammered that he wrote it but the barbarian told him what to write. The true words of Hui Neng's sutra had failed to touch him.

This is the tragedy of education. It fills one with motives, cleverness, and skill. The outcome of our education is violence, fear, hate, and a world in which money and distractions have become the god. There is no love, no virtue, no awareness. Only the outlets the system provides makes it possible for us to stand our falseness. Is this all mankind ever wanted – to be satisfied with outlets? It is shocking to see we have become so limited to thought and the body, and this is as far as we aspire. Very few people today have any connection with who they really are as God created them.

Outlets have become a trillion-dollar business because this life of routine needs outlets. Now that teenagers have buying power, they are being exploited. The unessential becomes important because industry must create new markets. In this way, a whole new lifestyle has come into being which did not exist before.

When the student told the Abbot the sutra was written by the barbarian, the Abbot asked him to wash it off quickly. Then he banged the wall three times with his foot. Hui Neng understood the Abbot wanted to see him at three o'clock.

Now there were two awakened people. The Abbot had the experience of mankind, which Hui Neng did not have. Hui Neng knew nothing of the wickedness of competition and status. When the Abbot met Hui Neng at three o'clock he took him by boat some distance away from the monastery, gave him the bowl and the robe of Lord Buddha, and told him to run for his life so that the others could not harm him.

How threatened is the world of ignorance, limited to the brain. The man-made, projected religion killed Jesus. And now there is the Christ in the child. What are the parents going to do? Divert him from his purpose? Are you going to declare your helplessness and go for expediences? If the child really calls for help, if you really call for help, it will be there.

For Hui Neng, the original sutra he heard was true. Here you must ask if your relationship with your child is true. If it is true, then your words have power and you lack nothing. If the parents see that their sole responsibility is to awaken the child who is entrusted to them and if they don't make a problem of it, it is done. That is the only thing required.

*   *   *

## THE TIME OF COMPANIONSHIP

The relationship between a child and his parents begins to change when the child is around seven or eight years of age.

The boy becomes more of a companion to the father, and the girl to the mother. How does the mother introduce her daughter to something more than physicality? How does the father introduce the boy to something more than the forces within the body?

Parents have to protect their children from body needs, body sensations, and body appetites. If the mother's life is focused on pleasure, she will invariably mislead her daughter. Who is really beautiful? Certainly Mother Teresa. Saint Joan. True beauty might be something within you that shines. It is not merely physical. What are you going to give your daughter? The consciousness that she must be pretty and draw attention to herself? Or will you draw her attention to something within her that bestows its blessing on all humanity?

What is of the earth is projected and pursued. This is neither good nor bad; it is just a fact. What is eternal is always discovered within yourself. Can the parents introduce their children to the awareness that they don't have to pursue or seek anything because they are already perfect? Do *they* have that awareness?

Is the father going to introduce his children to the lust for money, property, and possessions? Will he introduce them to a sense of lack and unfulfillment? Lack is unreal in God's world. Will the father introduce his sons or daughters to unreality and make it real for them? Or will he introduce them to their own inner gladness, the peace that is within them no matter what they are doing?

There are many things the father can do to nurture qualities of compassion and integrity in his son. He can impart the wisdom and necessity of non-waste to him. The child can be inspired by the flight of the bird rather than wanting to shoot and kill it. The father doesn't need a teacher. He just needs his own honesty, his own integrity. That is the awakening within the parent. They are both getting awakened at the same time at different levels. The sun shines for the little boy and the sun shines for the father.

In this way right relationship gets established in which there is no dependence. Right relationship is not of the brain. The brain says, "This is me, that is you. This is good, that is bad." Everything the brain knows is incomplete; it always has the duality of opposites in it. In relationship, there is only one life.

Around the age of ten, children should begin to be introduced to that which is outside of time, physicality, nationalism, and man-made beliefs and concepts. Start with the fact that everything mankind has done separates. Religion, the largest institution, has separated man from man. More wars have been fought in the name of religion than anything else. Politics divides man from man. There was a time when politics didn't exist; now it is all we know. We have almost completely lost touch with humanism.

Mr. J. Krishnamurti made a very strong statement when he said that our society has become "utterly corrupt and immoral."[7] See how ruthless the institution of education is. It isolates a person from Reality by making the externals real. *A Course In Miracles* reiterates for the Western mind what the Vedic scriptures made very clear: The world is an illusion; it is not real.

If it is the parents' intent to look after their child as a child of God, they will invite a very evolved entity to themselves. Can you imagine what free will must be? You have the free will to bear the kind of child you want. It is determined by the degree to which you will be responsible, by the degree to which you are determined to protect the child from getting immersed in the world of illusions.

The parents must correct their own misperception. That is their discipline. To see the false as the false awakens discrimination. First the child was under your protection. Now you must prepare him for the world by introducing him to discrimination. Before the child comes to adolescence, the parents can help him understand that everything he does has its consequences at the level of physicality. Can they inspire him to be an extension of Eternal Laws in which there are no consequences?

Mr. J. Krishnamurti said that before children reach puberty they must have some awareness awakened in them so that they are in control of themselves. Regardless of the external situation, they will not get taken over. A force, a clarity, a vitality is ignited within them that will not succumb to pleasure. This awareness must be present in proportion to the development of the new body sensations. Parents or teachers can turn the tide for the young, but they must live a noble life. They can only transmit what is their actual truth. Teaching and preaching only influence opinion. This parallel movement of awakening must take place if the child is to be balanced. This is a law of life.

If we really hear and understand this, we will start to undo and dehypnotize ourselves. We will activate those forces within us that are dormant. Our parents probably did not do it. Now it is our responsibility as parents. In order to heed true words we have to step out of time. When we only hear with the body's ears, the truth gets blurred again and we want to learn more. This activity of learning gives the illusion that, at some point, we will get the whole picture. Learning does not bring about change. It is a process of accumulation at the mental level.

Without having awakened their child, parents try to make him responsible in adolescence by imposing authority. If awakening has not taken place before puberty begins, when these new sensations come upon the adolescent, he won't know how to respond. His parents will tell him, "Don't do this, don't do that," while the fact is these new sensations are an involuntary force. He will soon forget all about his parents' admonitions.

Children obey authority as long as they are dependent and cannot get away. What a false position that is. I wish we would never do that with our children. They should never feel boxed in or compelled to comply. There is another light, another awareness that can be a real strength to them.

Parents have a responsibility to outgrow their own body senses so that their words are authentic. The parents must demonstrate that there is more to life than just the physical manifestation of the body. We must introduce them to the world beyond appearances.

It is especially important to make a young woman aware that she has one moment of freedom from which she will make a decision that will regulate the rest of her life. She will never be free again. When she says she wants to marry a man, her decision will determine who she is and what she values. How contained she is, how she vibrates, how wise she is, are all focused in that one split second when she makes the decision. Once the decision is made to be with a man, she is no longer a virgin and she will never be a virgin again. A cycle of cause and effect has started that will go on. It may take years, or even lifetimes, to complete it.

Can we prepare our children to be wise enough not to get taken over by sensation so that if a young man or woman is attracted to someone and wants to get married, he has aware-ness to guide him and she has awareness to guide her? They would know right away if someone tried to arouse them from the outside. They would see right through flattering words. The girl would know when it is desire. If anyone, either with words, with touch, or with presents, tried to seduce her or induce her to be false to herself, she would not have any part of it. For young people today, it is unlikely that they will find anyone to love them, nor will they be capable of loving anyone, unless they discover their own inner potentials and realize what they have to give.

Can you introduce your children to that simplicity in which there is no dependence? Simplicity comes into your life when you are wise. The benediction of simplicity frees a person from false values. We have to protect our children from getting into a life of consequences. The body wants pleasure and unless our children have their own contentment, they will go for it. We need to bring them to the awareness of the peace of God, but not merely as a belief. This peace is something pure within yourself, a gladness that is an ever alive, ever renewing joy within you.

What a responsibility you have. Your responsibility is to impart to your children that when your life is motiveless you are the light of heaven on earth. You will know no lack and all humanity will be affected by your presence.

## MY FATHER'S HOUSE

Hallowed my name. I am a Son of God
Who walks in stillness. I hold out my hand,
And from my fingertips the quiet goes
Around the world to still all living things,
And cover them in holiness. Their rest
Is joined in mine, for I am one with them.
There is no pain my stillness cannot heal,
Because it comes from God. There is no grief
That does not turn to laughter when I come.
I do not come alone. There walks with me
The Light that Heaven looks on as itself.
I am a Son of God. My name is His.
My Father's house is where my stillness is. [8]

If the parents do not have the ability to awaken their child, they can guide him to someone who is wise. They could find a true teacher the way Hannah found Eli [9] to awaken her son. Parents who refuse to compromise will never be deprived. First they do their part by feeding, protecting, and nurturing the child. In the next phase, they begin to slowly introduce the child to factors other than the body senses. Then may come a period when they cannot go further. Because they prepared the child, and that is their need, the teacher will be there.

You limit yourself if you say, "What can I do?" Until your child is sixteen, you have a lot to do. In many cases, even at the age of ten and twelve, a mentor or a teacher may come into the child's life because of your purity of intent. Your determination and your love for the child opens all the doors.

When this awakened awareness is nurtured throughout the child's life, he retains his wholeness. If he has managed not to get involved or distracted, then he will know his true spiritual ministry. Through this ministry he will extend the Will of God because he is one with that Will. And a new prophet, a new incarnation, is upon the planet.

# CHAPTER THREE

# 3

## IN LOVE
## THERE IS NO DESIRE

In ancient times, the wise discovered that certain times of the day and night were better for certain things. There was a natural rhythm for everything. Today we are seldom related to anything beyond our own survival and insecurity. Our only rhythm is when we go to work and when we come home. Life has become artificial. And as we have moved away from natural rhythms, our lives have become more and more personal. We have fewer families because we have isolated ourselves in special relationships.*

We do not miss holy relationship because we have never known it. We have never known what it means to lead an impersonal life. A life untouched by desire or fear must have its own resources, its own integrity. We think that mankind is moving forward, but it may be the other way around. It appears that we are progressing but, in actuality, we have lost touch with something essential.

Holy relationship is a state beyond gender, a state of complete trust. You would know instantly if there was ever a

---

* Special relationship is a term used in *A Course In Miracles*. *"If you seek to separate out certain aspects of the totality and look to them to meet your imagined needs, you are attempting to use separation to save you." ACIM*, I, page 290.

false note and would actually honor the relationship by mentioning it. Real friendship allows for vulnerability. It gives you the opportunity to discover the goodness and the giving-ness which are inherent in each one. I don't consider anything a friendship if it does not inspire goodness and charity. Any relationship that makes one dependent enhances a sense of lack.

True friendship embodies the newness of the impersonal. It soars beyond the resources of the known. Where the two become one, needs are already met. This is a discovery of the stillness within you. Friendship, too, is a fulfillment.

One would have to go back to the culture of India to get any clue as to what right relationship is. India is like the mother of the world. In India it is said that marriage is ordained. Because of the laws of cause and effect, we have certain relationships with people. There are consequences to bear, merits you have earned, certain obligations or debts you must pay. There may be a residue from one life to the next; therefore, the entity comes again and again to bring all relationships to completion. This is a law – not of the Absolute – but of the memory of human consciousness.*

In the West, people want to know who their soul mate is. Your soul mate is probably the person who is the most difficult to get along with. We are in relationship to learn lessons. Most of us want to teach the other person to change while not changing ourselves.

*A Course In Miracles* imparts the wisdom that chance plays no part in relationship, that nothing happens by accident. [1] If you run into a child on the street, if you meet someone in an elevator, it is ordained. You must find what you have to give in each instance. The opportunity is offered in every encoun-ter to come to holy relationship.

---

* For further discussion of the laws governing relationship, see Tara Singh's *"Love Holds No Grievances" – The Ending Of Attack* (Life Action Press, 1988). (Editor)

One of the most famous stories in India is the story of Savitri, the attractive and intelligent daughter of a noble king. The custom in those days was that princes from neighboring kingdoms would come to the palace to be considered for marriage. Garland in hand, the princess would look at each of them. When she felt something within – "this is the one" – she would put the garland around his neck and the wedding would be arranged.

We don't have that kind of intuition anymore. We have desire and lust. We know so little beyond the body. The body likes someone wealthy or handsome but it doesn't have eternal values. *I will not value what is valueless* [2] is not part of our thought system.

Many princes came to ask for Savitri's hand in marriage but no one pleased her. Naturally, her parents were getting concerned. They spoke to some of their relatives and friends from other provinces and sent Savitri on a journey to their kingdoms to see if someone there might suit her. No one interested her. Just imagine what kind of person she must have been to have such integrity and self-honesty. We would be impelled by our need, by a dream or projection, and then we wouldn't know what was dictating our choice.

One day when Savitri was returning from one of her visits, she saw a man who was a water carrier. Their eyes met and immediately she felt a contact with him. "This is the man." Her parents asked her when she returned if she had met someone. She answered, "Yes. I saw the man I am to marry. We never spoke but I know he is the one. He was in the village carrying water."

Her parents were shocked. They didn't know what to do. Their daughter was a law unto herself, but it somehow did not seem right for a princess to marry a water carrier. They asked the all-knowing sage, Narada, about the person whom their daughter saw. Narada said, "This man is a prince who has lost his kingdom. He is now taking care of his parents and lives simply. He is not an ordinary person and he is not a poor person." The parents were relieved to hear this. "But," Narada said, "there is one thing we must consider. This prince is only going to live for one more year."

When they told Savitri of Narada's insight, her response was, "I have given my heart to him. Do you think that I can give it to someone else?" Savitri knew deeper laws. This is real discipline. One would have to have integrity, conviction, one's own inner clarity and strength, to be able to say these words.

Because there were no choices and preferences in her life, they married. Savitri knew the exact day and time that her husband would pass away. They lived a very simple and happy life together. Finally the day arrived when he was to die. They went together to the forest. When he said he was feeling feverish, Savitri suggested he lie down and sleep for a while. During his sleep, Death came to take him. Savitri looked at Death and pleaded with him for her husband to live a while longer. Death said, "No one has ever loved the way you love. But this is a law. I am merely sent to administer the law. I cannot change anything."

Savitri implored further but Death insisted that he had no power to do anything. Suddenly, Death turned to Savitri and said, "Since your heart is so pure, I will grant you a boon, any boon that you wish. Just do not ask me to spare your husband's life."

Savitri paused for a moment and then said, "My husband is the only son of his parents. Who would take care of them after he is dead? The boon that I request is that my husband's parents have grandchildren to take care of them." Death said, "You outwitted me." Savitri's purity, wisdom, and thoughtfulness were honored in heaven. Her virtue changed the law and her boon was granted.

In ancient India, people lived a different kind of life in which they were not so often under the sway of physicality. Inner strength was deemed of greater value. Their lives were disciplined, not so self-centered. Discipline actually undoes self-centeredness.

Even today, when a girl is married in India, she bows before her husband and touches his feet. When I was married, I was horrified by that. I discovered, however, that this action of humility does something to you. It awakens something in a man that he never knew before. Of course it can be a ritual if the woman or man has had experiences and are preoccupied with desires. But what about a man and a woman who are virgin in their thoughts as well?

The purity of such a woman would demand that the man rise to protecting her vulnerability, rise to being touched by her humility. Desire automatically falls away. Self-centeredness disappears. All of a sudden you grow to be a man. Just imagine, you are nobody and your wife comes and bows before you, bows to the divine in you. It makes a very powerful impact. It is the first time you meet a woman. All things of the body just drop away and you rise to something else. You feel responsible for making the other person feel welcomed, not a stranger, not frightened. You are entrusted with this life. Would you rise beyond self-interest? Would you come to holy relationship with her? Would your brain give you that much space?

In marriage, one learns to be tender, gentle, noble, and caring. A transformation takes place within. You discover a part of yourself you will never know until that real marriage takes place. Through marriage, the woman is introduced to her womanhood. This is a gift she can only receive from a man who really loves her and not just her body. She discovers who she is in this atmosphere of deep caring. The man and woman share a stillness that awakens gratefulness for life which brought them together. It is the most glorious period of one's life. You cannot go for a walk without thinking about it. The happiness that accompanies it colors every cell in your body.

Everything changes in you and your spouse. You never knew you could love anyone more than yourself. You become noble because your wife treats you like a divine being. And she is grateful to you for introducing her to who she is. She finds beauty in yielding, in self-giving, in non-assertiveness, in being receptive. In this way the two polarities become one.

Another strength emerges that is independent of gender. It is possible for an atmosphere to evolve in the relationship over the years from which you can actually outgrow gender.

When I was a young boy, my distant cousin and I saw a book in town that said it could teach you everything about women and sex. We looked at each other, bought the book, and rushed out of town as fast as we could on our bicycles. We sat under a tree and read the book, which turned out to be quite extraordinary.

This book didn't tell about the stimulating ways of sexuality. No. It talked about kindness, gentleness, friendliness, respect. It said that when the woman is pregnant, the husband must provide a happy atmosphere with flowers, good food, and music, and they must not have sex during this period. I found this to be true later in life. Out of mutual love and respect, you are introduced to a very different part of yourself – a boundlessness, a generosity. After the child is born, you have also risen to a totally different level. Something else has become significant now and the parents have strength and security to give to their child.

Can you see what we have destroyed in our haste? The life unknown. The unknown is the only thing that is new. Something very different takes place when a woman and man discover this life unknown together. You are grateful to each other and you are grateful to life that brought some touch of wholeness to you. When sex is made a "body" thing, it will not have tenderness in it. When sex is of another spirit, it slows everything down and makes it possible to step out of time. It is actually sacred. There is no hysteria, no restlessness, no tension. It is a movement of life itself, a movement so spacious that it could never fit into a wanting. What is sacred offers the space and inspiration to make contact with the timeless – first in the marriage, then with the birth of the child.

We have lost something precious in this overly-stimulated culture – an innocence, a freshness, a contact with another potential in relationship. For example, when a young man and woman were betrothed in marriage, it was seen to be life's hand in arranging the marriage. This meeting of the unknown in relationship between the man and the woman is blessed by life. Thus it has a different significance. It has the potential to introduce the couple to a *sattvic* state* and the goodness and gentleness of each other.

The gentleness of a woman is inspiring – just the way her body is made, the way she walks and expresses herself. The relationship with her husband awakens a quality of thoughtfulness in her. It is a great strength for her to know her husband adores her, cares for her, is strong and noble, and doesn't lie or cheat. In actuality, she is his treasure. Their mutual care for one another inspires trust. Trust introduces one to relationship with life.

Could their meeting lift them beyond the body rather than drag them toward sensation? That is right relationship. Out of their fulfillment, they aspire to different values as a couple and as parents. Once the child is born, they become father and mother, no longer merely husband and wife. If this does not take place, they have become bound to the physical.

Once the couple has come to a sattvic state, they are more peaceful, less pressured, more fulfilled. It is like stepping out of time together to another kind of leisure and contentment, not pressured with wantings. It transforms their lives and brings them to having something to give.

If the wanting hasn't disappeared and the giving hasn't come into being, I would say that the marriage hasn't flowered. Marriage is a most intimate relationship in which two people complement each other and come to a state where

---

* An atmosphere of purity, balance, and wisdom.

givingness is discovered. The difference between giving and wanting is that one is a saint, the other is a savage. When you want, you abuse and exploit. Because you are self-centered, you can't step out of time or your own body needs.

There is no manipulation when you are giving. And by the time you come to orgasm, you have touched upon that creative action of life that is inherent in the sexual experience. It brings you to rebirth. Thus the meeting between man and woman, husband and wife, becomes something sacred and holy for which you only have reverence. In love there is no desire. With this approach, with this relationship with life, you produce different kinds of children.

What actually takes place in the atmosphere of the spirit – when the man and woman are sharing not bodies but life – is that the centers within the body awaken and introduce the couple to the unknown. There is nothing comparable in the whole world. You hold the other's hand with such feeling; you touch them as they have never been touched before. Caring civilizes a human being. A child who witnesses this harmony and virtue between his parents would make a different kind of contribution to this world for he would not be in conflict.

Many divorces result because the right atmosphere has not been provided. Separation occurs because we never really united. Instead of becoming sattvic, calm, pure, and timeless, we become more body-bound, pressured, needy. For the most part, sex merely serves as a release of tension. We have outgrown little, if anything. It is as if we are born at a certain level and rarely rise beyond it. Everything is reduced to sensation internally, and money and success externally. As long as we identify with the body, we are going to be insecure.

The man-woman relationship probably has more potential of becoming a holy relationship than any other because it is the first relationship in which one is grown-up and responsible. When you meet the woman or man with whom you are going to share your life, it is blessed.

Once our children have grown up, it is a time to simplify our lives. Having gained experience and known responsibility, we are free to be with a serenity that is superior to anything we can imagine. Old age is akin to young age in that it is innocent. But we fight the maturing process because we are unfulfilled. We have misery, loneliness, and sorrow of our own making. Yet, old age is probably the most blessed time of one's life in the sense that it is then we can discover the peace of God. If, when we die, we have brought our lives to completion, we can die forever to the physical.

For the brain to become part of the Mind of God, it has to be energetic. Dissipation of the creative energy prevents flowering. But if the energy is contained, another inner happiness begins to unfold, a current of joy that flows through you that nothing external can affect. That is actually why celibacy became important. Celibacy is not a denial. That same creative energy that produced a child is actually necessary to awaken other potentials within. That energy is the key to recreating yourself.

In India there are statues of Lord Shiva. One part of the sculpture is female, the other is male, because in him both polarities are one. That is what real marriage is. Could husband and wife both rise to that? Then they would have something to give to their children. Step by step the marriage should evolve to this so that in one lifetime all involvements, all consequences come to an end. Before the end of one's life, can we bring all relationships to rightness and real harmony.

A dear friend once asked me about how to bring some newness into her marriage. Although they both cared for one another, she had a sense that something was going awry. There is a wonderful African story which aptly addresses her question.

There was once a woman who was miserable because she yearned for her husband and often he didn't come home. She went to the medicine man and shared her agony, her fear that he was probably going to another woman. The medicine man said to her, "I can help you but, first, I will need some hair from a lion's mane." She didn't know how she would ever manage to get it, but she agreed.

I don't think we would do that sort of thing. We are so reactive. We have brought everything down to the lowest common denominator. Listen carefully. This woman wants her husband more than anything else. She feels that divine laws are involved in her marriage and she cannot be complacent. This is not merely an African story.

Although the lady tried for days to figure out a way to get the hair, she just couldn't muster the courage to face the lion, let alone get hair from his mane. But she needed her husband and she wanted to be his wife. I once heard the roar of a leopard. The bottoms of your feet begin to shiver as if the earth itself is trembling. Have you ever noticed that when the stalking tiger is absolutely sure that its prey is within range, he growls, and the animal freezes? You and I know that to go to get hair from the lion's mane is no child's play. What would you do if you had no option? This lady had no option and therefore other resources were available to her.

What came to her mind was that the lion might not eat her if she took a lamb for him to eat. The lion would be more apt to eat a lamb or a goat than her and she would still be safe. At least she entertained that possibility.

To implement this plan takes courage and intelligence. We are not adept at thinking for ourselves. We don't really know how to meet a challenge because we are taught to get a job and conform. There is so little newness in what we do.

Although she was terrified, she took the lamb and started to walk into the jungle. When the lion saw her and the lamb coming, he perked up. The lion loves food. He sleeps sixteen hours a day but he knows exactly when the lioness has made a kill. She can't ever get the first bite. He is there. The little lion cubs fly up in the air. Whoom! Nobody comes near him until he has had his favorite parts. Then he lets the others come.

That is the law of the jungle. So the lady let go of the lamb and ran away. The lion was very happy.

The next day she took another lamb. And the next day she took another lamb, and then another. She established a rhythm and slowly, little by little, her fear began to go away. Now she did not run away; she even stood there. The lion seemed to understand that this is some other intelligence and he started to purr when he saw her coming with his lamb. Gradually he allowed her to touch his mane and finally she was able to get a piece of his hair.

Jubilant, she went to the medicine man and said, "Here I am. I got the hair from the lion's mane for you." The medicine man looked at her and said, "If you put that kind of perseverance, that same intelligence, into winning your husband, you will get him also."

We need to learn to give everything we have to it. Then things will work.

In the county in India where I was born, a very great sage – a master of music – lived centuries before. When I say sage, I mean that he was an extension of eternity. Every year his anniversary was celebrated, and great musicians came from all over India to pay homage to his memory. Thousands of people would come to listen to their performances. Not a penny was charged and the little town provided the food for everybody since there were no restaurants.

India is a poor country but it is rich in friendship. Here we have lost contact with the truth of friendship and don't even know how to be a friend. Our friendships are merely expedient. We must find out why this is so. Why can't we be true to one person without any dependence or motive? We would have to be true to ourselves first.

I used to go to this musical anniversary which lasted for three days. One time when I went it was very crowded but some friends saved me a seat near the stage. When the master sitarist came onto the stage and sat down, our eyes met. The person beside me introduced us. The musician asked me if I ever came to Delhi. I said, "Yes." He gave me his telephone number and asked me to come and see him when I was there.

I went to Delhi not long afterwards and called on him. He greeted me like a long-lost brother and invited me to come to his home early the next morning for music. That is India. When I arrived around five-thirty the next morning, he greeted me at the door. Just the two of us were there when he played for me. The quality of goodness, the givingness, the refinement were so inspiring. That, to me, is music. After he had finished playing, someone knocked at the door and breakfast was served for us.

A year or so later, he was to marry the daughter of a great musician and a master herself of another stringed instrument, the surburhar. Everyone who was to come to the wedding wanted them to give a concert together on their wedding day. They agreed. As they started everyone was enthralled with her playing. It was quickly seen that he was no match for her, nowhere near her greatness although she was very modest. The next day the press raved about her performance and no mention was made of his. It really hit him. When she saw what happened, she never played music in public again.

She honored her husband and refused to be competitive. She never played again on the stage, although she became a renowned teacher. Who in this culture could have done that? We have brought about more divorces through our competition. I agree that man has been brutal and cruel, but there is no wisdom in being the equal of the brute. Why can't women rise to the height of their being? Today women are helpless. The only thing they can do to correct the situation now is to develop their own character, their own virtue, their own ethics.

\*　　\*　　\*

In a man-woman relationship, as in any relationship, there is a great deal one can learn directly. In most relationships between men and women, one person dominates the other. It may shift sides, but, fundamentally, that is how it is. It soon becomes an expedience and there are good times, and there are times which are not so good.

Right relationship between man and woman comes into being when you really care for the other person and you discover that you can be vulnerable. You no longer have to defend yourself. You are not trying to pose that you are different than who you are. You need no one's approval, you are as real as a flower or a tree, for you are totally yourself.

Wouldn't it be nice to have one relationship where you are totally yourself? We are afraid that if we let ourselves be, we would be mean, lazy, casual, and stupid. But I am talking about another spirit within you.

What would it mean for you to be totally vulnerable? Is it possible to shed all pretense? When you have something to give to another, you can be vulnerable for you are no longer dependent. You are who you are and you extend life. That quality of relationship between a man and woman would produce a child who would not know insecurity or wanting.

# CHAPTER FOUR

# 4

## TALKS WITH PARENTS
## Part I

I have been wondering, when does falseness come into the child's mind? How does it begin? In looking at my own life, I see that my mother never assessed, judged, or disapproved of anything that I did. I could be completely open with her about everything. There was no manipulation in it. But I did not have that same feeling of acceptance with my father, because I met my father when I was nine. He was forced to go abroad when I was less than a year old, due to his loyalty to India against the British rule. That is what brought my mother and me to the West – to be with him. I remember observing the process at the forefront of my brain censoring me with, "Don't say that to him. You will get into trouble." It is very swift. The information is sent quickly to the brain and comes out saying something more pleasing. Thus fear, manipulation, and dishonesty come into being.

We have fixed views about things – this is good and that is bad – but the child doesn't know that. The child is innocent. And so the question arises: what is the best way to impart correction? There are areas which need correction or the child may harm himself. But how can we prevent the process of censorship from beginning?

How can we be loyal to spontaneity? How can we ensure that the child feels secure in telling us everything? If there is even one relationship in which the child can be totally himself, then that relationship can provide the space to share any correction needed.

It took my father and I years to come to one mind but my reverence for him freed me from interpreting within myself. Today I feel blessed for having my parents, and twice a day I pray out of a glad heart for their loving care.

> PARENT: I know a young child, a year and a half or two, who is precocious and sensitive. Very quickly she has learned what brings her attention and approval. Prior to the development of language, what she has received from the parents has unwittingly started the censorship. Pleasing others has made her false so that even at this young age she is somewhat cut off from who she is.

Yes, that is very true. Children who are isolated, cut off, crave attention. The parents actually have no real contact with the child. We have to question, how did that falseness come into being? Why is there so little contact? How did the conditioning of the parents, which doesn't allow the space, come into being?

We have to be willing to make correction within ourselves. The potential is there for both the parents and the child to an equal degree.

> PARENT: Yes, the only thing is that the parents are so enamored with their child who is so beautiful and bright, that they don't have any point of reference from which to realize they are probably doing something harmful.

But they are suffocating the child by making her dependent. And then they won't want their child to be with other children, because they are afraid that other children will corrupt her. The problem is not with the child. In reality, the child has no problems, but she will develop problems because the parents have gone overboard. Often the father can provide the balance in families where the mother clings to the child. The whole function of the father is to introduce the child to the outer world – the glory of nature, the glory of God, and how things work.

> PARENT: So what would be helpful is for parents to really observe themselves and see what the dynamic is – what is actually taking place in their relationship with their child or children.

Perhaps someone reading this book may see, "My God, we're doing this to our child!" *A Course In Miracles* explains that unless you bring the error to truth it cannot be undone. [1] Whenever things don't work, one should try to find the cause of the error in oneself. This is difficult for the ego, the personality, to do. It is always going to look outside. Correction is not what the ego is seeking. It wants to blame someone else; it wants to evade responsibility. However, only by being factual and honest can internal issues get corrected.

We saw that falseness begins because the child can't say what he feels in a world of good and bad, in a world where there are consequences. We educate the child with our prejudices, fears, and views. We can't find the space for a miracle in our lives, nor can we find the space to give to our child. Our "knowings" prevail.

We need to recognize – and not merely as an idea – that the child is a part of creation. We may not be able to do anything, but creation would take care. Creation gave the child teeth. If we really knew the child is part of creation, we would know we are not limited to our own resources.

The child is actually a blessing in the parents' lives. Hannah from the Old Testament [2] said she enjoyed Samuel as a child. She did not use the word "enjoy" lightly. It never became attachment. You see, if she had a vacuum in her life she would not have "enjoyed" him, she would have clung to him. If Hannah became attached, Samuel would never have become what he was meant to be. But when she said she enjoyed him, she knew what it was; she gave the child to God and life gave her more children. Can you imagine? She had more joy, for joy multiplies.

If the parents are very wise, they will try not to make the child fearful but awaken his awareness. Correction is a good thing for the parents also. I have observed parents who, as if with a silent hand, cleaned up spilled milk without imposing any fear or guilt in the child who spilled it. That is the kind of correction we must make in ourselves. It could become joyous. Real correction would have to be.

Outgrowing is a great joy. We don't find it to be so, however, because we are afraid of the unknown. Undoing the fear of the unknown *is* the correction. Through that correction we liberate ourselves. The correction is always being presented as an option to outgrow, undo, and receive the miracle or insight. We need never be afraid of the unknown; we need never project. Correction brings one to another state of awareness where both fear and projection cease.

Can we awaken that awareness in the child by the time he comes to puberty? If we don't, the power of the body will be dissipated in sex, pleasure, and outlets. He will be of the earth. The power inherent in the body will start to recreate and reproduce children. But the wise would contain that energy, come to a different awareness, and step out of time and illusion. Without the power of that energy, it is less likely we will know that our Identity is timeless.

I can only recognize that creation is alive in me when I also become creative. Then the conflict ends. As long as I'm in conflict in God's world, I am suffering. The only correction that one needs to make is to discover how the separation came into being.

*PARENT:* That is a bit beyond my grasp.

Possibly, but it starts in a humble way. Can we see that there is always conflict? The conflict is always with the Will of God. That is a principle. We are promoting conflict with the Will of God because we want it to be our way. Yet unless we have the power of awareness intact within us, wanting won't stop because wanting is of the brain.

*PARENT:* Are you saying that when a child who grows up in awareness comes to adolescence, he naturally would aspire to complete awakening? Since that is the Will of God, he would not oppose it. Thus there is no impulse towards conflict.

Yes. And whenever I want to compromise, whenever the conflict starts that is not of God, I can undo it. The Will of God is what gives one the eyes and the teeth. The Will of God provides everything. Wanting things to be different than the way they are is where conflict begins.

*PARENT:* The key that I am missing in what you are sharing is the connection with the purpose of life itself. When that is not made, I cannot be aligned with the Will of God. If I haven't made that connection inside, I will always be in conflict. Parents are raising children to be in conflict with the Will of God because they themselves are not connected.

Yes, that is true. First, it is helpful to see that wanting and projecting promote conflict. If this is seen as a fact, parents can share it with their children, and miracles would be provided for both parents and children to awaken to the resources of creation which are available to them.

*PARENT:* By miracle, do you mean undoing?

Yes. It would undo the conflict within. Parents need never feel helpless. They need never undermine themselves. If they want to give their child something more, if they want to free him, then in trying to impart that, the miracle will happen.

The question that often arises is: "If I'm in conflict, how can I teach my child?" The fact we forget is that the child is not yours. You are the co-creator with God. You can have all the doubt you want about yourself. But if, in your heart, you want your child to be free, when you start explaining about wantings and conflict, the miracles will be given to you. The correction would be total – within the child and within you.

> PARENT: Children seem to have the capa-
> city to grow beyond their heredity and their
> environment. How do parents, in awakening
> themselves, facilitate that?

Parents just need to be receptive to inner correction and want to communicate that with the child.

> PARENT: Parents may not know what it is
> they need to communicate.

I think that the human brain will only know lack, regardless of whether one is a millionaire or a pauper. Yet lack is not real. Life is always expressing itself. Because we believe in lack, we limit our children. Since the brain only knows lack, it is best not to try to be perfect first. If your intent is to communicate to the child, that Creative Force of which both you and your children are a part will offer the miracles, and clarity will be there. Perfection is possible the minute you turn towards love and real faith. If you don't undermine yourself, it is there.

Observe how we create this conflict. Someone was telling me about the difficulty your son is having in school. But, you know, I just couldn't get concerned. I said that he is a bright child, an exceptional child. I cannot accept that the school is right and he is not. Don't you see? That doesn't mean we can't share with him. It is just that I am not going to start a conflict in communicating with him something that neither you, nor he, knows.

Other forces, other laws, are at work. In a strange way, people have destinies, and he has his own destiny. Why get panicky about some difficulty in school? Why blame him? First see that other forces are at work. We cannot do much about how those forces want to educate your son. But because we care, and he is entrusted to us, maybe we can find another way to communicate with him that doesn't start with conflict.

The minute I am in conflict, I am actually in conflict with the Will of God. I am in conflict with the child's destiny, with something over which I have no control. And now I want to correct it. You can only correct it with the knowledge that another Presence is invoked where two and more gather in His Name.[3] A different atmosphere is created with this knowledge.

> PARENT:  But I am not sure that doing noth-
> ing is the right thing. I am not sure what right
> relationship with this issue should be.

Right relationship is not to be in conflict. At this level of duality, there are other forces at work in his not succeeding in school. Seeing this, I relate with him differently. Then how it unfolds is something wonderful to witness because I am never going to depart from trust. When I want to let go of God's wholeness and start my own program, I am deviating from the Will of God.

> PARENT:  I always want to correct the
> externals, don't I?

Yes. That shows you think it should be some other way.

> PARENT:  I can understand it abstractly, but
> I don't understand it with the life of my child.

I will help you see how simple it is. If you are at peace with the way things are, you will say to your son, "It's okay. We can deal with whatever the issue is." If a child tells me he doesn't want to go to school, I say, "Don't go to school." That brings my relationship with the child to a different level. Once that relationship is firmly established – that *he* is important to me, not external rules – then maybe we can even end his conflict about going to school.

Since I'm not going to start an additional conflict, there might be some potential to end his conflict also. The guideline always is that you are not going to get into conflict with the way things are. "Thy Will be done." What power there would be. You don't appease the child, and you don't feel upset. And you're not going to deviate from this clarity because there are other potentials that you need to discover.

> *PARENT:* Yes. Because I'm not really in touch with the Will of God, it seems that…

Yes, but you are in touch with the Will of God when you say you are not going to start a conflict. Without the Will of God, could you ever succeed in that? Observe how it unfolds every single moment. At every step you are going to be with the Will of God.

I wonder if there are problems in the Will of God? Or, if one sees inconsistencies and problems, I wonder how It would solve them? Gandhi realized that non-violence is for those who have courage because they will remain consistent no matter what anyone else does.

Jesus said that if somebody takes your coat, give him the cloak also. [4] Can you stay with the perfection of the Will of God? Who knows: In the one action of being at peace with the way things are, you may give your son more than twenty universities could. We undermine the child, we undermine our own selves, and then we want to make correction. But that is not the way to correct anything.

We don't make demand of the power within the body to silence the brain, to undo what the brain is thinking, projecting, and wanting. And the brain's conclusions are meaningless. We must make that demand. The power not to deviate is there for us all the time; we can't limit it. If you've got it, then you've got it to give to your son. Do you think the Will of God won't help you? As you are helped, so is your child. Then he will pass on something that is far superior to anything the school will ever teach him. And maybe that is the only thing he needs to learn. It becomes something vast, even though it's very small.

PARENT: Yes, because it introduces both of us to a different potential.

Absolutely. And now you are making demand of that potential. The minute you react, or the minute you disapprove, it's a contradiction. The only way to be free of conflict is to be at peace with things as they are. That is actually what we need to impart to the child. If this is our intent, something else will take place involuntarily, but not through words.

PARENT: There are parents who have children twelve to fifteen years old and they may not have done certain kinds of preparation. If they could be receptive to making contact with God's Will in the situation facing them, would another energy be there to help them?

Yes, because by approaching it this way, you have already prepared the ground in which there is love, rather than fear.

PARENT: Just by not reacting?

Yes. When you are receptive, the atmosphere is not one of panic. It's not negative or hopeless.

PARENT: That contact does provide something else. I can see that. Then although the child is failing in school, or is involved in something that externally may seem quite alarming, if the parents can make that contact, other resources are available?

Yes, the parents must put away their judgment. Because we live only at one level, the children know exactly what we are going to do. Everybody is predictable. We resist stepping into the unknown that is not predictable. The only thing we do not know is love. Love is not in conflict.

I think the child would never forget that someone cared for him. It is really worth everything. What does it matter in the long run if he passes an exam or not? More than fifty million people got high grades. So what! A child who is sensitive will probably rebel against the regimentation of the system. Somewhere he needs a friend. The only friend is something called love.

\*    \*    \*

If I could see the fact that my conclusions, opinions, assumptions, and feelings are not reliable because they are partial, I would not condemn myself. I would be grateful, because this is the first sign that I am waking up. I would not move into "feelings" at all.

Feelings always evade facing a fact. Until we see a fact as a fact, nothing changes. What will happen when we see the fact remains unknown because it is something we have never done. This gets uncomfortable because we have always been shown a "carrot" to motivate us.

At this point the only thing we can do is see that partial attention cannot know truth. For a moment one sees, "My God, all my life I have so deceived myself with partial attention that now I'm not capable of knowing what is

Absolute. I don't know what truth, forgiveness, love, or real goodness are."

What I would like you to do is this: bring your mind to the fact. Then tell me, when you see the fact, is there thought? Are there feelings? I don't think so. What would it take for you to bring your mind to the integrity of stillness where it could observe the fact – the fact of your relationship with your husband, with your wife, with your parents, with your children? What is the fact of these relationships?

Partial attention has no integrity; it always concludes. The fact itself has the power to free us from any conclusion. Thought cannot touch a fact. The fact will introduce us to another intelligence, another energy called awareness which is free of personality and feeling. It is independent of hopelessness or enthusiasm.

Rarely have we come upon a fact and its direct energy. Love of honesty is not yet awakened in us. If you have seen a fact, your behavior changes. You would never need to advertise it or try to impress others; everyone will know by the effect it has had on you.

\* \* \*

## THE CREATIVE ACTION OF LIFE

Pregnancy is an involuntary, creative action of life. The body has very little to do with it. When the child is born, he becomes an extension of that creative action. If conception takes place at 11:37 p.m., from that moment on, for the next eighty years that the child is going to live, that same involuntary, creative action will go on in him.

During the nine months of pregnancy, the creative action goes on perfecting itself in the womb until the child is ready to be born. It is not just the father's seed that started it; it is not just the mother's womb that nourished and carried it. There is something much more significant in this involuntary action of life which also gave birth to the parents.

Without this involuntary action, there would have been no conception. When the involuntary action takes place, it is meant to awaken the parents to another Reality.

You can experience that involuntary action when the birth of a child takes place. Because it is your direct experience, you make contact with something that is eternal, something of life itself. Before you didn't know it, but now you do. How could you ever forget it? You would think we would yearn to be connected with that action again, now that we know it is there. However, we would have to be very wise and unselfish to maintain that contact.

Because our focus is primarily on the sexual experience, we are producing a civilization of mercenaries who exploit and destroy the earth. Isn't that what is happening? And now, this child whom you love so much is going to be conditioned, shaped, and molded by society. Where is your love? If the parents knew that this child was part of the involuntary action of life, they would be the custodian of that action of life in the child.

What will you give to the child who is entrusted to you? Can you keep his innocence intact? Who gives the child insecurity? The parents. We spend a great part of our adult life trying to return to innocence but it is almost impossible because our brain cells are thoroughly conditioned.

*A Course In Miracles* starts with undoing. And it affirms life by introducing you to being part of the Mind of God. [5] But we can't accept that. What have we done to ourselves? We are training our children to be separated. We destroy the innocence of the child and it doesn't bother us. Why is it that we don't need contact with the involuntary action that started conception and looked after the child in the womb?

> PARENT: In all my life until now, I never even knew what an involuntary action was.

Now do you see what it is?

*PARENT:* Yes. Now I see it.

One can see it very simply in the fact that when the child is born, there is milk in the mother's breast to feed it. Life protects the child. The mother and child need not worry, or ever be insecure. And when the child is ready for a different kind of food – which this involuntary action of life also provides in the garden – the teeth magically start to appear. Need we worry about anything when life is taking care?

> *PARENT:* I see that action clearly working in other people's lives. But I don't know how to nurture it in myself so that I'm living in relationship to it.

You will nurture it if you don't have options to recognizing its presence in your life. If you have options, then these words are just more knowledge.

We have seen the fact that partial attention has nothing to do with truth. If that is your fact, that fact will not allow you to accept options. Now you can observe how insecurity is going to convince you otherwise. Watch the drama. Fear is going to try to talk you into options. Pleasure will try to talk you into options. Watch it. This is the voice of the ego, the voice of the personality. Once you have come upon the fact, however, it will be hard for you to listen to the voice of the ego.

> *PARENT:* Does one need a teacher to awaken?

Yes. Without the relationships with Mr. J. Krishnamurti and Dr. Helen Schucman, the scribe of *A Course In Miracles*, or the teachers I knew in India, I don't think I would be anywhere.

First we have to recognize that we live by desire. Because we always want something, we are in a state of unfulfillment, partial attention, and half-truths. We want "something else" to achieve whatever we think we need. Partial attention is always seeking "moreness." Don't you want to read more, learn more? We always feel that if we had better circumstances we could do it. But partial attention and unfulfillment are one and the same thing. They are perpetually in activity.

Now this has come to your attention and you don't know what to do. I say, if you have no other option and you will not accept anything that activity is going to tell you, some other relationship will start to awaken. The activity of the brain is going to say, "I need more time; I need more education; I need a teacher."

With the attention you give it, the *little willingness* [6] can undo the options as they arise. You won't be so easily fooled by activity. You become master over the externals; they can no longer mislead you. When this clarity is received, it's a certainty. It's there before you. You become aware of it, and that awareness expands involuntarily and affects all the cells of the brain. A mutation takes place.

When you have no options your mind is still. Your little willingness will keep you alert and let the purity of silence work. Help is always a correction that takes place within if you have the capacity to receive it. The little willingness doesn't require that you do anything. It merely requires that you be aware. Awareness has the space to allow the correction to take place. There is nothing to seek. By seeing the fact, you purify your mind of all you learned that was not true. Then you have grown and come to your own newness, to rebirth. This is resurrection. Each one of us can do it if we so will.

It is of primary importance that we heal ourselves, that we come to correction within ourselves. The ego wants to do this at first. Then it says, "Well, maybe I can do it next week, next year, later on." But we are never in control of the "later on."

\* \* \*

Someone told me that because my mother gave me so much space and love, I keep on extending that love. They never received that kind of love from their mother. I said, "No, don't put me on a pedestal." You can't blame your mother forever, because every seven years all of the cells of the body change. By now you should have changed your view. Heredity can be undone. In America there is a trend toward blaming one's parents for everything. That is not so in other cultures. Here the errors are magnified and, therefore, they become blocks to your awareness of the Self. If you doubt your brother or your mother, you are magnifying whatever error you think they made and this becomes a block to the knowledge of your own God-created Self. You are only harming yourself.

We have to see that the only right response to life is gratefulness. Either you are grateful or there is ingratitude. Ingratitude is as detrimental as unwillingness. I don't think we realize how vicious it is. There is no way one can even think of salvation or sanity where there is ingratitude. Ingratitude is self-destructive, because it denies the good in the world. It cannot trust.

It is important to see that this is how the human brain works in the absence of awareness. We don't even know what awareness is. We just condemn ourselves. First you were blaming your brother; now you are blaming yourself. That is no improvement; it is not a release. The action that will make a correction will be born out of awareness, not thought. As long as you are not aware, your tendencies take over. When it becomes a real need for you to call on another power within yourself, you will put the energy behind it.

Very few of us discover the vitality of awareness, a state of being in which there is no interpretation or time. It transmits the creative energy of eternity and effects a change equivalent to rebirth. "Having the ears to hear" [7] brings one to full attention where the Given is received and instantly brought into application. Transformation is instantaneous. It is an awakening in which neither effort nor personality is involved.

\*   \*   \*

*PARENT:* Is it detrimental to use consequences to teach children? Sometimes I tell
Cliff, "Don't run away from me or you won't
go swimming tonight." Is that creating a
negative motivation for him?

It is easy to give advice, isn't it? First and foremost, could
we see Cliff as the perfect Son of God? Then we can see what
stimulation does to that perfect being. We can question the
factors that are detrimental to him and to you as his parents
but we have no right to question what God created. Then our
approach to correction would be very different, wouldn't it?

Now our approach has changed but we still don't know
what to do because, somewhere, we are so afraid of uncertainty. Because we are afraid of uncertainty, we must conclude.
We are like a drowning person in a sea of uncertainty; we are
not going to do anything intelligent.

Can we begin to see the virtue in uncertainty? Maybe in
uncertainty, you could deal with your fear. You cannot deal
with fear unless you have trust in something else – some other
perfection, some other intelligence, something called God.
Through uncertainty you can open to willingness, which
would introduce you to other forces at work in your life. When
I asked Mr. J. Krishnamurti, "Is it true, sir, that life takes care?"
he answered, "Yes, if you *completely* let go."

Let us leave Cliff alone for the moment. He is perfect. Let's
discover the factors that make me uncertain, make me panic
and feel helpless because I don't know what to do. Unless I
am at peace with uncertainty, I won't know anything other
than what I already know. If I go to the experts, they are going
to give me an expedient answer. There is no truth in
expedience. It has no relationship with life.

To be in relationship with life implies that you are not
afraid to be uncertain. Can we give that space to ourselves and

to our children? Otherwise, everything will be a conclusion – old advice.

We begin to see that this situation with Cliff is beyond you, beyond "this" versus "that." We want him to behave. But children who are not stimulated are not going to be any better than he is. It is likely their lives will also be false. The well-behaved child is also going to get drafted into school. We want to change the behavior of the child but we don't want to change ourselves so that we are free to be our own person. Both parents are victims of the world. And within that framework they want to straighten out the child so that he learns to behave.

Cliff is hyperactive. His nervous system is made that way. But if he was in a natural environment, with goats and sheep and mud and geese and rabbits, everything would get balanced. That would be a compatible environment for him. But now he is living in a city, and that is part of the difficulty. This environment excites and stimulates. Let's look at the impact of the environment first. It is wiser to be aware of the factors at work rather than to blame him.

There are always going to be factors in our lives that limit what we can do. The world is getting more and more that way. And so we have to prepare our children to fit into a world that demands conformity. If we become aware that these things are detrimental to Cliff's temperament, at least we're not blaming him. We will try to be helpful in a different way.

If you don't react to Cliff's hyperactivity, maybe in the evening when he's home and somewhat calmer you can have better communication with him. The pulse gets slower as the sun goes down. This communication has to be established with the child so that you can include him in whatever decisions you make. Don't impose a decision upon him. Let him see that you are his friend and want to help him. This is going to be very difficult, because children are very quick. They know from your tone of voice if you are sad, angry, or impatient. The quality of your voice has an effect on the solar plexus.* If your solar plexus is not receptive to the child, you can teach all you want, but he will only know that you are an authority.

The energetic quality of the solar plexus resembles fine, wiry hairs. It is a kind of light that goes out and encircles the other person. If I like Kenna, my solar plexus goes towards her. It envelops and comforts her if she is in crisis or need. Have you ever noticed that if you suddenly get shocked by something, you feel it in the solar plexus not in the head? It is not a faculty of the brain. Your son will sense the fact of how you are responding to him from your solar plexus. If you really care for him irrespective of his behavior, your solar plexus will invite his solar plexus.

When a baby nurses, the energy of his solar plexus is wrapped all around the mother, and the mother's is wrapped all around the baby. When you really care for someone, it takes place automatically.

The child is all right; it is the environment that needs correction. We also need to change so that our solar plexus reaches out, rather than our merely giving advice and threats. The child is going to get a lot of advice in the world. But at least he will know that somewhere there was something a little different.

If Cliff had a bath in the evening and a good massage with peanut oil on his spine and solar plexus, he would begin to relax. We have to understand his temperament to be able to help him. The other thing is both you and your husband should pray over him when he sleeps. Sit together beside the bed and very lovingly pray: "THE LORD BLESS THEE, AND KEEP THEE: THE LORD MAKE HIS FACE SHINE UPON THEE, AND BE GRACIOUS UNTO THEE: THE LORD LIFT UP HIS COUNTENANCE UPON THEE, AND GIVE THEE PEACE."[8] As you pray, the Presence that accompanies this prayer would slow his pulse and bring him to peace.

---

* The large network of sympathetic nerves situated at the upper part of the abdomen.

Make very, very sure not to make him too dependent on you. If you become dependent on the child, you are using him to fill your own emptiness. Attachment cripples a child. You are the custodian; the child doesn't belong to anyone but God. Everything has to be somewhat normal. Children love danger; they love exploring; they love adventure. If you deprive them of that, they will never be interested in anything. It is not easy to bring up a child because it demands that the parents fundamentally change.

Also, you have to have some space for yourself. If you don't have space for yourself you are going to get annoyed. Don't make the child the god. You are not any less important. You need time for yourself in order to transmit something else to him. That is why extended families are so necessary – aunts, uncles, grandparents, close friends.

It is our responsibility to provide affection for our children. Affection is *sattvic*.* Attachment is exactly the opposite. It requires tremendous discrimination to know which is which. When we are attached we demand conformity. Affection gives a lot of space to the child.

The solution starts when we change our values. We must begin to love ourselves. Unless we find our own peace and beauty within, there will always be problems. We will naturally begin to love ourselves, though, as our lives move toward virtue and ethics.

\* \* \*

*BOBBIE:* My son will be eighteen in May. He is leaving for college in September. I get caught in the guilt of the errors that I made, but I'm looking at the fact that I give authority to everyone and everything outside of myself. Everything I do is to please other people, to be acceptable. When I became a mother I became

---

\* An atmosphere of purity, balance, and wisdom.

an authority. I am caught in the conflict of wanting to have some authority of my own, but using him because I feel so worthless to others. I also feel, after meeting you, that my responsibility is to undo why I feel helpless and unworthy and to help him to undo that also. My biggest dilemma is that I don't ever let myself be okay and I exploit my son to reflect well on me. I have forced him to be something that gives me worth, and this has hampered both of us.

My dear Bobbie, failure, negativity, and resistance are of thought; they are not a fact. We can interpret everything. It may not be so. Truth is so far removed from our interpretations. I don't think any one of us have had a natural, gracious, and godly upbringing. We have bodies. And they present challenges. But we can be grateful that every seven years our cells change, and your son has the potential to change. It is so pointless to torment ourselves with the perfection we project. Our torment also gets transmitted to the child.

I am sure that you have made mistakes. And I am sure that your son has made mistakes. But I am also sure that there is love and there is care.

One can communicate with a grown-up child. We can share with him that we are not perfect and neither is the world. We all make mistakes. He will make mistakes, too. We can overlook them as long as we try to work with our tendencies. Do you know that I have enjoyed my mistakes much more than my virtues? Sure! I'm not going to be anti-mistakes. There are so many other factors in human relationship, and nature compensates for a lot of the wrong things we do. Life takes care. It becomes part of the fun.

It is natural for things to change. After your children are grown and you have more time, maybe you can introduce them to some peace within you that you have found by relating with something of creation, something that is not man-made. That is the biggest challenge in this sophisticated society.

Children today are not going to be all that receptive to wisdom because it makes demands on them. They will tend to go to the easier side of the easy, which is emotion, gratification, and sensation. We must keep a parallel movement going toward inner awakening.

\*   \*   \*

### "DO ONLY THAT"

The Text of *A Course In Miracles* states: *A wise teacher teaches through approach, not avoidance. He does not emphasize what you must avoid to escape from harm...* [9] A child may never know what harm is unless you make him aware of harm. Therefore, you are teaching the child harm, aren't you?

> JOHN:   I see that when I explain something to Crystal that has to do with avoidance, I fall into the pattern of explaining. "Do this, but watch out for that." Or, "Don't do this because this is going to happen." It becomes an "or else" situation. I think that if I tell her all of this, she will be better prepared if I am not around to protect her.

That is the assumption, isn't it? And we don't know any other way. How would love do it? Love would have space. But in the absence of love, there is not the space. And whatever you are going to do is going to be an expedience in your favor at the expense of the child. You use consequences as an expedience. You introduce fear and "or else" because you do not have time to give to the child. You've got more important things to do. For me there is no more important thing when Crystal is there.

> *JOHN:* Don't children need to know what
> the consequences will be if they deviate from
> what they were told to do?

This is what the Course is saying. It says, *A wise teacher teaches through approach, not avoidance.* A wise teacher would say, *"Do only that,"* [10] not, "Don't do that." Can you make that switch within yourself? Then when you say, *"Do only that,"* your love is going to give expression to it. When you say, "Don't do that," you are putting an "or else" into it.

Years ago I met a forest ranger in Tahoe City, California. He was a very wise person. He had two children and he was so gentle and spacious with them. If they were driving down the road and happened to see a car stopped, he would say, "Nathan, let's see if they need help." That child was learning to give, to observe, and to respond.

It is always best to include the child in exploring decisions beforehand. If they understand it, they will agree. If you want your child to find his or her own strength you cannot make the relationship with the child an expedience. The need to awaken strength in the child is essential. It's a joint venture, and I have found that children heed when they are included in the decisions.

One time I said to Crystal, "Please be kind to your parents, especially your mother." Crystal is very strong-headed, very determined. She has enormous goodness and she likes to help. I said, "Crystal, you have one of the best mothers. Please don't take her for granted." Two months later we were sitting on the staircase and I happened to ask her, "Crystal, have you been nice to your mother?" Well, she started to cry. She cried and cried inconsolably. I didn't know what had happened, so I just held her. When she finally calmed down I asked her why she was crying so hard. She said, "You had to tell me a second time."

Once I asked her, "Crystal, if I ask you to do something, would you want explanations, or would you just do it?" She said, "No. I would just do it."

I just have to say once to her, *"Do only that,"* and she listens. There is no conflict in her because there is none in me. By the same token, I don't point things out to her at every turn.

When the child has respect for the parents, he or she would cooperate. The mother and the father must have this quality of reverence for each other also because the child is impressionable. Reverence says, "Come, let's water the plant because it is withering. We will do it together."

When a child knows he can manipulate you, he loses respect. The child brings the parents to maturity. The primary needs of the child are met by life, but the child needs your wisdom. We never realized that we had to provide the wisdom and the integrity of true thought.

*       *       *

There are billions of people upon the planet and only a very small percentage are aware that they cannot trust their own voice or anyone else's because their words do not mean anything.

In order to have our own voice, we have to have something of our own that is related to Reality rather than to emotions, moods, advantages, preferences, choices, and circumstances.

How then are we going to read *I will step back and let Him lead the way* [11] in *A Course In Miracles*? Who is going to step back? Every single thing that the partial human voice is going to say is a lie. This is a realization everyone has to make. We are all the same, for there is only "one brain." The brain cannot say anything that is true; it can only say what it has been taught to say, conditioned to say. We have limited ourselves to the intelligence and energy of the earth.* How degrading it is! We do not kill animals and eat them raw anymore. But civilized man does worse by exploiting his fellowman. Look at the weapons he has developed. Do you think any animal would do what we have done?

Look at what the corporations are doing. If something goes wrong with a product, it is your problem. There are very few places where one is treated like a human being. There used to be some pride, some personal contact. Now there is utter lack of courtesy. As long as we are ruled by our body voices, it will be difficult to change this. But the world is crying for us to bring about something very different.

> PARENT: You say you cannot trust the body's voice. Do we need to get rid of the body voice or evolve beyond it?

If you were to see that your voice has no meaning, you would begin to ask yourself, "How did I become so distorted psychologically?" The animal is not insane, the plant is not insane, the moon and the stars are not insane – only the human being is. Psychological images and fears have damaged us.

Seeing this you would try to bring your child up in an environment in which there are no psychological pressures and projected fears. If you felt responsible for the elimination of your own confusion, your own images, your own opinions and assumptions, you would come to silence. That would be true.

We have to question and dissolve our own thought. This questioning is essential. *I will step back and let Him lead the way* means that I do not heed my own thought.

---

* For a detailed exploration of "earth forces," see "*Why Has There Always Been War In The World?*" in *The Future Of Mankind – Affluence Without Wisdom Is Self-Destructive* by Tara Singh (Life Action Press, 1992). (Editor)

Having discovered *My thoughts do not mean anything,* [12] you no longer depend on them. You allow a new light to come in. This outgrowing must take place before we can hear the voice for God. The rest is already perfect, already accomplished. The issue of insecurity does not apply. When our brain thought is silent, we walk with God in perfect holiness. [13]

> *PARENT:* Where did man's imperfection come from? He has this beautiful instrument, the body, but where did the imperfection come from?

Fear. When the psychological issues about tomorrow came in, fear came in. But, in reality, it does not exist. I am alive only in the present. Tomorrow is always a projection; it is not real. As long as I am preoccupied with the brain, I will never know the holiness and sacredness of my being.

We have to come to innocence for anything new to happen. We cannot seem to let go of what we know, and therefore we are caught in a trap. First, we must start with recognizing how the brain regulates us. Fear has a big family, a virtual Pentagon. Its many colors, shapes, and vibrations must be cleansed for our brain to come to newness. The action starts with you. And you have all the potentials and resources you need.

When the brain begins to see the deceptions inherent in thought, it becomes sensitive and wise. Then the Mind and the brain have a relationship because the brain extends that which is of the Mind; it is not preoccupied with its own fears and projections. Each of us is responsible for whatever we put into the brain. That is our first responsibility.

We have to see how heavily conditioned we are, how caught we are in insanity. Someone asked Mr. Krishnamurti, "How did you give up the whole organization surrounding you?" He said, "It was an action free of consequences." Can we come to that? No more consequences. I am not going to manipulate or be manipulated. *I will step back and let Him lead the way.* [14]

Could you observe the cleverness of the brain? Don't judge. Just observe how deeply selfish one is, how deeply regulated by habits. In awareness there is freedom. The minute you want to act differently, you have started the activity of the brain. Could you give yourself a day just to question? It would transform your life.

*   *   *

## STATUS QUO

The human brain resists seeing the *status quo*, the actuality of "what is." The brain does not know fulfillment. It does not know a state which has no lack. It must interfere. It must either possess or escape. And it is nearly impossible in this state of wrong-mindedness to correct wrong-mindedness. The brain will always project another activity, and we will probably die that way. Seeing this you begin to value the company and friendship of someone wise.

If I knew a wise being, I would not necessarily have a profound question to ask. I would not seek an answer to anything. I would just want to be shown the status quo without wanting to change things.

Five minutes with a wise person is all you need. If only you could get a glimpse of the status quo, the realization of it would energize you; the very truth of it would cleanse the earth through you. The status quo has energy. It does not have any wantings, any projections. It is just "what is." We want results, which require effort. When you seek a result you are going to get on all fours, labor, and struggle to get there. When you get there you will want another result.

A parent cannot have control over the child; nor would it be wise if he did. You just have to accept the status quo. Out of the status quo something new will be revealed that your brain did not project or know.

> PARENT: When you share something that has this depth of meaning to it, thought cannot really understand it. We think we hear you but we are hearing according to our own patterns of thought. It helped when you emphasized the importance of recognizing one's frailty – that we cannot bring about correction ourselves.

Yes. Arrogance would say that you can control the situation. This is folly. Within the realm of time and personality, the brain wants to make corrections, but these are not corrections at all, they are, again, projections of the personality.

> PARENT: You have pointed out that the brain, even at a subtle level, will always make a problem and then try to seek a solution. It stays within that range.

The minute the brain projects a problem, it must seek a solution. Being with the status quo is the only thing that doesn't seek a solution. It is independent of that.

> PARENT: I see that very few people ever move beyond the realm of problem and solution, which seem to have varying levels of contentment. But it is still coming from a place that will create another problem. I see if we could allow ourselves to acknowledge the status quo...

Which is difficult, because we cannot really be honest.

> PARENT: If we could allow that, however, then we would have let go somewhere inside, and another force could start to express.

Yes. Otherwise the only energy we have, the only force we have, is that of thought. The minute you go towards thought, you are denied. At the personality level – the level of illusion and time – we deliberately oppose the Will of God with thought. This is the only insanity.

We believe in helplessness; we do not believe in trust. We believe in everything the brain formulates; we don't believe in undoing the brain thought. Therefore, we are afraid to make contact with the Holy Spirit. The Holy Spirit would relate us with *I will not value what is valueless.* [15] It would relate us with Eternal Laws.

What is the status quo? It begins with the fact at the level of the senses. It starts simply. "I have a son who is sixteen. I want to direct him and I cannot control him. He is saying, 'Go to hell.'" To the degree you are attached to him, it is a shock. That is part of the status quo. The status quo is that the child is growing up in a society that is so externalized there is nothing you can do. And it is a society that is intolerant of anything that is different.

If parents do not know humanity, they will try to put the boy in a box. But he is not any better controlled by the parents than by society. It is the same thing. If the parents' control were good – if control can ever be good – there would be no danger in his being controlled. But external control is always dangerous.

The status quo relates you with all of mankind, until you begin to see that there is only one man in the world. Everyone has the same traits. All of society is separated. Who is going to protect the child from his parents?

When you learn what the status quo is you respond adequately to it because you are not seeking results. But we do not know what the status quo is and so we don't have an adequate response to it. We are so limited. If we knew the status quo we would be very inspired, and the brain could no longer make things little. We could cope, for our horizon has broadened.

This adequate response is the only relationship. It is a relationship between the Son and the Father – with "what is." It has no problems; it seeks no solution. It responds adequately and awakens you.

When you have seen the status quo you will not only have something to give to your child, you will have something to give to all other children as well. You will have understood something fundamental in relationship with the externals.

The status quo frees one of everything external to God. Then your response is not an individual response; it is the response of life itself to illusion. Without recognizing the status quo, no one is wise.

The world of illusion has opposites. The status quo does not have an opposite. You see things as they are. That is all. It will transform you when you no longer meddle in it. When you see the status quo and do not want to change it, it sets you outside the movement of time. You are not being affected by it or seeking to improve it. Because you are uninvolved you are the Light of the world. That state can only be known when you have gone past duality and see life. Then there is one person who is not affected by the illusion of time. You do not seek and you do not have problems.

*   *   *

Yesterday when we took the Indian sweets to the children, Scott virtually attacked the other boys, who are attending this Retreat with their families. They didn't react, but I thought, "Someday this child is going to meet someone who will teach him a lesson." We are all trying to prevent that. Otherwise, it is likely he will draw punishment to himself. We are too idealistic. It may be necessary to face the fact that although punishment is wrong, there is a need for correction. This opens up a different vista, a new perspective.

*LAURA:* I have been taking care of Scott and the other children recently. Are you saying that we should correct his behavior more?

I think we are limiting ourselves by thinking that correcting him is punishment.

*LAURA:* When in actuality it is not?

Yes. What you call punishment, I call correction. I want to question that set of words. Instead of punishment, let's call it correction and see that unless we help him correct, there are going to be consequences. If we neglect our responsibility there will be consequences.

*LAURA:* It makes me think of an experience I had with Scott when I took care of him on Saturday. He and the other children ran away from the dinner table. The rules were established that if Scott or the other children did that, then the rest of the meal was to be taken in his room. And so I took him to his room. I wanted to call my mother and have her bring our meals to the room, but every time I went to pick up the phone he ran for the door. I couldn't believe what I did. I picked him up, carried him over to the couch, and held him firmly, but gently, down. I told him I needed to make the phone call and that he needed to be still. Within thirty seconds he stopped struggling and melted into my arms.

It may have seemed like punishment but it really was correction. He tried it only one more time and then it never happened again. For the rest of the day he never again tried to run off. In fact, his sister started running off and he just stood there beside me while I went to bring her back. He responded so beautifully to being corrected, much better than any of us had anticipated.

One aspect of correction is that we always include the child when he is somewhat calm, not when he is hysterical or accelerated. We need to help the child be in charge of his impulses and urges, for he doesn't understand consequences. That is awakening natural intelligence. You and the child need to work together on awakening this new faculty of awareness or responsibility.

So you can tell Scott, "When you want to give in to your impulses and urges, we are going to help you stop. Would you cooperate with me and stop?" There must be mutual agreement that this pattern has to stop. After it is explained, I think he would agree. If he doesn't agree, you must try again the next day until he begins to understand. What he will understand beyond the words is that your action is born of love. That is the fact, and the correction is a strength to him. We want him to come to a point that when the impulse tries to control him, this other intelligence can be in charge. Then as he grows, he will become the master of himself.

You must include him and ask him how you can help him when the urges try to control him. In this way it will not be a surprise. Children have great strength to rise to something once they know you are not angry or unfair with them.

He will probably say, "I will listen when you tell me," but obviously any child is going to get taken over. And you have to patiently begin again so he knows that you mean what you say. We must act out of love, not reaction.

> LAURA: I saw it was helpful for Scott to know what was expected of him. On Saturday I told him that I really expected him to walk with me to the dining room and if it helped him to hold my hand in order to remember, he could do that. There was a time when he started to walk ahead. I stopped him and held his hand

and we sat down on the couch. He said, "Okay,
I'll stay with you." He has walked beside me on
his own since then. We have seen that change
is possible.

Punishment is a bad thing. But because parents love the
child they are responsible to make corrections. Without
discipline, life becomes irresponsible.

# CHAPTER FIVE

# 5

EDUCATION —
HAVING SOMETHING OF ONE'S OWN
TO GIVE

There is a lovely scene that the artist Nicholas Roerich* describes from his years in the Himalayas. He was in a village and met a young boy from the area. As they were talking, a man passed by. This boy, who was about ten or twelve, took off his little cap and bowed, offering his respect to the gentleman.

Roerich asked the boy, "Who was that man?"

The boy answered, "He is a teacher."

"He is your teacher?"

"No, sir, he is a teacher."

Without reverence, one cannot receive the truth.

Mr. J. Krishnamurti often remarked that teaching is the highest profession. We have little knowledge or understanding of the teaching to which he is referring. The role of a

_____
* Nicholas Roerich (1874-1947) was born in St. Petersburg, Russia. He came to America in 1920 and is well known for his luminous landscapes. The Roerich Museum in New York houses many of his finest works.

teacher is to awaken the student to the knowledge of his true identity as God created him.

*     *     *

Originally education started with the few who were wise and related to the sacredness of life. Because they knew that life provided, their slightest need was met by Divine Forces. They were not touched by a sense of lack; therefore, they had something to teach. What they taught was service – service to the Lord. They were a direct extension of the Will of God and they were serving that Will. They could receive the Given and instantly extend It in one action, for in it there was no memory.

As time went on and commercialization came into being, people lost the capacity to receive the Given. Today what is taught is only of the brain. It is not something we have simultaneously received and shared. What is received can only be shared; it cannot be commercialized. No one who knows the Truth can ever commercialize it, for they know that the Name of God cannot be sold.

The sages, the saints, and the teachers of God served God, and they served man by giving him True Knowledge. They transmitted their peace and created an atmosphere in which one could rest one's mind.

Wise parents took their children to such sages, or *rishis*,* during the Vedic age and the age of the Upanishads. In historical times the earnest student went to Socrates, to Jesus, or, during the time of the Pharaoh, to the enlightened High Priest, to be awakened from within. The student went with reverence to serve. He served the teacher who brought the Will of God and the sacredness of the student's own life to his awareness. He loved the holiness that surrounded his teacher far more than anything else on the earth.

---

* Ancient Hindu wise man of exceptional authority.

Reverence is the natural response for someone who awakens you, who shares all his wealth and the treasures of Heaven with you. Reverence is not something of the brain. It is not something you try to do. It has to be spontaneous, non-manipulative.

Once the teacher united the student with the sacredness of Life, the student became the teacher with something of his own to give. And so it went, on and on, as the Light of the Kingdom was brought to the planet. Kings bowed before these servants of the Lord who were in love with simplicity, space, and wisdom.

"GOD IS LOVE; AND HE THAT ABIDETH IN LOVE ABIDETH IN GOD, AND GOD IN HIM."[1]

Unity is a word we have lost contact with. All we know is separation. What the world calls education today is deadly. It has made man's greed more efficient. It has made hate and violence more competent and has imposed insecurity upon the human being. Individual human life has been made secondary. The violence, disorder, and fragmentation within the individual are increasing as there is more and more distance between man and man, between man and nature.

Today there are few teachers that serve. Our teachers are educated; they live in the realm of the illusions of the brain with its problems.

*     *     *

In ancient times, parents brought about a pure, sattvic atmosphere in their home. When a child was born they knew it was their responsibility to provide that atmosphere. They raised their children with a great deal of affection and tenderness. The essence of their relationship was givingness. Through their example the child learned the ways of reverence, thoughtfulness, and obedience.

The peace of obedience is merited by both the child and parents, for each inspires the other. It is an internal interaction, a bond between the two that makes them one. How lofty the parents would have to be, and by what rightness they would have to live, to merit the gentle purity of obedience.

The endearing words of an authentic voice strengthen the child so that he does not contradict or violate the impersonal holiness of the moment. As a child, I used to feel so elated to be obedient. It gave one such a sense of dignity. We no longer impart that to our children and our culture reflects it.

The work of the parents was to prepare the child so that he could be taken to the rishi, the wise person to whom True Knowledge came naturally. What heavenly Presences must have surrounded him. When the parents left the child with the teacher, they said, "We have given birth to your body. We have prepared you. But the teacher is your real father and mother because he will awaken your spirit and relate you with the wholeness of creation – to love, to light, to truth." The child lived with the teacher and he was introduced to a love unlike anything he had ever known before.

The parents could do nothing wiser than to find a teacher who would awaken their child. You may have had a thousand different parents but you will only know one teacher who will relate you to God. Even in *A Course In Miracles*, it is said that *God gives special gifts to His teachers, because they have a special role in His plan for Atonement.* [2]

Little Crystal came to see me yesterday but she was not well. When children are ill they have a certain peace about them. She sat on my lap on the staircase and told me she really wanted to go to school to be with the children. I said, "Well, we will have to replace that loss with stories." She laughed and was glad that there was givingness. I asked her, "Crystal, do you know what humility is?" It is very difficult to explain this to a child because we don't really know it; we just think we do. If we knew it, it would be one of the first things we would teach the child.

I said to Crystal, "Humility is beyond right and wrong. For example, Jesus said that if someone takes your coat, you should give him your cloak also. If someone hits you on your right cheek, you should turn to him the left also.[3] That is humility." Schools do not teach humility. Schools foster "me and mine."

Jesus never defended himself. He said:

"...RESIST NOT EVIL."[4]

That is sattvic purity. That is humility.

I have observed that as soon as a child attains a certain age, selfishness and manipulation begin to predominate. It is only a formality to try to introduce him to the sattvic. It doesn't get through. From a certain point on, you can't have that relationship with the child. They become clever because the impurities have set in. Of course you love them and care for them and there are always other factors beyond the senses, but it is much more difficult to impart something timeless unless they have been prepared and have reverence for truth. They are preoccupied with the senses and they are not interested in the sattvic anymore than you or I.

When I first came to Ojai, California, there was a river running near the main road. About fifteen years ago the river was diverted by a dam. Pretty soon the bed became overgrown with shrubs and bushes and now it is difficult to tell that there was once a river there. That is what has happened to our relationship with our real nature. We are taken over by the externals and have forgotten that there is a light in us.

Something happens in nature, however, at dawn and at twilight, that has the power to relate us to this sattvic quality. At these times it is easier to make contact with that state.

PARENT: What about those children who haven't been exposed to a sattvic atmosphere, or those who have been shaped by worldly values? Have they no chance?

We cannot underestimate the capacity of the spirit. Every child has a chance to come to detachment and awaken to values of the spirit when he goes through the world of experience and realizes it is nothing. At first nobody taught him but now he may read the Sermon on the Mount – "BLESSED ARE THE MEEK: FOR THEY SHALL INHERIT THE EARTH" [5] – and awaken on his own. Each child brings his own resources and potentials with him. Nothing is impossible.

> PARENT: Certain tendencies that we have seem innate or even *karmic*. If the undoing that you speak of takes place, does the change then become innate? For example, if I am a wasteful person, can something happen in my brain where the natural response will be non-wastefulness?

Actually, it doesn't happen that way at all. The mind is not the brain. In this culture today, man lives by the brain. In fact, there is no space for anything else outside the brain because we are so stimulated.

You were asking if these tendencies are innate or karmic. Karma* only exists in the realm of unreality; therefore, it can be undone. But it can only be undone by what is not of time. The personal cannot undo it. The brain, limited to the physical, merely perpetuates the limitations that it knows. Wisdom sees the fallacy. This seeing itself is the clarity, the light within your own being. This light is your God-created Self.

The question is, What happens in this undoing, this mutation?

---

* "The law that governs all action and its inevitable consequences on the doer." From *The Ramayana* by C. Rajagopalachari (Bharatiya Vidya Bhavan, Bombay, 1951), page 317. (Editor)

We are preoccupied with the brain and its knowing. We have emphasized the development of the brain so much that there is little space for the energy of awareness to step in. We have actually been trained through our education to block the entry of the energy of awareness. Awareness would correct any tendency, but the brain is so preoccupied it doesn't have the space.

We have taken the brain for the mind and we merely juggle things around at that level. But no problem can be solved at the level of the brain because its knowing is partial. There will be consequences no matter which way you turn. The brain cannot correct. About all it can do is deny. Thus we impose denial and conformity on all segments of society.

If you are with someone wise, he brings you to awareness. Then *that* energy brings about a mutation and changes your way of looking at things. Therefore you can adequately respond to whatever arises. The correction for any issue is insight and awareness. It has nothing to do with the brain and yet it is a gift *to* the brain. We want to correct our children – educate our children – with brain thoughts. They only become more conditioned, more like us and their environment.

It is necessary for parents and for teachers to make space within and invite the forces of awareness. When you do not accept what your brain tells you, then that other action is already there. It comes because you are not regulated by the brain. Something independent of and superior to the brain is then in charge of the impulses, urges, fears, and insecurities. The plans of the brain cease. Awareness doesn't tell you what to do and what not to do. It shows you the limitation of whatever you would project or conclude. Neither wisdom, nor love, nor truth can be personalized.

Whatever one does at the brain level is neither good nor bad. It is just wrong-minded. *A Course In Miracles* calls it insane because it is cut off from Reality. It is consumed with rearranging things in its own favor. Whatever seems to be in one's favor today has consequences tomorrow.

All of our education is based on "becoming." It is not based on the discovery of perfection, the glory of the moment. It wants to "become" at the cost of realizing who we are. "Becoming" is even encouraged in our society, given degrees and honors.

Whether you get a doctorate or a master's degree, if the brain is only trained with skills and relative knowledge, it doesn't necessarily mean there is intelligence or wisdom in it. This trained brain is only interested in becoming something other than what it is. That is the conflict within and the conflict without. Where there is fear, there is no intelligence.

Education was originally intended to awaken man's wisdom, to impart refinement and honesty so that he would be more himself, no longer ignorant. It was meant to relate man with God – whether through medicine, law, or philosophy. Now it is used to exploit. We have accepted the conclusion that we must learn a skill to get a job. Can you imagine, something is lost and we don't even know it!

> *PARENT:* Could you explain what you mean by intelligence?

Intelligence is not learned; it is impersonal. It probably has some relationship with how evolved you are. Intelligence immediately discerns the false from the non-false. This intelligence is not of the brain. It is something the brain delights in and receives, but it has its own ethic, its own moral principle, its own integrity. It undoes, unburdens, and revives something within one.

You wouldn't be reading this if that intelligence wasn't there. Life is not foolish; it doesn't experiment or live by speculation. It brings about an encounter where the awakening of intelligence can be brought to flowering.

\* \* \*

"Lord, somewhere we know that we are incapable of taking proper care of our children. Nor have we the wisdom to awaken them to their Divine Identity. But you have loved children and we invoke Your Presence and seek Your Guidance so that what is shared is understood and brought into application – not lost in the mirage of thought. Please be with us, for we need Your help."

A fundamental question is: what is the difference between punishment and correction? Certainty would know; but who can say he has certainty? That is why we start with a prayer. It is not sufficient to merely idealize that we should not punish the child. If you don't, a bigger boy or girl will; if you don't punish him, the government will. Our little piety doesn't go very far. We live in a world where all we know is punishment and reward, and we are asking: what is correction? That is the only thing we don't know. Because we don't know how to correct, we resort to punishment. Only a saint knows what correction is.

When a child is born he comes to extend something. And, with the birth, an involuntary feeling of love comes into the parents' heart. The question arises, how are you going to take care of the child? Are you going to awaken the child or have him conform? At every turn there is going to be a challenge and we are going to be tempted to compromise because that is all we have ever done all our lives. That is all our parents have done.

The child comes with a certain gift. It could be something as simple as making furniture. If status rules, you may not like it because he won't make enough money building furniture. Making money, however, may thoroughly corrupt him and cause unhappiness in all his relationships because he is not extending the abilities he brought. If our values are false, the abilities the child brought to express are going to be interfered with no matter what the child does.

There is a phenomenon that happens in nature where large sea turtles come out of the sea and lay their eggs in a hole in the warm sand. After the eggs are laid, the mothers cover them up and walk back to sea. Time passes and the young begin to break out of the shell. As soon as they are fully hatched they rush headlong to the sea. Not many make it, however, for there are birds who have known this cycle for centuries. They sit and wait and snap up the young as they scurry toward the water.

It is the same thing with our children. Very few of them make it to their true nature. Very few of them express the abilities they came to extend. And the situation has never been as dangerous as it is today.

During the sixties, the hippies were boycotted because they had different values. There was not the flexibility to incorporate them. Today, also, you see very sensitive children. They are exceptional, but one wonders whether society will be able to receive from them.

We thought education would help, science would help, democracy would help. Has it? It is a change at the same level. We were insecure and selfish when we were illiterate. And even though we are educated now, we are still insecure and selfish. We don't do anything that is not motivated by some personal gain.

> PARENT: When I met you in Santa Barbara, I asked you about kids and fighting and you told me that I would have to come to peace within and then I would never have to think – the response would come naturally. I'm certainly not completely at peace, but the continual awareness and attention towards that has helped me very much. My focus no longer is on them and everything they are doing wrong. It is on being peaceful with them so that I have a response rather than a reaction.

If you are not going to compromise, if you are not going to accept any option, then maybe the clearing away of options sets awareness into action until you come to a point where you can honestly say, "I don't know what discipline is, in truth."

If you really come to "I don't know," you have undone a lot of conclusions and assumptions. You recognize that whatever you or I think is going to be good for the child is still relative. You have come to the place where you see that you don't know anything beyond the relative level. When you come to that state, you have energized yourself. The intensity of awareness may make something very obvious. Where there are options, correction is going to be very difficult. If you have no options you have already corrected yourself. Then you would know what to do. But we would rather change the child without changing ourselves.

I go back to my relationship with Mr. Krishnamurti. How did he correct and not punish? If Mr. Krishnamurti was to have a serious relationship with anyone, he was going to be very confronting. In the documentary, *With A Silent Mind*, he says to a man he had known since the man was a child, "You're a good chap, but you're wasting your life." [6]

Can that gentleman hear those words as a law? Having read them, are *we* going to let them make an impact on us? He would not give instruction to a casual person. But to bring these words into application in one's life, one would have to heed them as if they were a commandment. Then one would merit relationship with such a being.

I heard Mr. Krishnamurti say, "There is a time for coop-eration and a time for non-cooperation." The child may think it is punishment, but you make sure it is non-cooperation. You extend the best of goodwill. Because you care for the child, you don't cooperate with that which is not in the child's long range interest. There would be non-cooperation when the child ignores correction.

> *PARENT:* I can see that when we were dealing with our son, it was really punishment. It was born out of our reaction rather than our love for him. The difference in our attitude is the difference between punishment and correction.

Yes. Punishment is when you try to make correction by force. Therefore it is loveless. I don't think non-cooperation is loveless. You're responsible to make the correction because you care for the child and you can't be indifferent. When you care, how could it be punishment?

> *PARENT:* Listening to you, I am shocked by how small the chance is for my son. Although we have some willingness to tackle the problem, we keep slipping. Last year you told us to do this. We do it for a little while and then we slip. This year you said the same thing. We do it for a while, then we lose focus. Soon he must go to school by law and the odds are he will not be able to get the one-to-one attention and patience that he needs.
>
> I see I don't really heed. And frankly it doesn't bother me a whole lot. It doesn't put me into crisis. I am amazed to see how thick my callouses are. It is one thing to ruin my life. But it is quite another to ruin our child's.

As parents we get started and our enthusiasm is short-lived. The children wear us out. We have to be in charge to master any tendency. *We* must be in charge, not the tendency.

Mr. Krishnamurti said to me, "If you don't listen to me, I will never see you again." Now that could be translated as punishment. But it is actually non-cooperation. Parents need never wait for the child to exhaust them. With non-cooperation, you are the boss. Once you've set that in motion, the children have to come around. We react, but that is false. It is wiser not to cooperate.

Mr. Krishnamurti's words are a law. He would never have said that to me if I were not going to do what he said. If I did not do what he told me, there would be no relationship.

> PARENT: That's very much what we do with our children. If something needs to be done and we've asked them to do it and they've refused or they're delaying, no other part of the day goes on until that is done.

Yes. *Do only that.* [7] Right relationship with a child is a way to come to enlightenment.

> PARENT: What are your recommendations about siblings fighting?

It is best not to interfere too much when siblings are having a rough time. Friction is necessary. Don't interfere beyond necessity; otherwise, we make children too fragile with our over-protection. Other kids aren't going to be so careful – "might is right" is the rule there also.

Let there be no "might is right" in the parents' relationship with the child. Among the children, you don't have to interfere until you see things are imbalanced. If one is pulling the other down all the time, that is a different story.

A little bit of friction is very natural and healthy. A child would need to develop different faculties to deal with it. For instance, some animals have developed speed for self-protection, others scent, others climb very high. Let's not deprive the child of a faculty he may need later.

The test of the whole thing is not to get involved in the externals. If you get involved, invariably there will be reaction or anger. How can you correct anything with reaction or anger? We must first correct these things in ourselves.

You grow wiser as you awaken other potentials within you. Then you can do things correctly within and without. We are one or two-dimensional people for the most part, but the times now demand that we be four-dimensional. Unless you have developed these other resources within, you cannot adequately meet the needs that present themselves. The challenges multiply as the child is growing up. Can you keep pace so that you are far ahead? Can you introduce your child to the resources he needs to take care of the problems of adolescence before they arise?

If you are not aware and responsible you cannot lead your children to maturity. You will be leading them no further than you have gone. But there is a very wide horizon open to both of you.

Another thing I want to mention is that we talk as if the child is God. We become so sentimental. But no one can be as cruel as a child. Our children are part of our heredity. We have to correct that heredity in ourselves and in them, too. Not to be taken over by a child is one of the basic lessons to learn. We get taken over by our own sentimentality. Sentimentality is just the other side of anger and reaction. *Do only that* is an extension of something that cannot be manipulated for it is not personal.

Where are you going to find a teacher for your children? If you have the need, then God provides. The tears of humanity produced the world teacher, Mr. J. Krishnamurti, as well as *A Course In Miracles*. The teacher for the children will be there if that is your need. How can you limit yourself? Have faith that if you remain with rightness, all will be provided.

* * *

Years ago when I lived in New York, I had a friendship with Orson Bean, the Broadway actor and comedian. He and his wife had a daughter whom they loved very much. On my return from an extended trip to India, I ran into Orson and asked him about his daughter. He said they had had a very difficult time finding a school for her. They went from one school to the next and couldn't find one that did not make the child conform. "And so," he said, "I started one."

I have always had a deep interest in education and I've seen that the problem is finding exceptional teachers. I asked him where he found the teachers. Orson said that he wrote to some schools in England requesting the names of good American teachers whom they had not hired. In this way he put together an excellent staff. I said, "Orson, you are really a wise man." This inspiration to have right relationship with his daughter's education became a gift to many children.

When I asked him the name of the school, I half expected a name like the Universal Mind of the Creative Child School. Orson said they called it by the name of the street where it was located. I believe it was the Fourteenth Street School. Isn't that beautiful? So factual and non-pretentious. He told me the school was housed in a three-story building. On the ground floor there were only toys, on the second floor classes were held, and the third floor was equipped for exercise and group games. No teacher was ever to ask the children to come to class.

Could you give your children that kind of freedom? We want them to fit into a society that is corrupt instead of helping them to become individuals who are untouched by society. Such individuals start schools like this, or do something else that is original, related to the eternal, something not of the earth.

Orson said that for quite a while some of the children didn't come to class. They would play upstairs and downstairs but never stop at the second floor. Months went by. The teachers were committed; they were never going to ask them to attend the classes but would try to discover the children's interests and work from there.

Such a revolutionary step! They had decided not to teach the children activities of the brain. It had to be their action. And slowly, after a few months, one or two children came; then another one; then a few more were interested. Orson said that the amazing thing was that at the end of the year all of the children in their particular classes were virtually at the same level. The children who had taken a longer time to enter the class eventually caught up to their peer group. Allowing the child to come to learning at his own pace did not hamper his growth. I only went to school for two years and I caught up. We have made our entire life into a routine.

Children need children and they need to play. Now they are all in school, and the play is not play anymore. It is competition. On the day that I visited Orson Bean's school something very interesting took place. The headmaster and several teachers had requested a conference with the parents of one of the children.

When the parents came, they told the school staff that their daughter, Jane, loved to draw and paint. The teachers and the headmaster said, "I'm sorry, that is not so." There was great tension at that moment. The parents kept insisting, and the teachers were just as sure. The parents said, "We have stacks of her paintings at home. We will bring them to show you!"

The headmaster was a born teacher and he had something to share with these parents. There are very few people in the world who are born teachers. The born teacher awakens the child's interest with whatever is at hand. It might be a squirrel, the singing curves of a tree, the joy of walking by the river, the rain. He connects the student with something beyond book knowledge. The earth is the best book. We think we can live in peace, cut off from the earth.

The headmaster said they didn't have to bring Jane's paintings, for he knew that they had paintings at home. The parents were puzzled, "Then why do you say she does not like to paint?" He said, "If Jane really loved to paint, she would do it here. Jane never paints at school. She wants attention.

That is why she does it at home. But that is not what her real calling is. "

Parents drool over anything the child does: "Isn't that nice!" The child performs because it is the only bit of attention she is going to get. The parents are usually preoccupied with their own thing. Had this meeting not taken place, the parents would have forced Jane to be an artist and her life would have been destroyed by being false to herself. Most of us are doing things that are false. There is always some other consideration besides finding our own inner calling.

*　　*　　*

> PARENT: My daughter just turned five and I'm struggling with what kind of education to provide for her. I read your book, *How To Raise A Child Of God*, but I don't know if I should keep her out of school and try to teach her at home. How do I teach my children what is really valid?

Quality education is essential for the child. But no matter where you send your child, they are going to prepare her for a career. Schools teach about things, not Reality. Wise parents face this challenge because they love their children. They don't want to send them to any old school that would condition them with fear and competition, or right and wrong.

There are not many schools where the teachers awaken interest in the child. The first responsibility is to find out if there is such a school. Your first thought may be that you can't afford it. Whenever you find you are limiting yourself, question *that*. You may discover the means to do the right thing. The child has his own destiny. You can't impose your limitations upon him. See if there are any schools near you that are authentic. Is there a teacher who loves children?

There are a few good schools. Look into them and remain uncompromising.

Exceptional schools welcome parents who want a different kind of education for their children. If you can't find a school, start one. Find other parents with similar values. Just don't limit yourself. Life will work through you.

If you can't find the right school for your child and it is not possible to start one, send your child to the school that is there and awaken him to a new awareness so the child himself can undo all that the brain projects.

Crystal used to say, "I don't like school, I don't want to go there." I said, "If I had it my way I'd burn the school, but then we'd both be in jail!" She would laugh. Sometimes she would not want to do things at school and the teacher would humiliate her by making her sit on the bench in the playground. I said, "Crystal, this humiliation is a bad thing if it makes you lose your sense of dignity. How come you can't outwit the teacher? If you are my student, you should be able to put circles around a predictable person like that." She never ever had to sit on the bench again.

As a parent, as a friend, you can give the child confidence. The most beautiful thing is that we all started praying for her teacher. Crystal learned how to win her with her goodness and non-reaction.

You can do a lot by yourself. Try to make the child aware of nationalism, tribalism, and how society is built. In reality, we are all children of God. Who knows, you yourself might turn out to be the best teacher around.

> *PARENT:* If innocence is protected, how do we deal with the abused child – the child who is a victim of drugs or of parents who abuse them? I expect to encounter children like this soon and I'm not sure how to look at it. How can I reach them?

It all depends on how much of your life you want to give to them. Partially, we are kind people. But our kindness only goes so far. Gestures never solve any problem. Until you are ready to take action, don't flirt with gestures. If you see a child who is abused, can you give your life, your whole life, to do something about it? When your life is behind it, you will be like Mother Teresa. When you are willing to compromise, you never find out who you are.

We have built a society that has so many pressures. Where do you stop? Maybe the person who abuses a child was abused, is abused. In the end, the wise person would respond to one human need and give his life to it.

People commented on the wonderful social work Mother Teresa was doing. She said that it is not social work. For that moment, with that person, it is an exchange of love. That person knows, yes, the Presence of Love, of Christ, is upon the planet.

If you are working with the abused, do it wholeheartedly and let it unfold, let it grow. Don't feel helpless. Don't ever get overwhelmed because it's such a big problem. No. It is always going to be one person. The Chinese say that no matter how long the journey is, it always starts with the first step.

The wise acts with what is put before him and with his own resources. He finds he is unlimited. If you haven't found out that you are unlimited, it is because you haven't put your whole heart into anything. The whole-heartedness of one human being can change the world. There is no force that can stand against such a being.

It is of first importance to discover your Self – to know who you are. *A Course In Miracles* gives such strength: *All the help you can accept will be provided, and not one need you have will not be met.* [8]

If the parents would accept the fact that their child has a destiny to know his God-created Self, then they would build a real home for him and everything they did would be helpful to him. I am not against school, but one has to stop and ask: In what way will it help in the evolvement of my child's awareness, in his inner awakening?

Because we are not really true to our destiny, there are all kinds of problems, deceptions, cruelties, and so forth. Your destiny is to know who you are as God created you. The few who succeed become a light to others.

*   *   *

There are certain things that take place in a life that represent its whole direction. A few incidents from the life of Gandhi demonstrate this principle.

While Gandhi was going to school his father died. The family was not well-to-do, but in India there was the extended family, so one never felt alone. The family would get together and provide what you needed. If you wanted to go to school abroad, you had someone behind you. If there was a talented child within a poor family, the whole family supported him in pursuing his interest.

They would virtually deprive themselves because they were so glad they could make it possible for the child to express his life's purpose. When he left the village to go to school, or to a teacher, the family members took pains to make sure he was dressed well and that he had proper food to sustain himself in a foreign environment. After his schooling was completed, he returned to the village and all of the family was strengthened by the fact that they made it possible for him to grow to be himself.

When Gandhi's father died, the members of the family got together and declared that since he would have to support the family, he would do well to go to England and get a better education. They had the means to cover his passage, school fees, and living expenses. Gandhi was thrilled. When they told his mother of their plan, she emphatically said, "No. I do not want my son to go to England." She was unlettered, but her voice had conviction. And because she said, "No," that was where it ended.

But Gandhi was young and youth loves adventure. It loves to expand. We rarely allow youth to expand beyond selfishness and self-centeredness into holiness. Our young people want to go from one place to another. They are ruled by a person, place, or an activity. Have you taught your children to be free of these projections of activity, person, or place? Youth must expand, but not as a mere shift from here to there, from one activity to another.

Gandhi's mother did not want her son to go to England and Gandhi would not contradict her. Few of us have elders to guide us, to help us shape our lives. Not only are most of our children on their own, they are actually being misled. But Gandhi's mother had some other purpose in mind. And for that reason her words were powerful. "No. I do not want my son to go to England."

Gandhi asked his mother, "Mother, why can't I go?" She looked at him and said, "I do not want you to come back puffing cigars, and eating meat. I don't want to lose you to whiskey and pleasure creatures. I have raised you to be virtuous and I want you to be true to that. I want you to be noble and honor Divine Laws." This illiterate woman had more to give than fifty universities. I hope she has dethroned something in your brain.

Gandhi thought about it and he could see the truth of his mother's words. And he had reverence. After some time, Gandhi said, "Mother, what if I promised that I would not do any of those things?" And now the greatest thing happened. She looked at him and said, "Very well. You may go then." She trusted her son. She knew his words were true.

Would you trust anybody? Do you trust yourself? Are your words true? Do they have any meaning other than self-centeredness? The whole family respected her words. Do you know a mother like that? Can you be that kind of mother? Instantly she agreed because she trusted her son's word. We all know what this son did. With the strength of his conviction, he uprooted the British Empire. He had the capacity to call upon another strength within because his mother taught him to be noble and true. [9]

He went to England. You have no idea how lonely one can feel in a strange country. He walked along the streets and didn't know what to do. He was not able to eat the English vegetables because he was accustomed to a different taste with different seasoning. He was miserable.

After some months of this agony, someone told him about a vegetarian restaurant. It was the first good meal he had, the first real prospect of companionship because the people were friendly there. One day an elderly person said to Gandhi, "Why don't you have some eggs?" "Oh, no," protested Gandhi. Eggs, to a Hindu, are not vegetarian. "You drink milk, don't you?" said the man. "Yes. I drink milk." "Well, in the same way that milk comes from a cow, the egg comes from the chicken. Eggs are like milk." He proceeded to order an omelette for Gandhi.

The order came and Gandhi said, "Sir, you have convinced me that eggs are like vegetables. But I promised my mother that I would not stray from a pure vegetarian diet and, to my mother, an egg is not a vegetable, it is like meat." That is conviction, inner strength.

*   *   *

## THE UGLIEST THING IN THE WORLD

In ancient times, there was a sage of the forest hermitage where luminous beings abided. They were the highest among men. Kings paid homage to them and sat on the floor in their presence. Their lives were sacred. They knew and lived by truth and everything obeyed them, even the plants.

A story is told in India about a twelve-year-old boy named Satnam whose parents took him to this sage to be awakened. Tradition has it that you make an offering to the teacher who takes on the responsibility for the child. The offering often consisted of a fruit or a piece of cloth. The parents started to present the offering to the sage, but he said, "Leave the boy with me. I will determine the offering later."

The compassionate sage, whose heavenly purity and peace charged the atmosphere, took away all anxiety from the child. The boy felt blessed to be in his holy presence.

At dawn Satnam asked, "Sir, what shall I offer to be accepted as your student?" The teacher said, "I would like you to find the ugliest thing in the world and bring that to me as your offering." The boy was somewhat startled by the request, but he left immediately, sure he could easily find the ugliest thing.

Satnam came upon many things which he thought would serve the purpose, but always there was the lurking thought: "Is this the ugliest thing in the world?" Comparison and duality intensified within his mind as he searched all day.

Finally, his eyes lit upon a crow which everyone in his village despised because it eats the crops, picks on the wounds of animals, and even takes food out of little children's hands. The householders had to guard whatever food was left outside so that the clever crow would not steal it.

Now Satnam was sure. The crow was certainly the ugliest thing in the world. But catching a crow has never been easy. The boy thought a great deal and finally found a way to put some grain under a basket leaning on a stick, which was tied to a string. He waited patiently in the bushes and eventually succeeded in trapping a crow.

As he went to retrieve the crow, a voice, as if of the crow itself, spoke with disdain, "Am I the ugliest thing in the world? Whenever I find food, I share. I caw and caw to call the other crows so they will not go hungry. And you think that I am the ugliest thing in the world?" Satnam, seeing his own selfishness, set the crow free. He started his search again and with it came uncertainty. The pressure on his brain of comparison and duality returned. He wandered around for days.

People have dreaded snakes in India since time immemorial. Very few people realize that some snakes are non-poisonous. "The snake would be my offering," Satnam thought and he was glad to rest on his conclusion while looking for a way to trap a snake.

After many hours his determination was rewarded and he succeeded in trapping a snake. Again, however, came the voice. "You think that I am the ugliest thing in the world? I hoard nothing and I never harm anyone unless I am stepped upon." Seeing the harmful nature of man, he set the snake free. But still, he was confronted with the challenge of finding the ugliest thing in the world or he could not return to his teacher.

In India, pigs are looked down upon and are treated as scavengers. They live off the excrement of man found amidst the fields surrounding the villages. They are much despised as dirty animals. So Satnam's mind went to the ugliness of the pig's habits of survival and he found a way to catch one. But again came the dreaded voice. "What? You deem me to be the ugliest thing in the world, when I am the one who cleans, while you soil?"

Satnam was tormented by the limitation of the brain. It knows nothing yet pretends to know. Faced with his ignorance, he felt helpless. But he had to find the ugliest thing to offer to his teacher, so he persisted. He was less sure now, cautious of his own conclusions. His trust in his little knowings was diminishing. He was tired and weary and walked about like an old man, burdened by the weight of thought.

The next morning, as Satnam went for his call of nature, it struck him that his own feces must be the ugliest thing! So he decided that was what he would take to his teacher. He got a wide leaf, and as he was wrapping up the feces, the voice came: "I was the fresh fruit that sustained you and yet you dare to consider me the ugliest thing in the world?"

Something happened. Satnam could no longer trust thought.

The boy came and stood before his teacher, arms down, empty handed. In the presence of the sage, it was as if time had ended. The teacher knew the boy had awakened his inner potentials and was ready for higher wisdom. This was education for inner awakening.

# CHAPTER SIX

# 6

## DEGENERATION AND INTELLECTUALITY

When I first came to America in my twenties, I was most grateful to learn the rules of etiquette from a refined friend. I discovered that opening the door for a lady was an expression of some inner beauty. A man's respect for women speaks of who he is. John, now that you are becoming a young man, it is important for you to understand that we are not just genders. The spirit resides within each of us. How important it is not to snuff the spirit, but rather to give it sustenance.

Thoughtfulness civilizes a person. What has happened to thoughtfulness and consideration in our culture? Degeneration is apparent everywhere. As parents and friends of the young, we need to bring to their awareness the dangers of degeneration and how laziness, sloppiness, and casualness are symptomatic of degeneration. We should bring it to their attention but not make it a personal issue.

> *BETTE:* Howard and I see that we have contributed to John's becoming more and more casual. Somehow we have compromised.

Bette, let me tell you something: You don't have to encourage sloppiness, it has its own momentum. You have to have a broom in your hand to keep it out! We are all a party to this. It is a collective movement. Degeneration has such a strong pull because it makes no demand. It's the easier side of the easy. But since John is your child, Bette, it is your responsibility to make him aware of the implications of casualness and degeneration without being negative.

When I lived in the village in India, a family was known by its breeding, its ethics. People knew that this family did not lie or violate moral laws. If you don't awaken this level of responsibility in John, then what good is all his education?

Parents must set a standard. That doesn't mean that children can't play normally. But we must not leave this area of virtue and ethics, manners and etiquette, undeveloped. If we don't impart an awareness of dignity to our children at a young age, it is somewhat more difficult when they get older.

Children will be exposed to degeneration as they grow up. They must learn its causes and, by contrast, what poise and dignity are. The renowned British author, Rebecca West, once said that the children in her family were not surprised when the war broke out because their father had been prophesying it for years. He had also said that it would not end in their lifetime because the state had taken so much power from the individuals that it did not have to consider the moral judgment of ordinary human beings. She said they were taught that great music was serene because it was certain of the values it asserted. She felt that in contemporary life those values were threatened and that it was not certain whether they would triumph in this world.

The child is not aware that the state is taking over the power from the individual. He is not aware that modern music reflects terror, panic, and hate; that drug addicts have become the heroes of our young people. If we don't expose the child to nobler values, something is amiss. We need to make the child aware that the modern music of today is an expression of hysteria, and then introduce him to refinement. If the family doesn't do it, it is unlikely that the school ever will. It is our responsibility as parents and teachers to inspire our children.

The media makes children very aware of what kind of jeans and running shoes they need, and we submit to that influence. But we refrain from exposing the child to something decent and noble because we don't want to influence him. Is this sane?

In ancient cultures it was felt that the greatest danger came from one's own impurities. If you did not awaken a new intelligence within yourself, your anger, your greed, your lust, or your pride would take control and mold your life. They were aware of the dangers that came from a mind devoid of spiritual and moral values; therefore, emphasis was placed on making inner correction. They were not so concerned with the externals. In the West, we begin with training the mind with skills. As skills proliferate, value for wisdom diminishes.

It is easy in the early stages to recognize tendencies as they arise in our children and to help them overcome them. The child is born to overcome these tendencies. He is always given a fresh start so that he can liberate himself from that which binds him to the flesh. Time and time again, he takes birth to be freed.

Awareness of this is the Given – the clarity that effortlessly corrects and purifies. It introduces the child to his God nature, where love, goodness, and truth are his forever to give and to share. This awareness gives him power over all that is outside of him, for he is the light that shines upon all creation. Awakened intelligence is holy, peaceful, and loving. It knows no lack, no problem, no sorrow. It is the power and purity of one's own stillness, cleansed of all impurities. That is one of the greatest gifts of God to humanity.

When I look at the lives of awakened beings I knew, it is obvious to me that they had dealt with their impurities in childhood. People who had greatness also had wisdom. They had outgrown intellectuality and made the contact within themselves.

A young saint like Joan of Arc was pure of mind, speech, and deed. By her life we are inspired out of our own littleness. And she could not even write her name. Our education has piled more and more information on the brain but it has not developed our character; it has not equipped us to deal with our inner impurities.

In ancient times, children were awakened by the wise because there was no other option to doing so. Children were guided and instructed so that they never got distracted into the meaningless or the sensational. They were introduced to their responsibility as human beings. Therefore, the child had reverence for his parents and his teacher. Today, we have very little reverence for anything.

How can any education be real that doesn't first take care of these basic things? The very fact that we think we need abstract education is born out of our insecurity and self-centeredness. If education doesn't make wisdom a part of our lives, it is meaningless. What self-sustaining values are there in our present society? Where is the light within man given the space to shine? Obviously, the greatest danger comes from internal, unresolved darkness. Without contact with God's Will there is little relationship with goodwill.

In the Sikh culture, the five basic tendencies are called *kam, karod, loveh, mo, and hankar. Kam* is the abuse of sexuality. *Karod* is ill-will, mulling grievances inside oneself. *Loveh* is attachment. *Mo* is greed. And *Hankar* is pride. These are the things we were taught to outgrow. It was like driving the demons out. That was our education. Being liberated from these tendencies made the space for the spirit to extend itself. It made the space for us to be a part of the Will of God. We want to be a part of the Will of God intellectually, without making any space within. There is great danger in knowing something intellectually without bringing it into application. One's life ultimately results in disappointment.

In each family in India, there was a wise man or woman to whom the child could go. In some instinctive way, the child trusted them more than the parents or anyone else. In their loving atmosphere, we heeded a voice of living truth and kindness. Their peaceful touch and counsel introduced us to an awakened dimension without the intellectual learning. It made human relationship spiritual. Through them we were taught principles related to divine laws which facilitated their integration in our own lives. True art is the way man lives. The art of living embraces every kind of skill because it extends something that is not of time. It represents perfection. Today, the art of living is all but lost.

We are owned by the system. It says, "Never mind the impurities, slaves, we own your energy and your brain. We will give you a job and deceive you into thinking that this artificial lifestyle gives you freedom." Our society has become so false that impurities are now the only basis for action in life. We have become so conditioned that we don't even know we are being cruel to ourselves.

Spiritual life is rooted in Eternal Laws. That is why India produced an unprecedented number of saints, prophets, and incarnations. Even in our times we have Sri Ramakrishna, Sri Sarada Devi, Sri Ramana Maharshi, Mr. J. Krishnamurti. Only the wise can introduce the collective to their moral responsibility. Since the advent of industrialization, moral values have not been of first importance. We want success. Without an awakened awareness, even education and religion become the means of self-deception.

John, you are a sensitive boy. And at your age you have all the space to bring about an inner transformation and to deal with these impurities. As adults, we justify everything. We think that because we don't like violence we are free from it, but inwardly we are not free. I am saying that while you are young, correct these tendencies. We have had to struggle to correct these patterns in ourselves, and now we want to make sure that you correct them. But we must help you, not bully you.

Bette, do you see that we are piling more and more education on children but we are not dealing with those things that
are going to completely shape their lives? What would John's
life be if he had no attachment to anything? What would his
life be if he never knew insecurity or unfulfillment? What
would his life be if he saw the other human being is just like
him, that they are both part of one life? An education which
merely promotes separation is useless.

> BETTE: Recently we have seen how diffi-
> cult it is to try to introduce anything to John
> without him feeling we are wanting him to
> conform to something that is not his own
> interest.

He is going to be interested in things that are easy, Bette,
just like you and me. He is going to be interested in things that
don't demand too much responsibility, but give an
instantaneous sensation and outlet. The correction of values
begins at home. Then he will have an atmosphere in which
other things are possible.

Every parent wants his child to be good. But we do not
know what good is. We know the good that has a bad on the
other side. There is a space within one's mind, however, that
goes beyond good and bad, right and wrong – an impeccable,
energetic space that is independent of thought. It needs no
education. It has some kind of inner happiness and joy that is
no longer dependent on anything external. One generation
should pass that on to the next generation. Since our
generation does not have it, we have passed on our phoney
education.

And then, because there is little likelihood of some other
direct contact within the child, he is compelled to acquire a
skill so that he will have a job. The job is a necessity because
he never did find the light and happiness within. True
education was meant to introduce the child to a motiveless
state in which there are no consequences.

The question is, how can we, as parents and friends, make the child aware? If we don't relate him with something different, the computer will take him over. Mr. Krishnamurti had warned us:

> "The twentieth century has had a tremendous lot of changes produced by two devastating wars, and the dialectical materialism, and the skepticism of religious beliefs, activities, and rituals and so on, apart from the technological world which has brought about a great many changes, and there will be further changes when the computer is fully developed – you are just at the beginning of it. Then when the computer takes over, what is going to happen to our human minds?" [1]

If you who are young make the demand to give some expression to the spirit within, it would give you a sense of dignity. You would enrich yourselves and everyone who comes into contact with you. John, you have to start with yourself. Find out why you feel isolated and become attached. Don't say it is bad. Just observe yourself. Become aware how much loneliness and attachment control you. Then you might observe that you don't really like spending time with some of your friends. Maybe you just hate to be bored. Until we find these truths, this new intelligence is not going to awaken.

If you were sitting with Mr. Krishnamurti, he would ask you if you like your friend, Toby. You would say, "Yes," but then he would ask you, "Do you spend time with him because you have common interests, or is it that you just don't like loneliness?" He would ask you, "If Toby wasn't there, would you find another distraction?" He would not tell you not to like Toby, but he would awaken another awareness so that you would not deceive yourself. Pretty soon you would have a light of your own because you do not lie to yourself. Krishnamurti stood for never being deceived, never being controlled by anything external. He stood for finding one's own truth within.

Do you want to know something that is eternal, John? That rock has been there for thousands of years and very few people know the reality of it. They just know the name. Don't you want to know something that is real?

*JOHN:* Yes.

Then you must be willing to put a little more energy into observation. Inquire. Ask questions. Start that way.

*JOHN:* Of my teachers?

Well, you can ask your teachers questions, too. Since you go to one of Mr. Krishnamurti's schools, you could ask them: "What would Krishnamurti say to my loneliness? How would he teach me that there is no need for attachment?" Then because you need Krishnamurti, he will impart the truth to you. He becomes the teacher to everyone who goes to his school when they need something the teachers cannot give.

We need to question because the question imparts space. Everything else is hereditary or conditioned. It is not yours. You have to give the energy to make these discoveries. If you don't make your own discoveries, then you will become dependent on someone else's energy.

Intellectuality has misled man because it has made application less possible. Now it is a challenge for us to live what we know. Even if we prayed: "Lord, help us," I don't think we would accept the help. Our own intellectuality would block it. We have learned to want and to ask for what we want. But we only receive what our intellect tells us. We have not learned to receive what is not of the brain. Intellectuality has intensified our sense of separation and made it difficult for us to come to disillusionment. What we know is of time; it is never whole. Achieving always starts with a lack. It gives the ego pride and vanity. Undoing is far superior to learning. Innocence is superior to knowing.

Because we intellectualize everything, there is very little that we know directly. We even put death and sex through the mill of intellectuality. This is the unreal world. "This belongs to you; that belongs to me." What is jealousy without our concept of it? What is anger if it is not put through the mental mill of thought? Everything is broken down to images and concepts, even our gender.

It is absolutely essential that we recognize the truth of this. There may be no such place as America, Mexico, or India. There may only be greed, power, and self-centeredness. Our cities are built on these concepts. The manmade, projected world is insane everywhere.

We have a responsibility to purify ourselves of these concepts so that we can love and trust our brothers. Trust is not physical, therefore, it can't be intellectualized. When we come to that fine energy, that subtle vibration, physicality no longer has its wants. Its energy goes into sharing something that is of God. Then we have something to give. When there is no love between brothers, we are violating something.

Now we are like orphans, hired hands. We've come to the cities to live and within us there is a kind of mental hunger and insecurity. Where that perversion exists, we can forget about faith and trust. We can't even trust ourselves. Can you imagine what this intellectuality has done? Everywhere there is this separation in a world where life is one. We want to trust as an idea, but it is all mental, all intellectual.

One of the lessons in *A Course In Miracles* is:

*I trust my brothers, who are one with me.* [2]

How is that possible as long as we intellectualize everything? We no longer know who we are and we don't know what to do. Still, we never cry out for help.

Any saint born today would have to deal with this issue. He cannot just talk about Jesus, or Buddha, or Mohammed. Without a being in our midst who can connect us with the truth of their teachings, we are isolated, fearful, loveless, unable to receive, and unable to give. We have become almost incapable of accepting love.

The loneliness of the western world is destroying mankind. Out of our fear of loneliness, we have invented televisions, newspapers, and fashions. We feel nobody loves or trusts us, so we are going to love ourselves. Consume. Buy. Is trust possible in this atmosphere?

Another lesson in the Course says:

*I place the future in the Hands of God.* [3]

We have to admit that this is just not possible for us right now. We are computerized with doubt, having substituted an abstract idea for everything real. Insecurity must be questioned. We will never know self-reliance otherwise.

If the parents could see that everything they know is intellectual, they would want to protect the child. They would not allow anything false to enter the child's mind. They would start questioning and undoing what they, themselves, have concluded. The space that would come from this process is what they would give the child. Thus, the birth of the child will help them undo their borrowed opinions and fixed views. The child has come to liberate the parents.

Parents may ask: "But our children are going to play with other children. They are going to be in this insane world. What do we do?" You awaken awareness in your children with which they can discriminate. It is not a very long journey. Parents can bring about that discrimination both in themselves and their children. You don't teach discrimination; you awaken it by introducing the child to the potentials within him. Then you would never send your child to a false school where his direct contact is annihilated. You would make sure he had a teacher to awaken him.

An exceptional dialogue took place between Mr. J. Krishnamurti and a boy at Brockwood Park, the Krishnamurti

Educational Centre in England, regarding the boy's clothes and the issue of conformity. Krishnamurti says:

> "I am asking. The pop singers wear purple trousers and yellow shirts – you have seen that. They say, 'I like these clothes, they flatter me' – is that why you are doing it? So hair, clothes, the way you think, the way you feel – is it because the rest are feeling that way? The rest are Frenchmen, Germans, Jews, Hindus, Buddhists, Catholics – and you become one or the other because that is the easiest. Is that why you follow? Or do you say, 'No, that is all wrong, I won't be like that.'
>
> "So first find out why you have long hair and clothes like this, whether you are American, French or German, so that you begin to exercise your own mind. You see, while you are young, if you are not revolutionary then – I don't mean throwing bombs, which is not revolution at all – if you are not enquiring, questioning, doubting, looking at yourself, finding out what *you* think, investigating the whole field of yourself, later on it will be much more difficult." [4]

We must make a demand of ourselves to come to awareness. Only awareness is incorruptible. In awareness there is no one to like or dislike, thus opinion comes to an end by itself, naturally. The lessons of *A Course In Miracles* can free us from this world of ideas and intellectuality. But we must want to step out of it.

To allow another to be himself, one must master non-judgement and all the conflict about right and wrong. Being oneself is the key to the awakening of the spontaneous awareness of reality. Few of us make contact with that space anymore, and we don't have that space to give our children. That is the problem.

When you don't have the space, you accept your opinion of another and falseness enters the relationship. The conflict exists in you because you don't have the space to give.

If we are ever to allow our children to outgrow the voice of influence within them, we must give them the space for an intimate sharing. Only then does the real voice of the child emerge. The child's real voice will undo all the borrowed influences and opinions. The human being is an extension of the Infinite. He is not a child of the world. Do not violate his wholeness or the all-encompassing sacredness of his life.

Intellectuality has no center. It is not in contact with its own true Self, hence it is always weak and dependent. When pushed far enough it is faced with its own helplessness. Such people cannot trust. They can never know the power of the still mind.

Your reality is only love. It encompasses everything in the stillness of the mind. If you don't bring your children into contact with the sacredness of life, to the awareness of love and truth, you abandon them to the world of jobs.

# CHAPTER SEVEN

# 7

## WORKING
## WITH CHILDREN
### Part I

"Taraji* works with me by first explaining things to me. Then he asks me if I would like to do it. He says that I can sometimes even put up a fight. He always is doing things in a happy way, but sometimes he is more serious.

"Sometimes he tells me very funny stories about when he was a little boy. Sometimes he tells me stories to teach a lesson. Sometimes he just tells mischievous ones. He teaches in a way that you have to pay attention.

"Taraji taught me never to be afraid of anything. He has taught me so many important things, such as how to be orderly so that I can find everything I want. It makes me feel good inside when I am orderly. I found out that it is much easier if things are simple. You have more space and you can do anything you want. I also saw that you think with

---

* Crystal Williams is introducing Tara Singh during a retreat on *A Course In Miracles* in Santa Barbara, California in 1988. In India, the addition of the syllable "ji" at the end of a person's name denotes respect, e.g., Gandhiji. This is similar to the use of "Mr." or "Mrs." in the West. (Editor)

more space if you are simple. Taraji taught me to be grateful for whatever I get. To be grateful for whatever happens or whatever is brought to me.

"One day Taraji asked if I would like to do a journal. I said, 'Yes.' I started it, but it was harder than I thought. It got easier for a while and then I saw that when I did not want to do it, it got even harder. I started a book of questions. Now I am on my second journal.

"Taraji also taught me music. He taught me to be able to tell what they were playing. I like classical music better than today's kind of music. It's a lot calmer. I think if some of the kids would listen to it and have Taraji there to explain the music and how beautiful it is, they would probably end up liking it better too.

"One time my mom and Taraji and I stopped at the bakery in Ojai. My mom said, 'Crystal, choose one thing that you like.' Taraji said, 'Oh no, no, no, choose everything, everything you like!' One thing I can say is Taraji always plays with me like a child. He always sees the child's side of something. Like when I was first introduced to sitting quiet, he said, 'Crystal, would you like to sit quiet for ten minutes?' And then it went up more and more minutes. He said, 'Now I'm not telling you to do this. You must see how you feel.' He always either asked me what I thought or he would say he thought it would be a good idea if I did something. But he never told me to do it. I've always appreciated that from him.

"If I had not come to the Foundation I would have been a selfish little girl, not being thankful for anything, always wanting something different. I would have wanted to be someone other than who I am. Now I like who I am. Being Taraji's student keeps you on your toes. But there are so many wonderful parts. We always have a good time together. I like being his student."

Crystal Williams
(at age nine)

\* \* \*

Crystal, I was wondering at what age a child learns to be disciplined. Discipline is not something that one is told to do. Discipline is really a direct learning of what is true and what is right. And then whatever you have learned comes through when you are attentive. This way you can learn something about yourself.

For example, you may learn that when you want something you become dependent on it. Very few people ever really learn this. They become more and more dependent on their wantings. Without discipline, one will not be able to find one's own strength. This is very different from someone telling you what to do.

People tend to teach children the way society has learned and functions, the way families function, the way they know. There is either punishment or there is reward.

CRYSTAL: What does reward mean?

Reward means that if you do what I want you to do, I'll get you something special, like a new dress. The dress is the reward. It is manipulating the child to get him to do something. It is not really honest. Manipulation is a difficult word. It is something like corruption, bribery.

CRYSTAL: Oh. Trying to make them do it?

Yes. For example, if I was going to give you money to do something, you would not be doing it because you have seen the rightness of it, you would be doing it because you want to get something.

That is how they train dogs. Give the dog a biscuit and he will do anything. That is bribery. Some people may say it is encouragement, but it actually makes them dependent.

In society, in the family, in the school, there is punishment if you don't comply. If you conform – which means if you do what you are told – then you are rewarded. You are not yourself, however, because you are always conforming. Who you are, what you feel, does not matter.

I question conformity because it takes freedom away from the child. Only might is right. The parent or the school is bigger, stronger. They know. Every generation does the same thing.

Crystal, from the time you were very young, you have been very much in love with Jesus. I wonder how Mary taught Jesus? I don't think she would have told him what to do. Or if she did, he would listen. She really loved Jesus and therefore she made sure that her words were honest.

Don't you find great joy when you are doing what you want to do?

CRYSTAL: Yes.

Older people say if you allow a child to do what he likes, then the child will do the wrong things. They need to be taught; they need to be told. Well, there is some sense in that, but not at the cost of taking the space and the freedom and the gladness from the child.

Some parents worry that children will get spoiled but I am not afraid that will happen because we are friends. Crystal, how you feel is important to me. We have known each other a long time. I am sure that I can talk to you and explain the circumstance to you. If I really love you, I won't tell you what to do and what not to do. I don't want to have authority over you. I'd like to see you grow up and make your own decisions so that you won't be limited.

When children are afraid they start to lie. They begin to do things to please the teacher, to please the parents, to please everybody else. And there is no more Crystal left. I do not think that you should be controlled by outside things. You must also be given the freedom.

If we love children, we give them the space and gently point out that what they are doing is not right. The less the adult interferes the better. I did not go to school until I was nine years old. But I learned a lot more than ABC by being given freedom and trust.

Crystal, wanting stimulation from the outside makes one very dependent. Real discipline comes when you learn that what you want controls you even more than your parents. It is very difficult to put the wantings away, isn't it? But if you don't put them away, you will never find the strength that you are. I want you to know who Crystal is, the God-created Crystal.

You need good food; you need good clothes; you need clean things. And you have the need not to be controlled by your wantings. You have the strength to say, "No, I can do without that." Then you will become very strong inside.

There is part of you, Crystal, that we do not quite know yet. That Crystal is the light of the world. That is the Crystal God created. That is the Crystal that has no wanting because she always has something to give. That Crystal loves every-thing that walks and breathes and lives.

Have you seen little drops of rain on the spider's web? They are so exquisite. You feel so glad to see perfection. The world God created is perfect, and the world of man is full of wantings.

We are controlled by body feelings. I feel this way, I feel that way. If you were not ruled by body feelings all the time, if you could go a little bit beyond that, you would discover the real Crystal. So few adults have ever discovered anything beyond their feelings. When you are sitting quiet, Crystal, don't you feel some other purity – that you do not want anything and your mind comes to quiet?

CRYSTAL: Yes.

We must move in that direction.

From now on you can ask yourself, "Can I do without that wanting? Is this really essential?" You don't have to say no. You just have to see it is not necessary. That which sees it is not necessary is not a feeling, it is a gift of God. There is another clarity inside you that helps you to understand you do not need it.

Could you and I start to awaken this new clarity inside? Could we say no feeling is going to have control over us? That we will question it and free ourselves from it?

I do not want you to do something because I am saying so. I want you to do it when you understand it and you are clear that you want to do it. You must have that freedom. If I do not give you that freedom, then we are not friends.

Nothing can compare with the happiness you feel when you understand something in a very clear way. It is like a light inside of you. It brings unbelievable joy.

*    *    *

## CRYSTAL'S DIARY

Crystal, this notebook is for your diary. Each day, I want you to write in your diary the wantings that lead you to sadness, the givingness that leads you to happiness, and the things for which you are grateful. Write about these three aspects daily. Happiness and gratefulness will change the quality of your blood, purify your heart and mind, and bring order to your life. This will make givingness possible.

Your education will begin with your relationship with God, your relationship with Eternal Laws. It will be an education of Absolute Knowledge.

Real education is related to something that is not yet known – the new, the whole, the undivided. Once you know something of the glory of creation, you do not need to worry about survival or consequences. Why should there be any other kind of education?

We are so insecure we cannot give space and freedom to our children. The basis of most parents' sharings with their children is not clarity but conformity, and we have not produced a single saint in America. What we call progress spends three hundred fifty billion dollars a year on armaments. Three hundred fifty billion dollars worth of human energy and resources of the earth for utter waste! Is that the fruit of our education?

Crystal should go to school to have a good time and play with other children. She needs children. She likes school but she is not under pressure. To do well in school will provide very little effort on her part.

I am never afraid to tell Crystal the truth, for I know it is not going to start a contradiction in her. She is learning geography at school. When I teach her, I will share with her that there is no geography. These are just names man has given to things. In Reality, there is only One. I am sure that she is not going to try to correct her teacher. The child must be intelligent and wise. My sharing with Crystal is not something planned. Life brings an encounter with her, and the sharing starts naturally.

In Crystal's diary, she will write every day about gratefulness. Not gratefulness for things somebody has given her. No, gratefulness for the truth that she has seen. Every time she is grateful, she has brought something of the Kingdom of God to realization in herself. It has nothing to do with the world of duality.

If she wrote, "My mother bought me a dress and I am grateful," I would say, "Crystal, burn the dress. Gratefulness is for that which is new, for what you did not know before."

That leads us to the question: What is giving and what is receiving?

Lesson 158 of the Course is,

> *Today I learn to give as I receive.*

> *What has been given you? The knowledge that you are a mind, in Mind and purely mind...*

If she does not live in the Mind of God, she does not know what giving and receiving are. Can you see how our giving and receiving confuse the child with ignorance?

> *The knowledge that you are a mind, in Mind and purely mind, sinless forever, wholly unafraid, because you were created out of Love. Nor have you left your Source, remaining as you were created.* [1]

There is nothing to learn. That Source is still there. We just have to make the child aware. We just have to awaken her to that awareness. What else is there to teach? It is a totally different process. It is a discovery of perfection, rather than learning from lack and *becoming* perfect. Learning has failed. Mankind is at the brink of self-destruction, and we still want our children to go to school in the same old way. We cannot stop. It's just as hopeless for the adult. Can you imagine, Knowledge was given to the child at creation, and we are not going to make the child aware of that Knowledge. We ourselves do not know it.

The real teaching-learning situation begins with the Absolute Knowledge that already exists in the child. It brings the child to the recognition of it. There is nothing else to teach.

\*    \*    \*

Childhood is given to correct the tendencies that surface. Tendencies help us to know what we came to master. The teacher sees that the body is built in a way consistent with its temperament. A particular body type will be drawn to certain foods. The tendencies were given as signs of the child's body type and mental make-up so that the parents and teachers can help the child outgrow them. If tendencies are not dealt with, the child will be left with them his whole life, and not know who he is internally.

*   *   *

## WHAT TO DO WHEN A CHILD IS IN A MOOD

Acacia, you have to be careful not to make Crystal too reliant on you. I notice that when she is denied something she gets into a mood. I would not do a thing for her as long as she is in a mood. Leave her alone. Tell her that she has to find the resources within herself to get out of the mood. You will make her dependent if you go on being the "good mother."

If she is in a mood then you are doing something that is not right. When she gets gloomy she wants you, and now she feels she must go through gloom to get what she wants. The tendency to get into a mood must be corrected now, or it will harm her and make her dependent.

> *ACACIA:* I thought I was taking steps to bring about that correction.

I think every mother feels that way. Most mothers fall for that unless they have six children. A mother with just one child is disadvantaged. It is better to have two.

The real question you must ask is: Where did her mood come from? As a mother, you should know where it got started. Then you will find that she manipulates you with it. And then you have to find out what weakness in you allowed her to do that. These are the responsibilities of parents. As you make the correction in yourself, she can no longer intrude upon your space. You don't need to be harsh or use harsh words. You are just not going to get involved.

You can say, "As long as you are in a mood, I am not going to listen to you. You want to cry, you want to lie down – be my guest." That is the way to awaken children to different potentials. I could talk with Crystal for you, Acacia.

> ACACIA:  It would bring a different energy. When you've explained things in the past, there was no one to blame. Then she and I can work together.

Yes, I can do that. But in general, it is best not to talk with her about things when she is in a mood. She is not going to listen. It would be asking too much of her. After the mood is over, talk with her until you come to some mutual understanding.

*　　*　　*

Crystal, I want to talk with you about moods – not your moods, but moods. Moods have to be understood. If we don't understand them deeply, they affect our life. Whenever there is a challenge, we get into a mood. Whenever we want something we can't get, we get into moods. Eventually it becomes a habit and our life becomes bitter. It is too great a price to pay and will affect your marriage later on and everything else. So we must understand what moods are.

Sometimes, Crystal, I get a pain in my chest that wakes me up at three in the morning. Then there is a war between sleep and pain. I have a bet on which one is going to win. I am determined that sleep is going to win. They fight it out. I sip some tea slowly. In about twenty minutes the honey in the tea starts to go into the blood stream and I do some breathing, and I win the bet.

Then I asked myself, "Where does this pain come from?" I found out when I ate turkey, I got the pain. Then I saw that

I got the pain when I ate chicken enchiladas. I discovered that these birds get injections that make their lives abnormal. Crystal, can you see that I am determined to find out what causes the pain? In the same way, you are going to find out what causes the mood.

Then I started to use a special cup that has a straw for drinking. I saw that when I used that cup, again I got the pain. Since I was determined that this pain was not going to win the bet, I discovered that when I drink with the straw, the tea goes straight to the tummy and doesn't mix with the saliva, and that is what caused the pain. I'll be darned if I am ever going to have that pain again. Sleep wins!

You are learning ballet and you love it. But when you get confronted with a challenge you will escape into a mood. What dance is a moody ballerina going to do? One day the battle is going to be between the dance and the mood. If you are not in control, then the mood will be in control. We have to do something about that.

Begin to see the workings of the mood within your head. You may discover that thought champions the cause of the mood. The solution lies within your own self. Do you see that?

CRYSTAL:  Yes.

Now we will discover how it works, how it controls and regulates you and makes you find fault in other people. That is an indulgence because it evades the correction. You would be a wise girl when you have learned to witness, to observe, to become aware. The power of awareness is the solution. Do you know why? Because there is no doing in it. There is no thought in it.

Crystal, see how the mood comes, but don't dislike it. Just observe how the mood manipulates you. Write it down. As you look at it you will become wise. I am confident that you can take this on and make it a happy exploration.

LETTERS FROM CRYSTAL

Dear Taraji,

"It's hard to realize and observe a mood when you are in one. I usually become aware of a mood after it has passed. Sometimes I will not admit I was in a mood. But if someone really points it out to me, then I realize it.

"This week I got into two moods and had a hard time later realizing that I was in a mood. My dad helped me a lot. A mood, to me, is to be very sad and quiet or really upset. I think what causes my moods is when I don't get my way or when I am upset at someone. I also think the reason I don't realize I am in a mood when I am in a mood is because I am upset, and not willing to accept people pointing it out to me or me pointing it out to me.

"These are some questions I asked and answered myself. Here are some more: How can I prevent a mood by not letting my wantings and other feelings control me?

"I will work on these things. A question I have is: What is a mood? Is it being the littlest bit upset or just sad? Taraji, I am very grateful you gave me this lesson."

Love,
Crystal Williams

Dear Taraji,

"It is hard for me to know what to say. It seems like I have already said it all, but I know if I had studied my moods while I was in them, I would have something to say. It seems like every time I write, I say that this time I will really watch my moods. But I never end up watching them when I am in them. I wish I could tell myself, 'Self, you really do want to watch and observe this mood.' It is like I am in another world, unable to tell myself the right thing to do. I am sorry I have nothing much to say. This is hard. Help me, because I want to be free of moods."

Love,
Crystal Williams
(at age eleven)

Crystal, the mood would teach you. Once you have that attention, you have the keys to everything. We either don't want to look at it or we justify it because we don't have attention. The mood takes place at the thought level, especially when we feel deprived. The only option we know is to get in a mood. The issue, Crystal, is not the mood. The issue is our lack of attention. When we lack attention, we are lazy, stupid, dull. All moods come out of dullness. Attention is not personal; it is not of thought. It is another energy within the brain. The brain is petty without that energy. Trillions of people have lived since the time of Jesus, Crystal, and not many have known the light of that energy. Until the attention comes in, one stays at a sub-level. Attention sees, but it doesn't condemn.

*   *   *

## CHALLENGE

We have lost a sense of value. We think that by sending a child to school, we have done our duty. But the school doesn't awaken. Since you and I are not awakened, we don't even know it is a need. We don't know that for that need to be met, we, as parents, have to live differently.

I brought a tape about Abraham Lincoln to share with Crystal. She listened to it, liked it, and put it away. I've noticed that she is doing that a great deal right now. Curiosity is there, but there is not the space to be with anything. If this goes on, she will get into a mood every time you don't do what she wants.

> ACACIA: Yes, that is definitely happening. She loses interest. When that is lost and something is not given, then the mood comes. She is a little more focused right now and probably more receptive than she was last week.

Do you know how I would start with her? I would say, "Crystal, what are the things that really bother you? What do you dislike? Maybe we can discover together and see if we can outgrow it."

I would be her companion. I'd say to her, "You are happy now. What could I say to you that would make you unhappy? Let's see just how unhappy you can get!" I would make it alive and really interesting. I would explain to her that if she gets into moods, she will have a lonely and sad life. She may as well buy a television right now to amuse herself, since she won't have any span of interest.

I would ask her what she didn't like today. What affected her feelings? I would help her to see how she need not be controlled by her feelings. Slowly, slowly, we would work together.

The tape I shared with Crystal of Carl Sandburg reading selections he wrote about Lincoln is exceptional. His voice is extraordinary, and he has great feeling for the man. The guard at the White House comes to Lincoln and says, "Mr. President, there is a woman sitting outside the gate crying. She wants to see you." Lincoln says, "Please bring her in." Is that possible today? The lady comes in and he is not the least sentimental. He has to make decisions. How can he be phoney?

I have to introduce Crystal to what sentimentality would do. Sentimentality would not ask the woman to come in. No. Sentimentality is too busy with its own program. It would only make a gesture.

When the lady comes, Lincoln is totally with her. She tells him she has lost several sons in the war and now there is only one son left. She would like that one to be home. He hears her loss and immediately signs the order for her son's discharge.

Lincoln takes care of all the details himself because this dear lady would not know what to do. Knowing human nature and the difficulty she is going to have, he is very exact. Because he is wise, not sentimental, he has a lot of space to give. What an extraordinary quality to introduce to children!

How many things we have to outgrow in ourselves along with our children. What a joy when both the parents and the child can make the correction. We have to explain to Crystal what a challenge is and how everyone evades it, including mommy and daddy. If you stop evading challenges you will be able to communicate and transmit this strength to her. Don't try to teach Crystal until you have done it, or else your words will be abstract and just create more conflict in her. Only when we've done it, can we be outspoken, straightforward.

When children are frightened, they go for the expedient thing to do. They say the right thing but they are not true to themselves. They feel obligated to please because they don't feel safe in being themselves. And so they are polite. They conform and we consider it good.

I would say to her, "You know, Crystal, I also do this. I don't like challenges. In the evening I will tell you all the challenges I tried to evade today. And then I'll ask you how many you tried to evade." I would do this until her need to evade is gone. What a wonderful relationship to have with a child!

\*   \*   \*

## HOW TO DEAL WITH A BULLY

A few years ago there was a little boy at Crystal's school who would pull her braid, kick her, hurt her. Every time she got pinched or pricked, she would get upset and the teacher would say, "Sit down. Be quiet." By now, the teacher was beginning to see that this child is a nuisance; she can't sit still. The teacher was getting more and more irritated about it. Wherever Crystal would go to sit down, the boy would go also. And it was becoming a real problem.

Her parents asked me what to do, so I met with Crystal. "Crystal," I said, "there are a few ways to settle this thing. I will give you some choices and you can see which one suits your temperament. One of the things you can do is to beat up the boy. I can teach you how. No fight lasts more than two minutes and you can easily have him on the floor." Well, she couldn't believe her ears. She thinks I am always loving and caring. I laughed, "Are you chicken?"

You may think I am contaminating her, but she doesn't listen that way.

"If you are chicken, then someday I am going to have to put some courage in you. Nevertheless, let me give you the second choice."

There is laughter and great joy. Can you see the spirit of it? Doing the right thing murders children, because it doesn't have any spontaneity in it. We've destroyed our children with our "right thing."

"The second thing you can do, Crystal, is don't react. You are a child who is never going to be controlled by the externals. The third thing you can do is outwit him. You ought to have enough intelligence to outwit this character. Sit in a different place. Find out where he sits, and go and sit down after he does. Use your intelligence to put circles around this kid. Prove you are my student."

She has confidence now.

"Crystal, I love mischief and I want to keep the mischief alive in you. Don't become so passive that you lose your childhood. Do something naughty."

We are so afraid to talk to children honestly, or even share a truth with them because we are undermining the child's intelligence all the time. I have a certain kind of care with children, but there is always this playfulness. And children like that.

When there is trust between you and the child, the child listens. Then you can say to her, "There is nothing to fear," and it is not your idea or projection. She can hear it. But if that trust isn't established, it is just words.

When Crystal was nine, I asked her, "Would you like to make your bed? Is it too difficult for you? Would you like to try it for a week?" She was so proud that she could do it. Then I said, "Crystal, maybe now you would like to make your mother's bed. If you don't want to do it you have the freedom not to do it. But once you have agreed to it, then you must keep your word."

Life without children is like a house without flowers. But we have to give them a lot of space, not constantly tell them things. More space. More love. Try to keep toys away from them. They can make anything into a toy. Once Crystal and her friend came to my home in the country. They found a long string outside and played with it for hours. We went walking for a mile or so, and they played with the string along the whole way. Children can play with anything. They certainly don't need hideous green teddy bears.

We need to be playful but we need not *try* to play with the child. If it is in you, it would naturally come out. The child knows it. If Crystal runs away from me I'm going to pull her pigtail. It's fun. But sometimes it is very serious, even austere. She knows that she can't get away with casualness with me. The relationship never becomes wishy-washy. I believe in inspiring a child to another level; otherwise, it is not a real relationship.

We have introduced Crystal to some wonderful books. The first one she read was *Opal: The Journal Of An Understanding Heart.* [2] The original edition is out of print but an abridged version is now available. There is no comparable children's story. Crystal cried a thousand times, and she laughed a thousand times, because Opal was very sensitive in expressing how she felt. And Crystal learned that Opal never reacted. She always had something to give.

Then Crystal read *Ishi: The Last of His Tribe.* [3] All his relatives were killed by the white man, and Ishi was the only survivor. She then read the lives of saints and many great beings.*

\*    \*    \*

## NO OPPOSING VIEW

The opportunity is given to learn about ourselves when we spend close time with children. Several of us were leaving to go to Cimarron, New Mexico, yesterday. The rock formations are so nice and the drive is inspiring. As we were leaving, five-year old Cliff, whose parents are attending the retreat,** asked if he could come with us. I don't like to say no to a child, and so although the car was packed, I suggested he could come and sit on my lap.

Cliff is a handful for anyone to deal with because he is hyperactive and extremely energetic; he was not still for one minute on the whole drive. He is so direct and forceful that you are likely to get into trouble if you ever say no to him. He simply refuses to listen. I like this quality of directness in him very much though, because there is no second thought in his

---

* See Addenda: Recommended Reading/Listening for additional material to share with children. (Editor)
** The second Forty Days in the Wilderness Retreat on *A Course In Miracles* held in New Mexico in the spring of 1989. (Editor)

actions. St. Paul also had direct, passionate energy; he was self-assured and fiery. The advantage of this temperament is that, with proper guidance, there is the potential to channel the energy in a compassionate direction.

We stopped at a restaurant in Cimarron to have something to eat. I very seldom go to restaurants with children, but I learned a great deal from everything that happened.

As we walked into the restaurant, right inside the door were seven vending machines with big gum balls, candies, and a variety of goodies for children. As soon as the child steps in the door, there they are. The first words out of Cliff's mouth were, "I want candy." I was shocked to see that I never noticed that these machines were there, situated right at the child's eye level. It then becomes the child's job to get your eyes there too, and your hand in your pocket.

Again Cliff insisted, "I want candy." I said, "Yes, Cliff, you can have candy." I started looking in my pockets to give him a nickel or dime for the machine, and he said, "No, it costs a quarter." I was shocked. I gave him a quarter and expected quite a number of these big gum balls to come out. Only one came out. Instantly, you see how the innocence of a child is exploited by business. There is no protection for the child's vulnerability. It is utter lawlessness.

When people earn money that way, how is it possible that their own children will know rightness? Earning money in a false way poisons your blood, your heart, and your mind. It is not possible to violate laws of rightness and know peace within.

As soon as he got one candy, he wanted another one, and another, and then another. We had to search all our pockets for change. Pretty soon, his hands and pockets were full of candy and gum balls. I didn't lecture, I just gave him what he wanted.

When the child says, "I want one of those," how do you feel? I feel the way the child feels. Why should I have a contrary feeling to the child? Why must I always oppose what he wants? We don't want to oppose the dictatorship of business; then why do we oppose our own children? Why don't we give them the space?

We interfere and react because we're afraid of what will happen if we let the child do what he wants. We always project a consequence out of our fear. Is that what we are going to give the child instead of the candy? I'd rather give him candy. Establishing a friendship with Cliff is far more important to me at this stage than right or wrong. Any adult who is interested in the child must have a long-range view. If you don't, then the wrong and the right will stand in the way.

I learned how beautiful it is not to have a contrary opinion. But I am horrified at what the system is doing. Those little balls don't cost more than a few cents each to produce. How much profit are they getting from cheating the child? Future generations will ask why someone didn't do something. We'll have to tell them we were living at a sub-level.

In the restaurant, all of the friends who had come on the trip to spend time with me sat down in the booths along the wall. Cliff said, "I want to sit at the counter." Where does one draw the line? Well, I don't draw the line. Even though everything he wants is contrary to the way you may like it, as an adult you have to have the flexibility to overcome your plan. Being with Cliff is a constant challenge. That is not what the adults like. They think something else is more important than the child. I don't think so.

I said, "Of course, Cliff, I'd love to sit at the counter. What would you like to eat?" He saw someone with a large plate of french fries and orange juice and so he said, "French fries and orange juice." Whatever he sees is what he wants. We ordered french fries and orange juice. Then, he saw a lady carrying milk and he said he wanted milk. I said, "Cliff, you can't have both because they don't mix well. It will make you sick." He listened. When your words are factual, they have their own energy. You don't become indifferent. We are supposed to protect the child but we are protecting ourselves.

When I told the waitress that we would like to change our order from orange juice to milk, she asked if he wanted regular milk or chocolate milk? I thought to myself, "Another trap." Cliff said, "Chocolate."

So we had chocolate milk and a pyramid of french fries. I asked Cliff if I could try one. He protested, "No!" I said, "What do you mean, 'No?'" I picked one up and ate it. He liked that – another kid, just like him.

I didn't have any resistance to him. He felt calm in that atmosphere because nothing was denied him. There was more space in his universe. Riding home on my lap in the car, he slept the whole way. It was such a joy being with him. I could caress him, notice how soft his hair is, and really love him while he was asleep. You couldn't touch him any other way. This was the beginning of closeness between us.

When we returned to the retreat center, he went and hugged his mother, Kenna. It was the first time in months that he had allowed her to hug him. She couldn't believe the change in him in just a few hours. His first duty was to show her all the candies he had bought. When Kenna asked him where he got those, he said with pride, "Taraji got these for me."

When the opposing view is not there, slowly a confidence, a friendship, can take place. Trust develops. If one was with Cliff in this way for a couple of weeks, his whole temperament would change because there would be no opinion opposing him. If we try to drop our opinion and be a nice guy, he will sense that we are being false. There must be a genuine change in you as a parent, or as a friend.

Because we are not afraid of the unknown anymore, we make contact with it. This increases Cliff's chances of making contact with it too. This is the highest education. No school, no teacher, no university offers this. It is worth everything if you could bring some other factor into your relationship with the child. This factor is the source of his life and your life. Can your interaction with the child emerge from that state? Then something else may happen.

*     *     *

In order for the parent to come to "no opposing view," he must first have established the right foundation with the child – one in which the child knows that his parent's words are true and dependable. The parent's fairness and integrity will nurture confidence and trust in the child.

*     *     *

## DO ONLY THAT

When I met with Steve and Kenna, Cliff's parents, some time later, we talked about *do only that*, [4] imparted by Jesus in *A Course In Miracles*. Children hear, "Don't do this, don't do that," all day long and eventually they stop listening. Have you ever wondered why one becomes deaf? Deafness results because one loses interest in listening. Or when one has failed to listen to the crying need of another, the consequences are one becomes deaf.*

Now apply this to continually telling children, "Don't do this, don't do that." We actually teach our children not to listen by telling them no all the time. For their own protection, they must block out the words and the electricity of attention goes away.

*A Course In Miracles* intimates that we should not use the negative approach with the child all the time. It suggests telling the child *do only that. Do only that* is a law; it is not the authority of the parent or the teacher over the child. When your yes is yes and your no is no, you have a right relationship

---

* "Deaf" refers to being unwilling to listen or hear, not congenital deafness. (Editor)

with your child. Because you have heard the words of Jesus, *Do only that*, you have the integrity of these words to transmit. When you say something, you mean it. It is not an opinion, something that can be changed one way or another. You, the parent, are with a fact, not with the habit or tendency. It may take some time to get this across, but parents must be the law that does not compromise. When the child burns himself with fire, he learns the law of fire. He is not going to touch fire again.

Shortly after our talk, Cliff's parents shared with me that when he got up one morning, the first thing Cliff wanted was a dollar to buy candy. He actually took his father's wallet to get the money himself. Steve insisted that Cliff could not have the money and succeeded in getting the wallet back. Cliff had a tantrum and turned the tables over, but Steve was firm. He was not trying to coax or convince him; he was a law. From early in the morning, until three o'clock in the afternoon, Cliff went on with his demand. Finally Steve could no longer stay in the same room with him so he went for a walk around the property and in the field. In bare feet, Cliff ran out of the room after him and doggedly followed him wherever his father went, over sharp rocks, cement, weeds.

At the point where Cliff broke down and realized his father was not going to give into his demand, Steve turned to him and said, "Cliff, we could have had such a beautiful day together but now you've wasted the whole day." He held him in his arms for a time.

As they were walking back to the room, Cliff's younger sister Nora came crying for money to buy candy. Cliff looked at her and said, "Don't waste your time, Nora. He is not going to give it to you." Some understanding had taken place and now Cliff could save time for Nora. Cliff recognized the power of *do only that* and he became an extension of it to Nora. How life always reveals what has been learned. It was a turning point for all of them.

Steve discovered that *do only that* has something else in it. When you are not going to waiver, your certainty gets transmitted. The law is something very different from opposing or complying. Gradually, Cliff discovered that his father was not going to budge and that became his strength. Where there is certainty, consistency is possible. The wise always acts out of awareness, hence, his words bear the light of certainty. Certainty in reality is impersonal.

If we could live by *do only that* in our lives, we would also discover another strength. *Do only that* applies to anyone who wants to overcome his habits and tendencies, his outlets and indulgences. It applies to anyone who wants to relate with Eternal Laws.

Cliff has the capacity to be a very idealistic person – somewhat like a mystic, somewhat like Saint Paul. He has the passion, the drive, the single-mindedness. He just needs a direction. Given his temperament, if one is not sensitive to him, he could become very disillusioned.

> *How can you wake children in a more kindly way than by a gentle Voice That will not frighten them, but will merely remind them that the night is over and the light has come?* [5]

Cliff and I would be some combination! If he can have his candies, he can have saintly people in his life, too. He would be very inspired by the lives of saints. We have to make the space for that.

\* \* \*

## SITTING QUIET

Crystal, it is fine for you to go and play. But first try to sit quiet for a short time. Your wanting to do it would give you the strength. See if you can discover that it is possible to be still. You know, the monkeys in India not only eat in a funny way, they also are never still. When you are not quiet, your hand goes here, your legs go there. You don't want to be a blond monkey, do you?

When you are still, it will teach you something. There is an energy that rises along the spine. As it rises, your mind will become quiet and peaceful. You will never want anything of the world. Nothing. Your mind will be silent and pure. The world needs you, Crystal, because you will be a light.

Sitting quiet is very important. Do you want to try it for five minutes? Sit with your spine straight; fold your legs comfortably. As long as the spine is straight, it is very nice. See, Lord Buddha sits that way. Sri Ramakrishna sits that way. Erect. Silent. Lazy, ordinary people are slouching all the time; they are like the monkeys.

Become aware of every movement the body makes. As you become aware, you will see that the body makes no movement. It is effortlessly still. You are not making it still.

Your eyes will become so powerful, you will see twenty times more than others. And then one day you will see lights around everything. That is real learning – the world of God, the world of light!

> *And let us receive only what You have given, and accept but this into the minds which You created and which You love.* [6]

This is something we have to learn over and over again.

So sit for a few minutes and then say, "Hand, I will not let you wander about. I am the boss. Spirit, you are in control." As long as the body is in control of you, you are ordinary. Do you know what ordinary means? Ordinary means that you are full of wantings. Once you touch upon that stillness, the wantings disappear. And then you have so much to give because you have found your happiness inside.

Acacia, whenever you sit in the morning and evening with Crystal, sit still with your spine erect the way Crystal is sitting. If you are still, she will be still. You cannot ask her to be still when you are not. *A Course In Miracles* explains that *to teach is to demonstrate.* [7] That is the way to work with a child.

## CHILDREN LOVE TO SERVE

When my children would come home from school, the first thing they would ask was, "Where is Papaji?" I could hear their feet running up the three flights of stairs to the terrace where I spent most of my time. When they got there, they would sit down and we would have great laughters.

One of the things I discovered with my children was that, although we had many servants in the house, if I wanted something, no sooner did I ask them, they would be off and running to get it for me. I thought to myself, "I have been in the wrong country, America. There the children have the parents doing everything! My children would feel deprived if they couldn't do something for me." So I took a better look at the Indian and other ancient cultures where it was emphasized that children should work. Mr. Krishnamurti said that children should be given work to do.

As I look back on it now, I begin to see that the joy of the child is to share, to do what the adult is doing, and to help. We merely distract him with nonsensical toys and stories.

When I told Crystal that she was my "butleress," something blossomed in her. It gave her energy, a sense of importance. She probably will never be subservient to anyone because she is learning to give. She loves to give. No world is going to put her in an office or make a demand on her inner freedom.

My children began that way. It was natural. And then I taught them to do it better, which brought us closer. If one of them brought a water glass with his hands dripping wet, holding the glass by the rim, I could say, "Papaji doesn't drink that way. Let me show you how to hold the glass." And they saw it. Whatever they were doing, they were learning that there was a better way to do it. There was a more gracious way to offer it. This kind of sharing strengthens a relationship. Crystal will be as gracious as a queen. She will know how to serve, how to train others to serve, and how to be served.

Today, she asked me if I would like some sparkling water. I said, "Half sparkling water, and half plain water, with this much ice, in a tall glass." She is learning what I like, and she is becoming particular. The next time I will not have to tell her. She finds so much joy in serving and she is energetic. Soon she will know what I want before I do. That is real love.

*   *   *

## CRYSTAL AT AGE 11 – FINDING AN INTEREST

The other day I noticed that Crystal didn't have anything to do or anyone to play with. She was very lonely. Nowhere in the world is there the particular kind of loneliness one finds in America. It is actually part of the vibration of the country. So often when great beings came here, especially musicians like Dvorak or Bartok, they were plagued by it. The cinema and television would naturally be developed here, as would nuclear weapons. Out of loneliness, people either become lazy or they get active. Loneliness is not very conducive to serenity.

In other cultures, where people are closer to nature, they are not so lonely. Their daily life is more balanced and normal and there are still strong bonds and human warmth within the family. Here so many children grow up isolated. There are fewer friends and so much transiency, and neither parents nor children know what to do. Children's lives become blank and empty. Other than television and going to school, they have no contact with anything which will set them free like wild horses, something that is not conditioned.

How can we respond to this fact that our children are lonely? We may not be able to change the situation so that there are more children in the neighborhood. We would have done that by now if it were possible. One would think a prosperous country like this could have had space for a children's park with fountains every few blocks. But it is not that way.

It is important that we deal with this loneliness now because as Crystal grows a little older and goes to high school, it will compel her to be false to herself. We are not fully aware of the fact that loneliness is a force. Children become dependent on what is comfortable and cozy, anything that can assuage this overwhelming emptiness. Out of dependence, havoc results. Instead of togetherness, we lean more and more toward an indulgent life.

Commercialized indulgence is a vast industry. Escapes and outlets have become the cornerstone of our modern economy. Lack of human warmth regulates our lives. Can you see the challenge we are facing? A child's life is extremely precious. To be integrated, the child needs grandparents and cousins and nature. Replacing them with television, candy, baseball, and movies will not suffice.

In the rural areas of India, where all the girls are considered sisters and all the boys brothers, there are various protections for the children. The families have been together for centuries, and parents don't have to pressure the children to get jobs. They are not going to get rid of them. Here "mind your own business" has isolated us to such a degree that it is beyond the control of parents to do anything. In the city, there is not so much to capture a child's interest. There are no trees to climb, or a variety of animals to care for and develop a relationship with. How many children have a garden of their own?

In looking at this situation, Crystal, what came to me is that the only way to cope with loneliness today is to develop, or discover, an interest – something that gives you energy, something that you enjoy doing. I don't know what your interest would be, but we must uncover it. No one can tell you what your interest is. It has to be your own inner discovery. The minute you get connected with it, everything else is going to become secondary. It will be like a friend. People who find their interest also find that their life is rich because they have made contact with life itself.

Your interest will free you from being dependent on the externals and will adequately meet this vibration of loneliness. It will relate you with other people who are also balanced, who have also been protected from this degeneration. We cannot fight degeneration today without discovering interest. Children who have no interests are distracted and the distractions lead to indulgences. Once the first step toward indulgences is taken, the other is sure to follow.

As a rule, children are not very interested. The task for parents and teachers is to discover how to awaken a child's interest. We can begin with whatever is at hand.

When I am interested, Crystal, I look at the color of this apricot and it melts my heart. Its color has a healing quality. It is so delicate, so lovable.

To appreciate an apricot you have to be hold it gently. Its skin is like that of a newborn baby. When you touch it and feel its warmth, interest begins to rise. Look at the shape of the apricot, it is not totally round. Where it is connected to the tree, it is shaped differently. Wouldn't you like to see if other apricots are the same?

Hold this apricot in your hand. Can you feel that there is a pit in it? Do you wonder what color the pit is? Now let's open the apricot. How does it look inside? If it is not ripe, then the pit will hold onto the flesh. If it is ripe, the pit will be loose. Why isn't the pit smooth? Crystal, that pit has the power to grow millions upon millions of apricot trees for decades to come. The pit of the apricot is part of the miracle of the timeless glory of creation. We cannot ignore it. What if there were only one seed in the world? That one seed could populate a continent. What would that seed be worth? More than the currency of nations.

When you look at an apricot now, can you see something timeless in it? You couldn't find anything greater than the apricot to relate you with your own eternity.

Let's discover the bell pepper now. Do you see the liveliness of its vibrant green, as precious as an emerald? Open it and look inside. It is spacious, bigger than the inside of the apricot. The seeds are tiny, white, and so many. Each seed has the potential to grow countless more bell pepper plants.

Now take the green onion; look at its beautiful shape. See the white root and how it blends slowly into the green stalk. It is creative, natural. When you see its perfection, something else is transmitted and you are inspired. That inspiration is just as essential as food or nourishment. When you see an apricot, bell pepper, or green onion in this way, then you would want to extend your goodness.

I would like to suggest, Crystal, that for the next thirty days, you find fruits, vegetables, and leaves, and write to me about what you see in them. You will find that you not only have new eyes to see, but you will have attention. And the stillness that accompanies attention will lift you out of boredom and loneliness forever.

I don't want you to write to me about the obvious. I want you to tell me what you discovered. If you tell me the onion is the color of rust and the upper part is brittle like paper, I'll say, "Big deal." Seeing the obvious is no miracle, because the eyes see that naturally. But when you look behind the appearance, you may see something that is not obvious. And then you may see the One Life behind it all. There is no end to seeing. Seeing may not even be physical at a more refined level.

I'm interested in starting with the obvious, and going further and further, until we come to a purer energy. It is not even a substance anymore but the spirit – the intelligence of creation itself. I want to see the creative action that produced the onion. So every time you tell me something, I will say, "Yes, Crystal, that is good. But what else is there?"

There is a wonderful story which illustrates this point of going beyond the obvious.

In the fifteenth century, there was a king who needed a new prime minister. The queen thought their son was best suited, but the all-knowing king was skeptical. He had someone else in mind whom he felt was more capable of being just and wise. Every day the queen brought up the subject in the hopes of convincing her husband. Finally, the king decided to put it to the test. He called his son into his chamber and told him that near the outskirts of the city there was a ditch where a bitch had just given birth to a litter of puppies. The son was to go and find the pups and bring the king a report of what he saw. After his son left, the king called in the other prospect for the prime ministership and presented exactly the same task to him.

Shortly thereafter, his son returned and arrogantly walked into his father's chambers. "Fine test this is," he was thinking. When the king asked him how many puppies he saw, his son said, "Seven." Then the king asked, "How many males and how many females?" His son was shocked. "You didn't tell me to check on that." So off the son went to make another inspection. Again he returned after a short time and said, "Three are male; four are female." "What is their condition?" asked the king. "Their condition?" Off he went on another mission to check the puppies.

In the meantime, the other man who was sent on the assignment was called into the king's chambers. He said, "I checked on the puppies, your highness. Four are female, three are male. They are all brown in color with the exception of two females which have black markings. Five have their eyes open, but one male and one female are not healthy and their eyes are still closed. It is not likely they will survive. The mother is thin, but in good condition." Thus, it was apparent who was the best choice for prime minister.

In the same way, Crystal, don't you be satisfied with the obvious and need seven trips to count the puppies.

We must bring you to that kind of inner energy where you will begin to make more demand of yourself. This is the process which leads to awakening. First there is the interest, then attention. Somewhere attention becomes awareness. Awareness is impersonal. To get to the impersonal awareness, you have to give the attention. Silence is the fruit of attention. So, Crystal, start with visible things and they will relate you with the perfection of life.

You know, Crystal, when you said to me, "I'm bored," I thought, "How glad I am to hear that." When I lived in New York, I was bored too. I came from another culture and did not speak the language well. I was painfully lonely and bored. I would walk several miles to see a tree like the one we had in India. For months, day in and day out, I was so lonely until I discovered literature, music, and architecture. I would read every evening from eight until two, sometimes spending four hours on four pages because I demanded of myself to discover the truth of what was written. This was how I taught myself to read.

Aloneness need not be lonely if you have interest. When interest introduces you to attention, you become your own pupil and your own teacher. Just being attentive would make you exceptionally sensitive. Let us see what this one month would do.

This exercise brought about the awakening of an aesthetic sense in Crystal. She was inspired to bring my meal on a tray with a fascinating beautiful arrangement of flowers and leaves. She has become so creative and particular about what she wears, what she says, and being a student.

ACACIA: How should we help Crystal find her interest?

You can read Lao Tzu to her. Just his simplicity will bring about a pure space. Within one stanza he lifts one to timelessness, like the calm serenity of twilight and dawn. Read the story of John Muir's boyhood and youth, as well as Dear Papa, [8] letters between John Muir and his daughter Wanda. Now and then read Krishnamurti's Commentaries on Living, [9] The Secret

*Life of Plants* [10] by Bird and Tompkins, and Nehru's *Glimpses of World History.* [11]

Crystal should see paintings of Rothko to appreciate the dignity and vibration of color itself. Show her Nicholas Roerich's paintings of mountains. Books and postcards are available. Look at the painting of St. Joan of Arc by Bastien-Lepage. The purity of the expression in her eyes is not of the world. A barefoot walk on the beach close to the surf is something money can't buy. It is one of the lifegiving moments of leisure.

There is so much to introduce her to, Acacia, but it should not be imposed upon her. If it is imposed, she will isolate herself. I have seen people who are naturally gifted and drawn to a certain expression, but when they have to do it, it eventually becomes competitive and is no longer an interest. It becomes vanity, drawing attention to oneself.

Crystal, you will know right away when you make contact with your inner calling. It will absorb you and give you energy and direction. Then you won't be part of degeneration. In degeneration, people become sloppy. They don't dress well, and they are casual and vulgar in their speech and their manner. When we don't make contact with the spirit, we become more earthy.

The external environment is not helpful because there is no joy in it. It has made children dependent on buying things from shops. In itself, it has nothing. With so much dependence on the externals, few children flower inside.

Until you find your interest, do the things you enjoy – baking, violin, ballet. Also sit quiet morning and evening. You can tell Jesus, "I don't know what to do. What is my interest? You love children. What do you want me to do?" He will open doors for you. You will bring something of God to earth and you will enrich other people's lives.

In India, Crystal, they have great love for God. And they express it by making their altar in their home very beautiful, with fresh flowers every day. This is a wonderful thing for you to do – make an altar in your room and decorate it in a very nice way. Spend half an hour sitting quiet, half an hour fixing your altar, and then when you have done that with all your heart, you will sense that Jesus is there. How would you move if Jesus were there? Not casually, would you? Someday, you may even see Him.

\*     \*     \*

## TAKING ON A RESPONSIBILITY

Since we talked about interest, Crystal, I am beginning to see that it may be wise for you to take on a responsibility so that you never have time to be lonely.

Without taking on a responsibility now, loneliness would rule your life and degeneration would start. Eventually you will find you are not in control. Then you will give in to whatever you think fills the gap. That is the illusion, however, because it will never really meet the need. You will feel abandoned again internally and each time it will be worse than before. As long as we don't find the happiness inside, we look for pleasure outside. Everything that gives pleasure comes from the earth. But happiness comes when you want nothing of the world. Where there is pleasure, there is also sorrow. They always go together. People like pleasure because they are essentially in sorrow. If they were happy, they wouldn't want anything.

All outlets are an attempt to escape sorrow and loneliness. Out of sorrow, we go to the movies, buy things, kill time. Modern society has done nothing to dissolve sorrow, it has actually intensified it. Until we have found the happiness within us, however, there will be no peace.

I don't think anything distracts Mother Teresa. Because she has the happiness within, her brain doesn't chatter. She sees the light of Christ in every single person. Whether you are a good girl or a bad girl doesn't matter to her.

What we are seeing, Crystal, is that by the age of eleven, children must develop a sense of responsibility. First, I want you to see the wisdom of this. Without responsibility, you will not be able to deal with distractions and impurities such as laziness and selfishness. The responsibility will introduce you to the strength inside of you. Laziness is going to say, "Never. Never." Selfishness is going to say, "I want to go to the movies today." And boredom is going to say, "I don't want to do anything." Everything is going to try to take you away from responsibility. But if you can still be responsible in the face of laziness, then you are something of a law unto yourself. You are in control. This strength has to be found by each one of us – parents and children alike.

Because schools don't really know how to impart this, teachers give you homework. But homework doesn't make you responsible. When you are responsible, you would be able to see something through. You will be reliable. You will have confidence because when you say you will do some-thing, there will be certainty in it – no doubt, no conflict. Certainty relates one to something of God.

*   *   *

## LETTERS FROM CRYSTAL

Dear Taraji,

"I have been thinking about responsibility and what I could do. I came up with the idea of keeping the incense bowl clean at the altar at the Foundation. I do not know if this is too small a thing? But if I could do it, I would really do it, not just a little time here and there.

"I have also been thinking about interest. I am still wondering if I should add to all of my other interests of ballet and violin. I am very happy to add another thing, but I am wondering if I should just be more focused and regular about them (ballet and violin)?

"I am very happy. I have been sitting quiet every day. School is ok, still lots of homework, but much better the past two days.

"Thank you, Taraji, for all of the lessons you have taught me."

Love,
Crystal Ann Williams

\*   \*   \*

## GHOSTS

Dear Taraji,

"I love you very much. For the past few days I have been scared at night. It's not because I don't like the room. I love the room. It feels like a real room. I bought a big pot and some flowers that I am going to plant. I have three trees that I also got pots for. I have my altar set up right next to the window which is real nice.

"But at night I get scared that there are ghosts in the room. I don't know why I thought of that. But my brain keeps thinking of scary things. It is like my brain or my self turned against myself. My Dad told me there are no such things as ghosts. That helped a little. I don't know what to do. Is being scared a mood?

"I know I have to start to get much better and not have moods and jealousy. But I don't exactly know how to work on jealousy. I know you told me not to not be jealous – that it is ok to be jealous. But when I feel jealous, I don't feel ok, I feel bad.

"I thank you so much for showing me and teaching me everything you have."

Love,
Crystal Ann Williams
(at age twelve)

Dear Crystal,

"If ghosts were driving the buses and selling candy and popcorn to kids at the cinema, even if they were shopping at the supermarket, I can still assure you that no ghost dare enter a room where there is an altar of God. Even fire cannot enter a sacred place where the Presence of holy pictures is alive.

"You are fully protected. Ghosts are in the head and fear puts them there. There are no ghosts but if there ever were ghosts, they would be in the beauty salons where superficial women have their hair turned to foxtails.

"Crystal, you are a child of God. You are blessed and protected, because your life is meant to be a light in the world and to serve those in need.

"Crystal, if possible, it would be good if you went every Saturday to the Missionaries of Charity with the other people from the Foundation to help feed the poor. It will inspire you. You have a direction in your life. It is the one thing very few other children in the world have.

"My prayers surround you, Crystal. No harm can ever come to you. If you see a ghost, give him my address."

Much love,
Tara Singh

*   *   *

Dear Taraji,

"I wanted to write and thank you for the phone call. I will work on the fruit and eye exercises daily.

"I am sad now because the girl next door is playing with little Crystal, and I have no one to play with. But I know little Crystal has been in this position before too. But when I think about you and what we talked about, I feel a little better.

"I have been going to Mother Teresa's (Missionaries of Charity in Lynwood, California) every Saturday. I like it a lot. I love to help them. It makes me feel good.

"Taraji, I am wondering about the jealousy. It hurts me to be jealous. But sometimes I get angry. But all that disappears when I think of the time when I was with you in the dining room at the Foundation, and we were talking and no one dare enter the room.

"I love being your student. I wish I could be with you every day and I could talk to you and over-come my moods and jealousy. You give me great strength, Taraji. Now thinking about all this, I feel much better. I am going to live my life as your student. I will always be honest with you. Thank you. You have given me the greatest gift – the ability to be your student. I love you very much."

Love,<br>
Crystal Ann Williams<br>
(at age twelve)

# CHAPTER EIGHT

# 8

## WORKING WITH CHILDREN
## Part II

*The following sharing took place during the Forty Days In The Wilderness Retreat, held in New Mexico from April 1 to May 19, 1990. These parents attended the retreat with their children. It was the second Forty Days Retreat which families attended, and provided a blessed opportunity to bring clarity to the fundamental issues which they, and most parents, have to face in raising young children.* (Editor)

### INTRODUCING A CHILD TO HIS OWN STRENGTH

"Lord, You have promised that You will always be there when we ask for Your help and make space to heed. You have said:

*If it helps you, think of me holding your hand and leading you. And I assure you this will be no idle fantasy.* [1]

"Knowing that You are here, we pray,

*This holy instant would I give to You.*
*Be You in charge. For I would follow You,*
*Certain that Your direction gives me peace.*" [2]

A child is entrusted not only to parents but to all of us. And we have to introduce him to what is of the spirit. If we fail to do this it is unlikely he will ever know he is anything other than a body. Limited to body senses, he becomes isolated. His behavior becomes abnormal and correction is difficult. This is the situation with your son, Scott. Often we get confused when it comes to the point of correction. But we have to make corrections.

Some people may say this is just how the child is. I say, "No, we just don't understand him. He is of God." We *can* understand, however, that what he is doing is going to lead him to consequences, and it is our joint responsibility to prevent this. Whether the child is Stephen, Tara, Lisa, or John, it doesn't matter. These are only names.

When it comes to bringing about correction, punishment and reward have become the only resources we know. But we are here because we want to find a way that is different from punishment and reward. That doesn't mean we will not be austere. Austerity is not punishment.

We also know that at the level of cause and effect there are consequences. The child is unaware of this but we, as adults, are farsighted. How could we let the child go on, knowing that at the level of cause and effect he will be a victim of consequences? If we love him, we cannot do that. It becomes more difficult when we think he is "bad." What is "bad" is our lack of clarity. And all of us, adults and children alike, are very unwilling to change that. This is a challenging situation, but it is only difficult to the extent that we have options.

*PARENT:*   What do you mean by austerity?

The austerity I am talking about is when you use *do only that*. [3] That means you are not correcting the child incessantly. Your words must have the strength of authenticity behind them. The austerity of keeping it simple would help.

Last year we discovered the wisdom of having no opposing thought, and giving children space. But that doesn't mean you are never going to be firm with Scott, especially now that he is six. You and I are responsible for that balance. If that balance is not kept, we can't blame the child.

It is more critical now because if we don't introduce that balance, direction, and guidance to him – if we don't set limits – his obstinacy will be strengthened.

Scott now assumes the role of the ringleader, but fundamentally he is not courageous. Probably it is just the opposite. And that is what is going to get him into consequences. Now he has Jonathan as his sidekick and they are both affecting the other children. We can't be indifferent but we can't be harsh, either. There has to be the strength of *do only that*. He may think it is cruel, but that is only his definition for this moment. It is not a fact.

One day Scott went into the transcribing room where Melanie was concentrating on something. He began to disturb her, and she turned to him and said abruptly, "I am concentrating on this! Please don't make any noise!" He left the room, closing the door with a gentleness you would not have believed. I feel confident that *do only that* will work. In these words, *do only that*, there is something of the Christ. Other forces are with you if you don't compromise.

This is an age where words have lost their meaning. Your words, however, are going to have meaning. If you don't deal with this now, you will wind up blaming him, so correction is a benefit to your whole family.

There is no mystery with someone who is predictable. And Scott is predictable. You know what he is going to do. Wherever you are, he will try to run away. You have to lock the door ahead of time, but you can cope with it.

You must be firm with him until he really hears it and knows that when you say something, you mean it. It is a law. First there is going to be a fury. He'll want to break things, hurt the girls, or lash out at you. You gently say, "No."

*FATHER:*  You don't allow him his reaction?

Absolutely not. If we allow the reaction, what will he grow up to be? Once you are sure you are not going to compromise, that clarity will stay with you. You are going to be firm. That's all. Scott won't listen as long as he is filled with reaction. And you are not going to let him get away with the reaction. It will take a while. Just stay with it.

He will fight you – possibly for hours – and you will not give in. At the end of the struggle, he will come to a point where he sees that he can't do anything. Then you will be loving to him. If you don't impart that strength to him, you are not being true to your function as his parent. This is austerity. Austerity becomes something beautiful. He may translate it in a different way, but you are extending something to him which only his parents can give.

It is still possible to correct it now although it might take four hours to get one little point across. But as the days go on, it will take less and less time. Someday four minutes will do it because he will know once you've said something, you mean it. It will begin to get across to him that there is nothing he can do; that he is making it difficult for himself; and that you are not angry. But you are not compromising either. You are austere but not angry. Talk to him in a loving way when he starts to weaken, not when he is reactive. I know he will begin to listen.

In most situations like this, the solution inevitably comes to the "or else." Behave or else leave. To me, that is not meaningful. When you are headed in that direction, why deceive yourself? Take the "or else" away from us and we don't know what to do, because we are not related to Reality. We don't know what love is. We don't know what responsibility is. These are just ideas to us. We want to go beyond the ideas. We are dealing with life.

If we don't correct this in Scott now, just imagine the kind of difficulty he will have in school. The teacher will not be able to cope with him. He is too provocative. He will wind up seeing a psychiatrist.

We said don't have an opposing thought against him in a situation that is not harmful to himself, to you, or to anybody else. Those are the parameters. The discrimination is yours. When you use *do only that*, let it be a law – no matter what he does. Reaction can never change the law.

It is only difficult to bring about change when we have options. If you don't have an option, you have to do it. If we don't find the strength within ourselves as parents and as teachers, how are we going to introduce Scott to his strength? The rightness of this is good for him and it is good for you and me. Rightness is independent of circumstances.

> *FATHER:* It seems that it will be important that whenever we start with *do only that*, it has to be something we are fairly certain we can see through – something that is a sure win.

You've got it. You need a victory. That way you are in charge.

In the present situation he is harming himself and the other children by being disruptive and teaching them to be disrespectful. You have to respond. You can't afford to sit back and say, "I can't do anything." It is unfair to him because that is not who he is. It may be wise to eat together as a family in your suite for a few days. Start with teaching him that there is order when you eat. First, establish ground rules for meals. Once these are honored, then join everyone in the dining room. Now the disorder is too much of a strain on all of you.

> *FATHER:* This is one we can win.

Now whenever you ask him to do anything, his first response is "No." As we begin to work with him, we have to change that no to a yes. This is called reverence.

There is something of a sacred atmosphere at this retreat. And you have come with your children to be touched by this atmosphere. This correction is part of that. We have the Prayer Vigil going all day and all night. Your children and the other children love to go and sit in the Prayer Room, even just for a short time. Make sure that both of you pray over Scott when he is asleep. Every day. The heavens are with us.

Right now we can correct this misbehavior and disobedience in a week. Later on, seven years won't correct it and the consequences will get worse. Adults have the advantage of knowing the whole picture. Children do not. In actuality, Scott may have little to do with the fact that he gets stimulated. There are forces within him that get activated. It may be beyond his control.

You have to be clear about one thing. You are not changing Scott – you are introducing him to his own strength. That changes the whole thing. It takes away the guilt and will give you some conviction. The order you bring in your lives will bring order in Scott's life. Always pray and ask for help. He is a child of God, and one day both of you are going to be proud of him. He is very talented. His energy merely needs to be turned in a different direction.

We are doing this to introduce him to his own vitality, his own inner strength. I wish that was the intention of education. Schools today merely teach skills. The only ones who can help the child make these corrections are the parents. Yet we are more isolated from the right way of life than he is.

It is understood that Scott will react, especially in the beginning. Don't you react. Just be firm. You are not dealing with the externals, with what he wants. You are dealing with *do only that*. Thank God there is an end to all emotions and all crises. Because they are of time, they come to an end.

Give your whole mind and heart to it. Once you are committed, let him throw a fit. You be at peace. Whenever he wants to come to you, you are at peace. Say it once and no more. You are going to teach him that your words are not meaningless.

> *MOTHER:* Could you explain to me what
> the role of the mother is?

It is very simple. Because the mother has a stronger bond with the child, her love, her atmosphere, is to introduce him to something that is not of the earth. Through your love for him he will know that he is not just physical. He will sense that within the physical there is another Reality.

What can a mother do? Awaken him to his eternity. The nature of a child is identical to the nature of God.

*   *   *

## THE CHILD AND THE PARENTS
## WANT TWO DIFFERENT THINGS

You and I may want one thing; the child wants another thing, and we don't know which is which. We want a life that is one-dimensional, over-simplified, in which there is no challenge, where we can do the same thing every day. The newness of life is a challenge. It confuses us and we get lost.

Acacia, we want to explore the situation that arose when you and Crystal were going to see the ship, the Queen Mary. You have to be here, Acacia, when there is a class at the Foundation because what is shared is vital. And it is just as vital that Crystal not be ignored merely because she is a child. But we don't know how to think in a whole way. Then the parents get frustrated and tell the child no because that is the easiest way. They don't have to think, and the child accepts that this is how parents are. "Might is right" prevails and the child is *told.* With Crystal, we are trying not to do that.

You cannot always deny the child, nor can you always acquiesce to her wishes. Maybe you could make her aware of the whole situation. You could say, "Crystal, if I had a job somewhere, do you think you could call me on the phone and ask me to take you to the Queen Mary?" We have to see this as a fact. When you were working at Lockheed, Acacia, Crystal couldn't call you and ask you to leave your work and take her somewhere. At the Foundation there is more freedom but where total freedom is given, responsibility goes with it.

Acacia, could you be sensitive enough to see that you could take Crystal to the Queen Mary, or you could tell her the truth? Could you tell her that this is an important day for you? And Crystal, could you see the whole picture and say to your Mommy, "If that's important, I don't mind not going to the Queen Mary." I have trust in you, Crystal, because I know that you will be honest with yourself.

We all say that we want to go to the movies, to the museum, to the Queen Mary. It is neither good nor bad. Everybody wants to go somewhere. In reality, nobody ever goes anywhere. They are really just running away from their own emptiness because they haven't found happiness inside of them. Because we don't know what to do, we want to run away. So you're not going to the Queen Mary, you're running away from the fact that you don't know what to do with yourself. Do you think you would want to run around if you had something wonderful happening within you? Happiness is inside. But we are always trying to find it outside of us. When the emptiness inside doesn't know what to do, it wants to go out and get busy.

Very few people are not afraid of the emptiness. But that emptiness can be filled with God's love. That emptiness can be filled with great happiness. And it is that happiness that we give to everybody. If you don't have it to give, then all day long you will be busy wanting. This is the only education. All other education is merely part of the running away.

Now tell me how you understand the emptiness.

CRYSTAL: I understand that I go out to get something to entertain me, so that I have something to do in the day.

Yes. Now could you say it so that you don't blame yourself? Could you say people go out to be entertained? Otherwise one starts, "I'm bad." I don't like that. Nobody's bad. Everybody's beautiful. People go out to be entertained because they don't know what to do. In this way we are understanding something called a principle or a law. It's not personal anymore. We are all taught to go out to entertain ourselves. And all of us must first see this is how we live before we can change.

If your Mommy had a lot of money, she would go to buy a dress. And Daddy would want to buy a car. We don't know what to do with ourselves. And now we're learning that we can't tell you, "Don't go," because we are also always running away from our emptiness through stimulation. Isn't it wonderful how the child brings the parents to a different kind of integrity? And when we make the correction in ourselves, you will find it easier also.

Most people love their children only if the children conform, if they do what the parents tell them to do. Then they say, "I love you. You're a good girl." Try to do it the way you want to do it, and they don't like it. Then they punish. Do you know what punishment is? It is trying to control the other person with fear. I don't want that.

Often parents won't allow their children to be honest. If I told my parents I went to the movies and not to school, they would have taught me a lesson. The important thing to me, Crystal, is not that you agree with me. The important thing is that you know you can be honest with yourself and honest with me.

When parents say no, the child becomes afraid. We are always teaching fear and control. To cope with the fear the child becomes clever. I don't want you to be afraid. Because I love you, I don't want to give you fear or lies.

The wonderful thing is that you understand right away, Crystal. Knowing I am not going to say no to you, you can afford to be honest with me. Then you are coming from your own strength, your own light. Persuasion is manipulation. I won't do that. We must provide a different atmosphere.

Of course, there are times that are somewhat pressured and require a quick agreement because there is not room for a lot of explanation. When there is trust, the child understands. I can say, Crystal, I can't explain it right now, but I will as soon as there is time. And because she trusts me, she doesn't argue, she doesn't make a fuss.

Crystal, did you know that fifty years ago there were no televisions and very few radios? When I grew up there were not even electric lights. At that time, especially in the East, people tried to find out what this emptiness is. They wanted to know God. They wanted to know what it is to be honest. Today emptiness is driving people crazy. They don't have their own resources and therefore they feel they must always look outside themselves for satisfaction. But in you, Crystal, we are going to plant a flower of interest in the emptiness so that you will know your own self-reliant, uncontaminated Self.

When we are born, Crystal, there is a part of us that God has guarded from fear. If we knew that, we would never be afraid, we would never be bored, we would never be lonely. We would always have that to give. Then we would be giving what is of God to everybody. This is what the world needs. And the world will not be the same because you lived here.

*   *   *

## WISDOM IS BORN OUT OF SHARING

In the Indian culture, the mother was always understanding and giving, and the father represented the law. He would say no when that was necessary.

It is possible in the single-parent family for the mother to represent both polarities, but it is far more challenging. She must be very well integrated to do it. Often the child assumes the role of the father, establishing the law of the household. He can put up tantrums, he can blame, he can be demanding because his whole energy is fixed on what he wants.

But by telling the child no, the mother is not saying, "I do not trust you." She is letting the child know that she is not going to get taken over by the child's wanting. And then someday, the child and the mother can talk freely about it in an objective way.

You both become friends. You can see his point of view and he can see yours. It is possible for that sharing to take place.

We are moving toward genuine sharing. He wants it his way and the parents want it their way. Parents have a right to want it their way because they have a broader view. But the whole purpose of the parent having the broader view is to bring the child to sharing, so that the child feels he can talk to his parents.

With real sharing another kind of reason and logic come into being. Something else becomes the determining factor until, in the end, both of you have respect for that other factor and that is what decides. That would be wisdom.

Wisdom is born out of sharing. It is not born of one telling the other. But where are the parents who are moving toward wisdom? They are going to tell the child they don't have the money to buy what he wants.

If parents cannot bring the relationship to the sharing of wisdom, they will find some reason to justify depriving the child of what he wants. That is not good enough. That may give the child a better picture about their circumstances, but wisdom takes one out of circumstances. That is what needs to be shared.

I don't think Crystal would put up a tantrum for what she wants with me because she knows I would get her anything. She also knows that when I say no it is no, and for good reason. But it is not set in her mind that I am going to say no. I am going to be more unpredictable than she is.

*   *   *

## STIMULATION

Crystal, we were talking about stimulation, and that everyone has something to master, something that gets the better of them. It could be stimulation, as in your case, or it could be something else. One person may be controlled by greed, another by fear, another by desire or wantings.

It is neither difficult nor easy to deal with these, but once we have given it the label "difficult," we believe it is so. This belief then rules our lives. That is why the wise person doesn't believe in anything. Because once you believe in something you are controlled by it. You are limited to thinking with the brain, thinking with thought.

Our thought is just memory. Everything you memorize is what you know. For example, you know me because you remember me. That is Taraji. He is a good man or a bad man.

To know the truth the brain must be silent. Haven't you ever felt this sitting in meditation or in prayer? You feel more quiet.

CRYSTAL: Yes, I have felt that quiet.

The more quiet the brain becomes, the closer you get to the Mind of God.

Crystal, do you see that stimulation is something you must learn to master? There is a strength in you that is stronger than the stimulation, but when you are stimulated or tired, it is more difficult to call upon it. We must discover together what to do, so that strength is always available to you.

Sometimes, in the evening, after I have talked all day long, I have difficulty sitting quiet. The more I sit, the more I feel how tired I am. So if I want to sit quiet, I had better stop talking earlier. This is called wisdom. You have a more complete picture and you have the strength to be true to yourself.

I was wondering what we could do to help you not to become so stimulated so that you can call upon the strength you have. That way you would not get taken over by those things from the very beginning. It would be wonderful, Crystal, if you always have a space in you that is your own, a space that doesn't get taken over. What do you think would help, Crystal?

Wanting is a stimulation too. You can never want anything if you haven't seen it. All the shop windows stimulate wanting. Stimulation does not only occur when you play and get wound up. Stimulation always wants more. And therefore one gets limited to what Tara or Crystal want. Then we know nothing else. All we know is that we are controlled by this stimulation.

Do you think that when your Mommy says you are getting stimulated, you could hear her and immediately say that you will stop? If you can't do it right then, you will be that much weaker the next time it happens because you will become clever in order to get your way. It might be helpful if you would listen to your Mommy and Daddy right away. Do you think that is a wise way? Would you be able to listen, Crystal?

*CRYSTAL:* Yes.

I know that strength is in you. You are the only one who doesn't know it's there. God has given you parents and a friend who is a teacher. We can make sure that the strength is stronger than the stimulation by making sure that the stimulation doesn't get to the point where it is more than you can cope with.

The other day when I was in Los Angeles, we were talking and everything was very nice. Then you laughed over something. I knew from the quality of your laughter, from the tone of your voice, that you were getting stimulated. That is when I suggested that you should go home with your Mommy. Your parents can observe those things, too.

If you can do this at your young age, you will feel happy all day. You won't have to worry about getting stimulated because you will know that you can step out of it instantly. Then you will have confidence in yourself. Right now you know the stimulation but you don't know your strength. My job is to introduce you to your strength.

What should we do, Acacia, to help her before she gets taken over?

> ACACIA: I think the word stimulation is something that she identifies with right now. If I approach her and tell her that she is becoming stimulated, she knows what I mean.

It is something you both understand.

> ACACIA: Is the next step determination on her part not to be stimulated?

Yes, but we must also see that there is a reason the child has parents. Discrimination may not be necessary for her yet, because you have it.

> ACACIA: So she doesn't have to be thinking about whether she is stimulated or not?

Right. But she knows how to cooperate. It will require that she have respect for her parents because she knows that what they are saying is true and necessary. What a responsibility for the parents!

When she is getting stimulated and you point it out to her, what do you expect her to do then?

ACACIA: To recognize that this is what is happening.

Yes. But we have to have a clear outline of what nonstimulation is. We need more understanding of what is entailed in stepping out of stimulation. We just can't leave it at telling her to stop it when she is becoming stimulated. She may stop, but it is our responsibility to see what else she can do or not do.

ACACIA: Should we lead her to something else that is less stimulating?

It is our responsibility not to just impose something upon her. We must help her with the second step also. We cannot afford to leave that unresolved. Then we would be making a demand on her without giving anything of ourselves. When she is cooperating, we must ask in what way are we cooperating as parents in the second step? We can't leave her out in the cold.

ACACIA: If I can be there with her in order to find some way to wind it down, it helps.

Yes, we can't tell her she is getting stimulated and then abandon her. At that moment, she needs human warmth, she needs a friend. Just to tell her to stop is too tough. I wouldn't want to be a child then. If I tell Crystal she is getting stimulated, I give myself to Crystal. I won't isolate her. This kind of response requires a lot of love.

Acacia, suppose she is getting stimulated. Can you notice it and ask her to come and help you do something? She likes to work. Can you include her in something? Together you can find out what brings about relaxation.

Crystal, I know that if I start washing my clothes by hand, it relaxes me right away because I love to do things with my hands. Acacia, maybe you could suggest some time that both of you clean the pictures in the Prayer Room. They have not been cleaned for a long time. Doing this lovingly, in a slow manner with attention, will bring your brain to silence and you will see how quickly the stimulation will go down.

One of the finest music teachers in the world was Madame Nadia Boulanger. She was a great master. She taught the finest contemporary conductors, composers, and artists and made quite a contribution. When she would teach a class, she would say, "Everyone says that this particular piece is impossible. Let's practice this impossible piece until we master it, and then we will take on another impossible piece and make it ours. Then we will take on a third." That is how she taught music to her students. And that is how we are going to master our tendencies, Crystal.

It's a tremendous responsibility to talk with a child. She has her whole life ahead of her, and we have a responsibility in how we communicate, in a joyous way, something that's very demanding.

*　　*　　*

## TEACHER/STUDENT RELATIONSHIP

Crystal, do you understand what a law is? A law is like when the night comes, we sleep. Under certain conditions, it rains. Laws are not manmade. Rules are manmade and they are different from laws. A rule is that you have to be at school by eight o'clock. But laws are laws of life. Summer, spring, autumn, and winter are laws of life. They never change. Man-made rules change all the time. All laws come from love.

The teacher/student relationship is a law. In our relationship, I am not going to talk about man-made rules. Those you can learn in school. We are going to talk about laws that God created. Schools do not teach these laws and there are very few teachers who directly know them.

So then I ask, "What are the laws of the teacher/student relationship according to God?" The law between the teacher and student is that the student must learn something when it is pointed out. The student must ask questions. I love it when you question and question until you are sure you understand what we are sharing. Then I am not influencing you. You have discovered it for yourself and it is your light. And because you have understood it, you can change.

The law between a teacher and a student is that once something is learned, it is learned for all times. It has its own energy and nothing can take it away.

Then maybe sometime you will make a mistake. I will explain it to you again until you understand it better and feel confident that it is clear in you. When you are clear, then you are not dependent on me. I like clarity. I like understanding. I like questions. I don't like laziness or feeling you can't do it.

The law is that the teacher will tell you three times. The first time maybe you didn't quite understand, the second time maybe you forgot, but the third time will be the last and you must master it. If the student wants to learn, then three times are enough.

Don't ever be afraid. If you don't understand something for a whole month, that is alright with me. I will work with you because I love you. There is no pressure. When you learn one truth, it will give you so much energy, so much strength, so much joy because it is something of God. We will have learned one truth together. It is the most beautiful thing to share.

\*　　\*　　\*

## SELF-CONSCIOUSNESS

Acacia, I want to talk with Crystal about something serious, related to other laws that take place in a person's life. I have observed that she becomes very self-conscious. We have to help her free herself from self-consciousness because it is a torment. It paralyzes her.

> *ACACIA:* Are you talking about the self-consciousness that comes when you are too shy to ask a question?

That is one kind. The other is when Crystal is asked to join a group of us in a cheerful dance, she becomes self-conscious. Her life won't be happy as long as this is so. She will go through inner torment if self-consciousness isn't outgrown now.

I want to talk with her but I don't want to tell her what to do. I want to share the pain and the difficulty she goes through. I know what it is. You would really like to participate but you just don't know how to overcome the torment within. I have suffered a lot over it.

We have to help her master this before she enters puberty. Because it is there, it makes her false and her life is meant to be true, through and through – always honest, always direct. If her life is to be noble, we have to help her undo this.

\* \* \*

Crystal, a student has the capacity to hear a truth instantly and bring it into application because she is receptive. Receptivity means that she can listen without like and dislike. Her receptivity gives her the strength of True Words. A student would never say, "I am going to try." No. Those words don't exist. For her everything is direct, simple, and uncomplicated.

Self-consciousness is a human disease. A child cannot be blamed for it. You really love to dance. One day you may not want to, but now you do. But self-consciousness is coming in and you feel shy, although dancing is natural for you. No one is trying to embarrass you.

> CRYSTAL: I know that I have to overcome being scared in front of people. It is important to overcome it while I still can.

Yes. You see, now you are ten years old. God has given you the energy to overcome it. When you are twelve and thirteen, you will have other interests and you won't have the energy to deal with it. The past drags on for so many of us because we never did things on time. We want to free you from the past so that you don't have to be self-conscious.

Talking about it is a help because then you will understand it. Suppose I had talked with you two days ago. Then yesterday at the party when you were so self-conscious, feeling you just couldn't do it, I would have been able to say, "Just do it." And you would have been able to do it. Slowly, you would discover you didn't need that pain. You can be yourself. A student would discover that self-consciousness is a painful thing.

> ACACIA: A beautiful example is when we were on the telephone with you and I mentioned that Crystal was concerned about whether she was speaking up. Before your call, I had given her some instructions about speaking up on the phone. You told me that I was having her conform. Now I see conformity increases self-consciousness.

We want her to conform, which makes her more false. And then we blame her for the mistakes we are making. I don't want her to conform to anybody – not to me, nor to anyone.

Few parents can teach a child. They can sustain the child and give comfort, but very few really know how to teach. The teacher can teach. The teacher can say, "Do this because I am telling you so." And the child gains strength from those true words. That would be one way of curing self-consciousness. If you as parents tell her to do it, you are making her conform. If I say it to her, I am giving her energy. She has trust in that. I can say to her, "Crystal, do it, baby. Conquer it." She would do it because my love is there; the true words are there. All three of us have to cooperate: the teacher, parents, and the child. Now everything is piled on her.

> *ACACIA:* I see that to blame the person shifts the responsibility onto the one who suffers. It doesn't resolve anything.

Talk with her, but don't make it a problem. I would spend some time with her and ask her, "What are you self-conscious about?" And she may say, "When I put on a bathing suit, I am self-conscious." I would then say, "Put on the bathing suit and see if you can do it without becoming self-conscious." Simple things. But I wouldn't have her conform. The two of us could take away the self-consciousness and the fear.

> *ACACIA:* Another kind of situation arises with children at school who may want her to do something. She may not want to but feels the need to try to conform in order to overcome the feeling of fear or whatever might be holding her back. How would she make a decision that isn't necessarily going along with the group, nor going along with self-consciousness?

At this time I would say go along with the group even though it is conformity because she would be overcoming self-consciousness through it. When she overcomes self-consciousness she need not conform to anybody. Her no would be no and her yes would be yes.

Crystal, I would say if self-consciousness arises when someone asks you to do something, then do it. Now you are using self-consciousness to hide. Later, when you have mastered it, your true Self may not want to do it, and that is beautiful. You don't need to conform.

Other Forces will help you. I want to introduce you to something that has no limitations so you are not controlled by anything external. There is just your honesty. You want to do it, you do it. You don't want to do it, you don't do it. How do you understand it?

> CRYSTAL: I see that when you don't want to do something or are self-conscious about what you are going to do, then go ahead and do that to overcome it, to break that down.

The teacher's job is to introduce you to the strength in you. The other person may say, "Never mind. If she doesn't want to do it, it is not important." You may love that for the moment, but it will weaken you.

*　　*　　*

## PUBERTY

One wonders how Crystal will cope with the external situation when she is thirteen or fourteen. Before reaching puberty, she should be brought to an awareness, an awakening, that there is a force, a clarity, a vitality in her that would not succumb to pleasure. That no matter what the situation may be, she will not get taken over. Parents rarely impart that awareness because they themselves are still full of lust and desire.

We have to start not with Crystal but with Acacia, her mother, so that her words are true. Then the Divine is there, and the blessing would bring something very different into the world. We are all blessed by a woman who is holy, who has given the world a child who is intact, whole. We can't teach Crystal not to be controlled by her wantings if we are not in control of ourselves. Where man, woman, and child have come to rightness, that is where right relationship begins.

What are you going to do with your beautiful child, Acacia? Teach her doings, opposites, conflict? Some day both of you will have great regret that you were moving at a pace that was much too slow. She is strong-willed. If that strong will could be directed one way, it is helpful, but the other way it is not. Right now she is not so much controlled by the body.

Before the other sensations awaken in her, we have to help her not be controlled by the body. What is possible now will not be possible later.

Start in a gentle way with something she is fond of either doing, wanting, having, or eating, and take it on to outgrow and undo it. The strength that it would take to undo it would be your treasure.

\*     \*     \*

## TOO MUCH HOMEWORK

Last night I noticed Crystal was sad. When I asked her why, she told me about all the homework she is assigned. I said, "Don't do it if you don't like it. Stand up for something!" Her parents felt that she needed to do it and it was causing some friction.

I said, "She needs warmth and friendship. She needs you on her side. How can homework be so important? You both did your homework for more than sixteen years. Did it contribute anything to your life? And now Crystal is humiliated in the class if she doesn't have it finished. It causes her anxiety, and that is doing much greater harm." What a wicked thing to do – to embarrass a young child in the presence of other children. She won't have any shame left.

We decided that it was necessary to go and talk with the principal about the homework, without blaming the teacher and without reacting. Deal with your child and the homework. That is the issue, not anyone else.

Whenever you want to meet with another person about a cause, find out first if it is a reaction. How wise you would have to be to know if you were moving from reaction. Instantly it would be corrected. Then even if the principal doesn't agree with you, at least you have come to something. Rightness is always right. It doesn't need proof.

What a heart that has no blame in it! Then you raise the question, "My child feels this way. I talked with other parents and they are also feeling this way." The issue is homework; it's objective. Go with the approach that the teacher has the best interest of the child at heart. Always bring it around to that.

When we shared this with Crystal, she started leaping on my bed. She felt here is somebody who will protect her. She felt safe. In five minutes, she was asleep.

*　　*　　*

## AWAKENING A SENSE OF AESTHETICS

I would like to talk about what is entailed in invoking a sense of aesthetic value in the child. Aesthetic means that whatever you do is beautiful, and you put your heart into it. It encompasses everything that represents the spirit.

A person who has aesthetic values is refined, dignified, thoughtful. He is mature and wise. Therefore, he would not be greedy or selfish, nor would he take advantage of anyone. Most people have very little aesthetic sense. Their homes reflect it, their dress reflects it, their speech reflects it.

Let's start from the premise that the child knows very little of aesthetic values, but as we start introducing them to the child, we will learn also. Parents do the best they can, but because their lives are crude, their children are crude. It's a tremendous challenge. We have to awaken other potentials to deal with our resistance and unwillingness to change. Nothing is going to be easy.

People who have developed an aesthetic sense have vitality. In their bathroom, the towels would be straight and if they are not, it will bother them. Any disorder, internally or externally, will bother them. They extend themselves in a very different way. Their home is beautiful, their dress is beautiful, the way they relate with another human being has ethics in it. Do you think it is easy to say, "I will not take advantage of another?" Without an aesthetic sense, one would invariably take advantage. If you met a person who has a refined, aesthetic sense, you would know immediately that he lives differently. Every single thing would reflect his values.

The child is going to be like his parents. He grows in that atmosphere and he has his own particular face. The wise person could look at a young adult and see whether he made his face by developing his inner potential or if he still has the face he was born with. When you've developed aesthetic values, your face has character. Very few people have their own face, or their own voice.

Parents have to teach their children appreciation through their own inspiration over seeing the clouds. They communicate their own aesthetic sense, not the beauty of the tree or the sound of the stream. If the parent is inspired, he would sit with the child beside the stream and listen to its murmur. The parent would then share what it does to them, not just what is visible.

*     *     *

## ST. JOAN OF ARC

Dear Taraji,*

"Thank you for sharing the Joan of Arc book with me. I like how they start the book. It begins by telling you where she is, what she is thinking to herself in a very calm, beautiful, and different way. Joan seems to be a very kind and caring person."

Now that is a mature outlook. That, at your age, you can see that she is calm, beautiful, different, caring! How perceptive you are. You are a little Joan of Arc yourself, and you are going to do great things.

"She is also a very determined person."

Now, you probably think you are not determined but when the time comes you will know that, too. First you have to hear Crystal's inner voice.

"I think I would like to be somewhat like her."

I love the way you don't say, like her, but "somewhat like her." Because you may have to do something totally different.

"I think I would be too scared to do all of the great things that she does for many people. But I would do the things she did if they needed to be done."

For you to write that you would be scared takes more courage than to fight the war outside. I am so pleased that you can be honest. To say that you are scared takes a great deal of courage and conviction.

You are not any less than Saint Joan. You will demand self-honesty of yourself and make everybody shiver. A person with conviction, who would not lie about how she feels, is a

---

* Crystal Williams reading her letter to Mr. Singh. (Editor)

unique being. There is a state of being that is not afraid and you are going to know that state.

You have to eat the right food, you have to get rest, you have to keep a very strong body. And we have to protect you so that you are strong in conviction. No compromises. One day you will find the truth that you are. Nothing in the outer world could stop you when you have made contact with the Self that God created.

# CHAPTER NINE

# 9

# THE MIND OF THE AGE — TALKS WITH YOUNG ADULTS

In our culture we spend sixteen to eighteen years in school and come out of the assembly line with skills by which to earn a living. Presently it is almost impossible to step out of this trend. From a very young age, children are told what to do. Very few people question this pressure to conform, even though the child has brought his own potentials to express in this world.

The result is that the gifts the children have are not nurtured by the system. Children are conditioned by our values and the school system to have careers. Thus competition and conflict are intensified.

One would think that parents would love their children enough to question this. One would think the religious institutions would call attention to the fact that this kind of education defies wholeness, humanism, and wisdom.

As a rule, students do not learn to question even in college. They might meet other students who are frustrated and reactive. But they have never sat next to a wise person. In fact, there are very, very few wise people today.

> JEFF:  Why are there so few wise people in the world today?

Life would produce a wise person if we had a need. Life does meet needs. For example, during the winter time nature produces hard fruit, like apples. During the summer when it is dry, it produces melons, peaches, coconut milk. If we really recognized this fact, there would be no sense of insecurity. We would trust in the intelligence of creation. When wisdom is not needed, wise people are not going to be around.

*JEFF: Why don't people need wisdom?*

Because they are conditioned from childhood and this conditioning shapes their perception and their aspirations. They don't have any choice, no matter where they are. Everything is reduced to manmade institutions, manmade rules. There is no need to be related with Divine Laws. How is it possible that we no longer value wisdom? Our highest aspiration is a career which will get us to the top. The collective values power.

The wise person would stand back and see what the mind of the age is today. What does it value? The wise is not concerned with the French, or with the English, the Americans, or the Russians. He sees the common factors. That would be real thinking.

Broadly speaking, we are only taught how to improve our self-centeredness. Now that we see ourselves as separate, we've got to take care of ourselves. We are not related to wholeness and this leads to expedient solutions, and then to consequences. The wise person can predict what the consequences are going to be before they occur and he doesn't go that way. When a whole society is limited to expedience, it doesn't care how much of the world's gasoline it burns.

The present world has not evolved toward humanism. As long as we divide the world into segments, there must be internal conflict; and where there is internal conflict, there is violence also. If we could understand this, then we have understood the mind of the age. We are brainwashed from childhood. The child is born with his own capacities, his own abilities. If he were allowed to flower, he wouldn't be so easily controlled.

There was a time when people had their own work, their own expression. Now most of us are owned by the corporations which don't care what we do in our personal life as long as we perform for them.

The hippies didn't like the system, but they didn't know what to do. Their expression was not welcomed and they felt rejected. But in order to be integrated, society has to incorporate the vitality and aspiration of the new. The giants of the industrial age demand conformity and control. They humiliated the new spirit and snuffed out a certain enthusiasm for different and peaceful values. The hippies hardly had a foothold in the system. Isolated, they could not do much. But the nation lost a treasure. The hippies became reactive and lazy and nothing in their lives flowered because they were not productive. Productivity is essential.

> JEREMIAH:  That is where I am. When I was young, I saw what the system was and I reacted against it. I gravitated towards punk music and all of that anger.

Yes, it is a reaction! If those in government were farsighted, they would realize they need to value young people more than their own control and help them make their own unique contribution because they have different ideas. We get so fixed that we cannot see what we are doing any more than the Romans could see it.

Why do we react? Would you be interested in that? First we have to see that everything we think is a reaction. We either like or dislike but we are always reacting to something external to us. Maybe there is no such thing as the external. If I am affected by the externals, then I don't have my own voice.

> JENNIFER:  Is my joy a reaction? I always thought joy was good.

Yes. But what we call joy is usually just pleasure. And pleasure is the opposite of pain. They are inseparable, like two sides of a coin. Pleasure is always at a price. Sooner or later we are going to have sorrow, too. We waste our whole life in this cycle, limited to the body which loves sensation. The body has a greater hold on us than the government. We are controlled by our physical senses and therefore we don't need the wisdom of intelligence. Indulgence satisfies us.

Why don't you ask me how I live alone? It takes great wisdom to live alone. Aloneness is totally free of indulgence.

*JENNIFER:* How so?

It has a richness within, an inner happiness that is not of the physical. Because it's not of the physical, one may say it is given if there is the capacity to receive it. When you come to that space, you're happy. Pleasure and pain no longer matter. You do the right thing naturally, for you are a law unto yourself.

Yesterday I had some small pieces of broken cashew nuts. There were not many. I went and threw them in the field for the birds. Because you are related to everything in creation, you just cannot waste. Those little cashew pieces aren't worth a nickel, but your thoughtfulness for the birds and the ants can never be bought. We are all part of the same life. We are children of this planet at the level of flesh and blood. But when you go beyond the physical senses, you are part of the whole. You can no longer belong to anything.

Do you know what you notice when you have something of your own to give? You notice that nobody really wants wisdom. They want something that suits their self-centeredness. They don't think that wisdom is necessary, even though it is free.

*SUSAN:* I can see that I don't have a true yearning to bring *A Course In Miracles* into application. Intellectually I want it, but every cell in my body resists it. How can I change this?

Susan, you must see that there is one "how" that demands a technique and leads to dependence. And there is another "how" that makes you aware that you are not here to learn the Course. You only think you are. That awareness may correct something. Techniques and doing will not.

That awareness is not readily available to anyone lacking discrimination. You are blessed that you have touched upon it. Awareness is the only thing that may do it. Nothing else will. The blessing of hearing words that awaken awareness is the greatest good fortune on this earth.

I do not teach. I merely bring things to awareness. The only "how" that is valid is the one that makes you aware of what you are doing. If you see the deception, then it is up to you to do something. It is not for me to tell you what to do.

> SUSAN: So by being aware of what I think, what I am doing, I can undo my own thought system?

Do you see that when you need confirmation you have not received the energy of awareness? If you had awareness, you would not ask this question. And if I give you confirmation, then I am a false teacher and you would have to pay me. But when I have said this to you – something that awakens your awareness – you cannot pay for it with all the money in the world.

You want confirmation; you do not want awareness. You must ask yourself why you evade contact with Reality. You say, "No. Confirmation is good enough for me." Then if I am a false teacher, I will give you confirmation, won't I? And it would take discrimination to know the difference.

*   *   *

## TEACHER-STUDENT RELATIONSHIP

Each of us has some areas within ourselves of which we are not conscious. And even though these areas are not apparent, they rule and determine our lives, for they limit us and form our life patterns. If they are not dealt with while we are young, they gain strength and become tendencies which are often difficult to overcome.

The teacher who does not commercialize True Knowledge begins to introduce the student to himself by awakening his inherent potentials. It is not teaching but sharing of clarity and light with the student. I want to meet someone who could speak to me of Reality, beyond learning, without being awakened themselves. How would he or she know or undo those factors which rule their life? The ancients have said: He alone teaches who has something to give beyond words.

Our tendencies are tyrants. They are the vast forces behind the personality, the ego-self that pretends to know it all. Without a still mind, we can look but we do not directly see the tragedy of personalized life. Very few people can see it. Those whose lives are personal find safety in these tendencies and remain isolated in their own world of illusion.

This is a different, rare, and probably holy perspective – a state free of interpretations. It transcends the understanding of words and feelings. From this space, a new action begins in the lives of those who are students. If you are a student, you are wholehearted and resolute, knowing fully well that partial attention will never relate you with Divine Wisdom. Inner awakening is demanding. It cannot be put in the second place.

Who is a student? Obviously one who is grateful for the newness that has begun to light his mind with insights. These insights transform the very cells of his brain. I don't think we know what gratefulness is because we don't know what responsibility is. Our knowing consists primarily of the understanding of abstract ideas. But ideas, in themselves, are meaningless.

Being subject to skills, we excel in thought-knowledge. This is *about* truth but not Truth itself. Without clarity, there is no certainty. The student is one who is lifted out of himself by the joy of clarity that energizes his life. Everything of the world has now become secondary to him. He has heard with ears he never knew he had. He has touched upon the Unchangeable within himself and he can no longer live without the reverence for Truth that envelops him.

The student is not hampered by mundaneity and calculations. Nor is he satisfied with the profane intelligence of the senses. He is now a student who values insight above learning. He knows how much there is that yet needs to be shed and undone.

Little has meaning for him except relationship with the teacher who effortlessly and naturally awakens his appreciation and reverence. This relationship brings solace to the student's heart and mind, as if for the first time the light of day begins to dawn on his life. *A Course In Miracles* becomes his Noah's Ark for, to the sage, that is what it is in actuality. It is timeless and divine. The teacher who offers the one-to-one relationship does not commercialize True Knowledge. He awakens the student's own potentials. The teacher is more significant to the student than his parents, for although they have given birth to his body, the teacher brings the student to rebirth.

Right relationship is holy. The ancient scriptures say that a true teacher does not teach, but awakens the student's awareness. How is this done? There are no techniques to it. Surely the past does not intrude; it is free of preconception, strictly individual. The whole of humanity is enriched by such a relationship.

Meditation is most essential, for it quiets the mind and allows space to renew the brain. Only the renewed mind communicates with the Holy Spirit. The Holy Spirit is your true Self, ever guiding the abstract, physical self to know the reality of your own sacredness.

*A Course In Miracles* points out:

*Let me not forget myself is nothing,*
*but my Self is all.* [1]

The teacher is fully aware of the student's capacity to receive. To the degree the student is attentive, he has the ears to hear the true words of the teacher without interpretation, for the vitality of True Knowledge and meditation has stilled the student's mind.

To the teacher, the student is only a student if he has the vitality of interest and the purity of intent to listen. By listening, he receives the very light of the teacher's words. Thus, in the final communication, they both meet without thought, out of time, where the internal interpretation no longer intrudes. How blessed is such a moment that is infinite. It transforms life.

In the true teacher-student relationship, there is the sharing of Love. This relationship is not based on authority or conformity. There is no dependence in the sharing of awakening in the moment. *A Course In Miracles* is a curriculum for those who yearn for the Presence of God in their lives. Yet few people undertake the uprooting of unwillingness which makes the external real and the sacred valueless.

*I am determined to see things differently.* [2]

*I will not value what is valueless.* [3]

It is not possible to weed out deceptions without having an attentive mind that is precise and factual. To be exact and precise are qualities that accompany a sense of responsibility for our thought, deed, and action. How little we know of inner integrity and conviction. We know much about effort and striving, choice and wanting.

The teacher knows that attention and awareness are needed to qualify for: *My single purpose offers it to me.* [4] A loveless life, with all its indulgence and conceit, has no notion of the power and purity of willingness. Without genuine and spontaneous willingness, who can remove...*the blocks to the awareness of love's presence?* [5]

Without the peace of God, it is usually difficult to be discriminate or to know one's function in life. It requires a heart that is pure in its intent to welcome what Life puts before it. Wisdom offers the discrimination to see the difference between idea and fact. Wisdom makes detachment possible. There is no duality of choice in true responsibility. The truth is: If there is one person in the world who loves you, you can make it.

*    *    *

## SEX AND CELIBACY

In *A Course In Miracles* it is made clear that minds are joined. At the level of the mind there is no gender. Gender only exists at the physical level, the level at which we reproduce. When I was younger, I used to wonder why saintly people advocated celibacy. How could they impose it on themselves? I later found that it is possible to relate to another at a level where gender doesn't interfere at all.

JEFF:  When you repress something natural to the body, does it create a preoccupation?

Yes, if body wantings are denied, then you have some vested interest. And if they are not denied, one may also have a vested interest. Where there are opposites, it is not absolute. Only in the absolute is there no opposite, no good and bad, no denial and no pursuit.

JENNIFER:  What does one do in the mean-time?

Outgrow the identification with the body so that we don't get caught at the level of cause and effect.

I used to feel that if I denied my attraction to someone, it didn't seem right. I was going against my own nature. I also saw that if I pursued the person, there was some motive in me. When you love honesty you can see the motives behind what you do. If you love pleasure, you wallow in self-deception.

> JEFF: I see that it's wrong to pursue it in any way and yet it is there at some point. What is it that is not a denial and not a pursuit?

That's a very good question. Anything that we resolve at the thought level is going to have an opposite in it. Anything. This is not a quick answer. You can never know the Absolute or truth at the thought level. You can never know love. But you can know what is *not* love, what is *not* truth. That is where the wise person would start.

> JENNIFER: Is that where you are able to make some space within you?

Yes, because you're questioning. It is best to start with a question. If someone tells you that you must be celibate you would question, "Good God, that's the one joy in my life and I have to give that up, too?"

I would not accept it without finding the truth of it myself. But I wouldn't deny that there may be some merit in what the other person is saying either, especially if the other person is someone like Mr. Krishnamurti.

You must be responsible to keep the question burning in you. If a great being said to you that you can't come to this other awakening while engaging in sex, then you try to find out, in an original way, if this is true. You would not accept anyone's authority, because you want to make the discovery for yourself.

> JENNIFER: Will something then be imparted to you so that you don't have to figure it out?

You don't have to figure it out as long as you don't let motives rule you. In the meantime, watch out for the motives. If you are contained and you don't let anyone exploit you because they have a motive, some revolution is going to take place in your life. You will not exploit or be exploited!

> *JEFF:* How can I be independent of these forces within the body?

The fact is, Jeff, we only know denial or taking the question just so far. There is no solution at the relative level. One is as good or bad as the other. At the level where we think, everything is duality. I want to step out of duality, not just be celibate.

Start this way. Somebody has said that there is another state of being outside the physical senses. For the moment we could call that Divine Intelligence. The preacher who preaches about celibacy may not have realized it. He merely brings it down to a relative level and talks about it as an idea. Those who deny sexuality are just as bad off as those who pursue it.

At the level of duality there is no such thing as a solution. It would always be a preference, a choice, a wanting. When it's a preference, you're self-centered. That is not bad. I just want to see the fact as the fact. Then what does one do?

If you think you need sex – and we all think we need it – why don't we observe how the brain does its propaganda? Let's observe how it brings forth images; how it lives and wallows in the past; how it always wants to repeat the same experience over and over again. Observe that. There is no need to condemn yourself for anything. Just observe how the body likes pleasure.

There are two factors. The body likes pleasure but the fact provides insight, which is by far stronger and superior. No indulgence stands a chance. What we have to watch out for is intellectuality. There is no integrity in it.

Observing is the action that frees one, not denial or non-denial. If you don't observe the fact, then you are under my influence and I don't want to influence anyone. I want to share the creative moment which doesn't know sex or duality.

When you touch upon that creative moment, sex seems primitive. In fact, what the whole society is built on seems primitive. The creative moment introduces you to why that force exists in the body. This is new and creative, isn't it?

The sexual energy is in the body to rise from center to center and finally awaken you. In the Bible the centers are referred to as "seals;" in Yoga they are called *chakras*. The depth of this is shared much more thoroughly in Yoga.

The sexual energy is seated at the lowest chakra, at the base of the spine. This chakra is the only one from which the energy can go out. All the other chakras emit something within the body. If the sexual energy is conserved and not released, it begins to rise within the body and awaken other potentials within you. It can bring you to the Absolute.

What the ancients knew is that you can't have pleasure and the Absolute as well. If you have pleasure you will have sorrow also because you have limited yourself to the body. If you see that, then you have a responsibility. When you're responsible, you are not led by motive. You are wide awake. The same energy that can produce a child also has the potential to bring *you* to rebirth. Inner awakening takes everything you have. When you have mastered the body, you have your own inner strength.

Sex is one of the few direct experiences we ever know in our lives. A direct experience is contact with the creative force of life. It is not the body that produces a child. At the moment of orgasm something takes place that is creative. The conception of a child is sacred. Whichever way you turn, responsibility is there.

If eternal values are of first importance you would be very careful about the man or woman you marry. You would be attentive and responsible about the conditions surrounding the conception and the birth of a child. You would be certain to provide a peaceful atmosphere to welcome the child.

It would take a great deal of moral courage to say, "I am not going to get involved until I know, from the inside, that this is the person with whom I am to share my life. I will give myself to no one until that knowing is direct. I may never meet anyone, or I may meet someone, but I will not be dishonest to myself."

People who are that responsible go beyond pleasure and indulgence. They have a face that is their own. We all settle for any little crumb, but everyone deserves a lot more. By being responsible you will find your own potentials and know how rich and beautiful you are. Those of you who are young have a different potential, a different destiny. There is urgency for you to awaken, for your contribution is very much needed.

Each one of us has the capability of being a unique being in the world. We don't need wise people; we need to become wise. Seeing that is what is needed in the world. Let us meet that need.

JEREMIAH: Why do we undermine ourselves?

Indulgence is easy because it doesn't make any demand. But to have some ethics and virtue in your life, you have to give your whole heart to it – that you will never conform, no matter what the circumstances; that you will not be regulated by the five senses or deceived by your enthusiasm; that you will be responsible for whatever you do, responsible in a timeless way.

JEREMIAH: One has to relate to something that is beyond the known?

Yes. To meet the unknown you have to contain yourself. If you go for gratification and diversion, you become your own enemy, preventing yourself from flowering. The inner awakening takes place inside you. Once you are awakened, what a blessing your life will be – not as a citizen but as a human being. As a citizen you live by cause and effect. The consequences are apparent to the whole world. If you see the whole nation is going that way, isn't that all the more reason to step out of it?

You can make contact with your own God-created Self. We either identify with what God created or we identify with the physical body. Ask yourself, which are you going toward?If you don't identify with the body, then your values change, your whole direction changes. Responsibility becomes important; having one's own strength becomes important so that the externals can't affect you. What we call external is time-bound.

Then you'll have a voice of your own. Otherwise you are a mere echo of somebody else. This action involves stepping into the present that has no past or future in it. It's not difficult to be in the present. The challenge comes in letting go of the known to which we are attached. Even though you are young, you've seen enough of the other way.

It's going to take courage but you would love yourself so much more for what has awakened in you. If you got married, you would be true to who you are and you would be a worthy wife or husband. You would make certain that it is something more than the brain and the physical that attracts you to the other person. A woman yearns for the seed of a noble man. And a man yearns for a woman who inspires him with her goodness and serenity. Now everything is reduced to the lowest level imaginable.

> LEANN: I've understood that there is no use in denying these energies in me. Denying it doesn't help and indulging it doesn't help. Am I just to see what the mind does?

Yes. Unless the brain revives the experience of it, you will find that you don't get excited. When we are lonely and filled with a sense of lack, the brain will always project the opposite. It starts thinking about that nice boy or girl and how wonderful it would be to be with them.

The body, independent of the brain's perceptions, functions in a different way. If I have slept well, when I awaken, all the centers in the body are totally relaxed and the lower chakra is charged with energy; however, there is no desire in it. This is the natural function of the body. If that energy is not there when I wake up, then I know my body is not fully rested.

When the body is rested it is alert. That energy wakes me up but it doesn't wake me up with desire. I don't let the brain project desires. Then, when I sit quiet, it doesn't intrude. I am over seventy and it still happens the same way. That is the natural function of the body. We don't know the natural function of the body because we don't allow ourselves to be that rested. We activate desire through our thoughts. The end result is that, through abuse, we damage spiritual centers in the body. If you abuse the body through sex, what kind of child do you think you will bear? He will only be capable of half-truths. There are consequences for everything.

There are people who are true to themselves. They are a strength to all of us. I knew a young woman once who said to me one day, "I always take care of things right in the moment because if I don't do what is required of me now, I will be that much weaker tomorrow."

The only true education is the awakening within one's own self. The mind of the age has gone wrong because it still believes in learning and teaching what is of the past. Because it is not of the living moment, not of the present, it is not truly creative. In the present you are whole and intact, and you bring something of the Kingdom of God to earth. That is what we are attempting to do.

*    *    *

## IDENTIFICATION WITH THE BODY

The real work of adolescence is for boys and girls to become responsible for what they say and what they do – that they would not abuse another person because they feel the urge of desire within them. Body identification prevents right relationship between young people. As long as you identify with the body, you are nobody's friend and your words are not reliable.

> *LEANN:* Are you saying that as long as we identify with the body, it is not possible to honor what we are saying?

Let's talk about the power the body has over you. This is dealing with facts and not theories. We may see the wisdom of not identifying with the body, for even one's own body is an illusion. But this identification with the body has gone on for thousands of generations. We are part of that heredity. That is what our brain wants. In fact, that is all we know.

In order to learn that our identity is not the body, we have to contain the strong urges and swift impulses of the body. If they are not contained, we won't find another strength within. To find that strength, that self-mastery, you contain yourself. That is really right discipline. There is no guilt in it, or any of the other connotations of suppression.

The first step is to find out how much you identify with the body. It virtually owns you. See that you cannot be a friend as long as you limit yourself to the body because you are controlled by your enthusiasm.

We are trying to find another strength. Is that possible? One thing I can suggest is that, as students, it would be wise not to distract each other. Be a strength but don't distract. Now that you are a student, your work is to find your own vitality. Your work is to awaken your own inner strength.

In his essay *On Friendship,* Thoreau shared that Confucius said, "To contract ties of friendship with anyone is to contract friendship with his virtue." There should be no other motive in friendship.

> *JEREMIAH:* Why do we always identify with the body?

Thought always does, no matter how much man has denied himself. But now *A Course In Miracles* is here and one of its first actions is to free us from the concept of sin. It dispels our concept of guilt. Separated man identifies with the body. That is a fact. We want to awaken to know that wholeness where we are not separated.

Suppose you long for another person, what do you do? If you didn't long for someone, there would be something wrong with you. But now you are becoming responsible. You are now realizing you have no right to make your appetites real at the expense of someone else. As a student you do not attract or distract another person. Don't try to help the other person, just contain *yourself*. That is help. No scripture has made it as clear as the Course that the body is neutral and our thoughts are images that we have projected.

The teacher knows human nature; therefore, he knows Jennifer better than Jennifer. For the first time she realizes she has a real brother who will prevent her from getting entangled in those urges the moment the body darkens her. I would say, "No, dear, that is not it." Right away the impurities would get corrected until, eventually, the impurities would have no power over her. That is why relationship with a teacher of life is the most precious gift. This one relationship can correct all relationships if one has reverence for truth.

> *JEREMIAH:* If one was unkind to someone in the past, how could one heal that unkindness? What is it that purifies the impurity?

That is a beautiful question. The only thing that corrects impurity is your awareness of it. The teacher brings it to your awareness. In awareness, there is no thought. Thought does not lead to wisdom because it knows no intelligence.

Intelligence is of the Mind and therefore it brings correction and purifies the brain.

The teacher will help you discern the difference between awareness and thought so that it is your own clarity. That is awakening. You would speak from that clarity and everybody would learn. We would enrich each other in holy relationship and become part of wholeness.

Either one relates with the ego or one calls upon the Holy Spirit, the Christ within. We need to ask the Holy Spirit for help to see any person or given situation differently. The Holy Spirit is the teacher. The ego is the alternative and always points to the external issue, while the Holy Spirit undoes illusions and relates one to the Christ within. That is its only function.

> *The best defense, as always, is not to attack another's position, but rather to protect the truth.... Innocence is wisdom because it is unaware of evil... It is, however, perfectly aware of everything that is true.* [6]

We must learn to make the call for God within. If you recognize the truth of this, it brings learning to an end. The unfortunate thing is that we all get involved in learning and thus miss out. *A Course In Miracles* is not to be learned, but to be lived.

> *All real pleasure comes from doing God's Will. This is because* not *doing it is a denial of your Self.* [7]

We meet as students of the Course to know there is another way of looking at the world and to make contact with the Holy Spirit.

As long as impurities are present in the body, it is our responsibility to be cleansed of them. The only thing that can cleanse them is becoming aware of them and being responsible. Then you would not do anything that would be born out of motive. You would deal with the facts of the body. The body needs sleep; the body needs food. You would make your life productive, not to amass money but to become self-reliant.

When nothing external controls you, impurities are gone, opinions are gone, reactions are gone. Then you will remain the student, purifying your thought system. Whenever your knowing starts taking you away, awareness will help bring you back to innocence.

When you separate from the body at death, some of these impurities get cleared and you think, "Oh, this is wonderful. I don't want a thing in the world. What a damned fool I was! I could have used the Will to awaken myself. Now I see I need determination."

When you are in this other state – after leaving the body – you long for a body because it is only through a body that you can be liberated. You started the separation, got into the body in the first place, and now you have to outgrow the body.

Prior to birth you may say, "I can manage now. I will never listen to the body needs and all its sensations again because now I know how it deceives me. I am going to confront thought."

And you wait and you pray to get a body so that you can be liberated to complete your work and be a shining light in the world.

Today, there are many highly evolved beings who are yearning for a body in which to be born, but the kind of purity they need in the parents no longer exists. Because those beautiful beings can't come here, there are no teachers anymore. What a tragedy!

JENNIFER: Do we have a responsibility to open that up for them?

Be grateful that you have a body and you are not going to be controlled by the body. Our work is to come to heaven right here while we are alive so we don't have to come back again.

Before a person is born, he is very sure he is not going to get taken over by the body. But when the glands start to change and puberty comes in, he forgets everything he decided "upstairs."

So be glad you have a healthy body and a healthy mind. Let us be determined to have something to give to our fellow beings. We will extend the Will of God when our lives are dedicated to service. Then we will extend the peace of God which the world needs desperately.

*   *   *

## DIVINE LEISURE

We have long forgotten what wisdom is. We are so stimulated and our brains are so pressured. We have no idea how to prepare ourselves for sleep or what to do when we wake up. Neither do we know how to invoke the Presence when we pray or how to be grateful.

All of these require divine leisure. This means that for some time during the day we are less troubled by things of time, personality, and the brain projections. There are very set times in nature, in creation, which bring one to that divine leisure which renews one's whole perspective.

Each morning the day is born anew. The dawn comes with its energy of stillness and the awakening of light. That is the physical light, but it also can awaken the eternal light, the absolute light within us. It's not a light the eyes see; it's a light that is the source of creation. It is within you. You could sit for ten minutes or five hours. Actually the ten minutes are the five hours. It just extends its own peace, its own serenity, its own renewal. But ten minutes is all it takes. It might be difficult at first because the brain won't leave us alone, but it is possible.

We don't even have two seconds, much less ten minutes. But if that is what you are interested in and it is more important to you than your job or anything else that you give value to – when you fall in love with stillness – then the issue is settled. If it is not important you will do it for some weeks or days and then go back to your old self again.

When you are honest there is no conflict. When you say what you mean, more of you is alive and awake than at any other time because one part is not opposing another part. All of us can do this. If you could give ten minutes each day to being quiet, you would witness an awakening within. As the energy itself silences the mind, you are not going to dissipate it by letting the brain take over after you get up.

Your first response is gratefulness. All day and night. You wake up in the morning. You give thanks and you mean it. You had a good sleep and now there is a divine leisure ahead of you. No rush. Nothing to disturb you. The night is like a mother. It caresses you with its tenderness and affection. The day comes with another energy and you are thrilled. You give thanks and sit quiet. All your movement is a movement within stillness. Just picking up the glass with a still mind would still all of you.

We must have this divine leisure and not wake up with pressure. We never question how much we have lost in this accelerated culture. Our "progress" has shattered us all.

When you awaken, there is not a thought in your mind. You want to sit quiet rather than get busy. So you invoke the Presence with the Lord's Prayer. You start with adoration. "HE GAVE THANKS AND BROKE THE BREAD." [8]

"OUR FATHER WHICH ART IN HEAVEN..."

See? There is no sentimentality.

"OUR FATHER WHICH ART IN HEAVEN,
HALLOWED BE THY NAME.
THY KINGDOM COME."

Thy kingdom come *in* you.

## "THY WILL BE DONE..."

You are prepared to receive the Will of God. To be one with the Will of God.

## "...IN EARTH, AS IT IS IN HEAVEN."

Heaven is the Spirit. Earth is the body. When you identify with the Spirit while in the body, you are in heaven. You are not in the world of the body. Knowing this as an idea doesn't introduce us to heaven within. Only recognition does and it is direct. It is not a learning but an awareness.

## "GIVE US THIS DAY OUR DAILY BREAD." [9]

No job is going to give you this bread. The job is going to take your energy. It's a barter deal. Whether you're a pauper or a king, the Giver of bread is God, not a job. And out of your joy and out of your gladness, you will also give to your brother. There is abundance. No insecurity.

Someone offered Sri Ramakrishna* food they had prepared for him. He liked it and ate a little bit but he didn't take the rest. The man said, "Please, take it with you. Maybe you will eat it tomorrow." Sri Ramakrishna was shocked. Tomorrow? How could he think this way? He doesn't know lack, so how could he hoard for tomorrow?

## "GIVE US THIS DAY OUR DAILY BREAD."

This is the daily contact and there is no lack.

---

* Sri Ramakrishna was a God-lit being who lived in India from 1836 to 1886. For further information on Sri Ramakrishna, see Chapter Ten: Talks With Parents – Part II, reference No. 4. (Editor)

# CHAPTER TEN

# 10

## TALKS WITH PARENTS
## Part II

*PARENT:* I am very shaken by all of the stimulation and violence our children are exposed to today.

We live in a world where we are all too well acquainted with these things. We assume we are the victims of the world we see.[1] But in reality, we are not.

Until you have liberated yourself, you cannot liberate another. As a mother, take on the responsibility to surround your child with sacredness. Unless you live the words you use, your child will not trust you. Your virtuous life and your goodness would inspire trust. You would have an inner richness – you wouldn't manipulate, you would be true, you wouldn't fall for temptation, you wouldn't want advantages. All these things that you are would inspire trust. Once you have inspired that trust, the child will listen to you and not to his own thought, nor to the external pressures and values.

If you have reverence for life, and if, for you, the human being comes first, this will be communicated to the child. Once you have inspired this reverence, you have freed the child from the externals. This is the parents' responsibility. Later on, the child may need a teacher, but you have prepared him.

Now we prepare a child to go to school and fit into society because our values are of the earth. When your values have changed, you won't be looking for a school. An authentic teacher will be there. That being would introduce your child to a motiveless life and bring him to his spiritual ministry where he becomes an extension of God on earth. If you prepare the child, the teacher will help him outgrow everything of the world.

Both *A Course In Miracles* and Mr. J. Krishnamurti start with the undoing of illusions. The wise begins with doubt. Doubt everything external. That which doubts everything external is awareness, the light that is within you. It never gets entangled.

It is as if we are lost in the forgetfulness of His forgiveness and His love; the forgetfulness of our own holiness; forgetfulness that our Identity is protected. All our concerns are unfounded. We don't have to do anything but protect ourselves from the artificial and the false. There is nothing to achieve. We just need to protect ourselves from anything false which intrudes. There is nothing to acquire. We are already perfect, sacred, and holy. Every day I give thanks to the Father for *my everlasting holiness and peace.* [2]

> PARENT: Is it necessary to praise the child,
> to build his confidence through praise?

I think that flattering the child can almost become an indulgence. One should teach the child not to undermine himself. We have to do things that are honest and true. I am not talking about behavior. Behavior is sentimentality.

Give the child space. Some encouragement is necessary. It is important to know when it is necessary and when you are doing "your thing." If the parents are doing their thing, it is like paper flowers; there is no fragrance in them.

When I was growing up in India, all the peasants would go to the county fair. The young people would all go together. In Punjab where I lived, physical strength is highly valued. All the young men do push-ups and lift weights. Sometimes at the fair, people get drunk and take offense at very minor incidents. Before you know it a fight breaks out. If you are in a fight and someone else from your village is there, he calls out in a loud voice, "I am with you!" Everyone's blood freezes. You feel so much stronger because you have his life behind you. You know that he is going to back you up. Other friends shout, "Don't touch him – we are here!"

That sort of thing does not exist here in America. When you encourage another, your energy must be there. It is not merely a verbal thing. Your words can't be false. Could false words encourage?

In *The Ramayana*, Lord Rama said to Sugreeva when he needed his help: "I shall make your cause mine and I, who say this, have never uttered a vain or a false word in my life and never will." [3]

PARENT: What is the relationship between the abilities the child brings and his potentials?

The abilities the child brings are backed by his potentials. Often status is more important than the honesty of the child's life, and we totally ignore the child's potential.

He may have a gift for something, a specific ability, but our concern for status may never allow it to flower. Because the family values the privileges of being a doctor, he may never discover he loves designing or botany, or being a tailor or a carpenter. We are not going to recognize the abilities he has brought.

Sri Ramakrishna [4] said that a "breadwinning education" has wrong values from the outset. If we want to bring the child to a place where his abilities and potentials can be awakened, as parents we have to value Eternal Laws. The heavens do not know any other laws, but society has its own corrupt and immoral values.

Whenever the child feels he can go the easy way, the parents should help him not to undermine himself. Bring him to the truth of what Lincoln discovered, "Rightness has its own strength." Society will always lure him with false values, but you will strengthen him when you help him make these corrections.

   *PARENT:* Now parents have false values.

Yes. If they are part of society, then society is right there in the home. It reminds me of what Rilke said, that for nearly five years he had done nothing more than try to get the remnants of society out of himself. [5]

   *PARENT:* What is the father's role with his son?

The father must introduce his son to greatness, to examples which arouse his manhood, awaken his faculties, and give him another vision. Examples are very necessary.

It is essential to introduce him to the lives of great men and women. There are people whose lives were impeccable, who did things outside their own vested interest. When some other force was awakened in them, they stood up for a law, for a principle, or for a friend – not as politicians who make causes, but strictly through their own nobleness, their honesty to themselves. The politician offers false promises. He is dependent on votes and so he becomes clever and persuasive. Such a person is not capable of doing anything great.

The great person always has something to give. His greatness would be in the eyes of God. The politician's greatness would be, at best, in the newspapers. There is nobleness in one; there is falseness in the other. Abraham Lincoln embodies genuine greatness. Here was a peasant boy who had the moral strength not to compromise. He had the capacity to listen. Without his handling of the Civil War this country would be divided to this day. When he didn't know what to do, he turned within. Every politician and president who "knows what to do" is acting out of arrogance.

The child needs to be awakened to watch out for arrogance and recognize humility. Arrogance is always of personality; it is always self-centered and false. Although it may be temporarily helpful, there are consequences. What about the one for whom the real can never be threatened?[6] Can the father inspire his son with the truth of: "Rightness has its own strength." Can he introduce him to real heroes?

Thoreau lived a life of utter simplicity. He was never deceived and he never made a cause. He went to jail because he protested paying taxes to support a government that believed in slavery and war. That is ethics. That is courage. The father must introduce the boy to moral courage, which is the only courage. The other is assertion and aggression.

Thoreau said: "Peace and security of the world lies not in inventions, but in men's hearts and men's souls. That to sustain life we need less, rather than more; to protect life, we need courage and integrity, not weapons, not coalitions."[7]

John Muir missed the coach in San Francisco so he walked all the way to Yosemite. How much he liked that. These are not people who are busy going somewhere. They are always where they are. They are not pursuing anything. The one who is pursuing never finds, because he is always projecting. To be present is the greatest gift one could give oneself. You will always find yourself in the present – not in the future you seek, nor in the past you go back to. If you want to know holiness, it's in the present.

We find examples of certain kinds of valor: John Brown gave his life to free the slaves. When they were taking him to the gallows, they had to have a military escort to protect him from the farmers who wanted to shoot him because he was freeing slaves.

Also, we can't forget the wisdom of the American Indian. In the book, *Touch The Earth*, [8] there are verbatim accounts of Indian commentaries on their relationship with the earth, their feeling for their fellowman, and the devastating impact of the white man on their way of life.

The father can share with his son about Socrates and Whitman. Also the story of Saint Peter is very inspiring. Saint Peter was on his way into the temple when a beggar asked him for a coin. Saint Peter came to crisis because he had no coin to give him. Some other force awakened in him and he said to the beggar, "SILVER AND GOLD HAVE I NONE; BUT SUCH AS I HAVE GIVE I THEE: IN THE NAME OF JESUS CHRIST OF NAZARETH RISE UP AND WALK." [9] What he had to give was not of him.

We have so many examples of the awakening taking place in adults. On his way from Damascus, Saul was hit by lightning and was made blind. He heard a voice speaking to him, saying, "SAUL, SAUL, WHY PERSECUTEST THOU ME?" [10] A total awakening took place in him. The Lord told him that when he got to Damascus a man would meet him and give him sight. Here is a man totally transformed. His values have completely changed. This unique action demonstrates that it can take place if you are receptive.

This inner awakening can take place more easily in the child because he is still innocent. But it can also take place in the adult. Parents must not limit themselves. When they want to give the child that which is of God, it will take place in them.

*PARENT:* What would the mother teach?

The mother would teach about Mother Teresa, St. Francis, Florence Nightingale, Joan of Arc, and even Antoinette, the queen of France. Young Antoinette was totally corrupt. But when she was put in prison her hair became grey overnight because of the shock. When this pleasure-ridden woman went to speak before her subjects who were mocking her, her voice was the voice of a queen. In crisis, one rises to something one never knew was there. She said that she would be a true daughter of her mother and face death with courage. A calm descended upon her as she realized that to live required more courage than to die.

> *PARENT:* How can one resolve this inner conflict – the guilt that I made a mistake in separating from my husband and breaking up our marriage?

First of all, one must recognize that even though it is not the child's fault, the child is the one that is going to be affected. This factor alone could bring one parent, if not both, to some sense of responsibility for their own peace.

We see more and more today that we can hardly take care of our own sadness, loneliness, and isolation, let alone think about the child's needs. How can one be so enamored by a culture that perpetuates this situation, where one cannot even be true to one's own child?

If there is any sanity, then through humility that reunion could take place, or harmony could again be restored. Finding fault in each other is pointless. Certainly there are things which will make you want to react, but that is not going to bring the two of you together. How much wiser to bury the hatchet. One partner may be more attached to the other, more insecure; likewise, one may be more receptive to coming to humility.

In the end the deciding factor is honesty. If you are using the child as a means of getting your wife or husband back, or getting the house or more money, it will not work. But if you are objective and your interest is solely in the child's welfare, God is with you. Other forces that accompany you can even affect your partner, with whom you may not be seeing eye-to-eye.

You will not be able to do it if you have a motive. Who is going to have that discrimination? These are not easy things. Easy things are never true. They are false. They are born out of partial attention and are basically self-centered. That is what we have to outgrow. If the child needs both a mother and a father, and you speak from this impersonal, objective tone of sanity, then the universe is with you. The other parent would heed those words. We can't undermine that. We can undermine our intentions, but we can't undermine the power of truth.

The power of truth would correct. Lawyers won't. Marriage counselors won't. Only truth can end separation. The awakening of the child within necessarily entails the awakening of the parents within. When all three of them are awakened, something in the world awakens.

If the other person refuses to listen to you, it is not your concern. Do not seek results. You have mastered your own honesty. That is all that is required. If the child needs the other energies of the male or the female, life will provide. Your child will not be imbalanced. That is guaranteed because the child is innocent. Since the child did not bring about the friction or the divorce, why should he suffer? If both parents see that they are responsible, they would mend the situation out of wisdom, not arrogance. Whichever parent the child is with can do it.

> *PARENT:* Do women have a specific role or
> function?

Wisdom refrains from dividing the human being into genders. The division of gender exists at a much lower level. At the level of the spirit, there is only one gender. We have to come to a state where separation doesn't exist. If we are trying to solve all the physical, mental, and psychological problems of human beings, we are not going to get anywhere. What has taken place over millennia is that man dominates. The woman reacts if she identifies with a gender. Then she makes a cause, wants equal rights, and destroys her marriage and her child, too. If she is uninvolved, she becomes like a saint.

Naturally there are apparent differences and tendencies in the woman – little things – but we must bring all people to that gender-less state which God created. Feminine and masculine only exist at the physical level. Only by awakening from within will you know that state of being where there are no genders and no conflict.

\* \* \*

## VANITY

One incident about your child will reveal everything if you have the eyes to see it. In fact, nothing is discrete, but we cannot see wholeness.

Your son, Stephen, is now twenty-five and he is fascinated by a young woman who is more mature, more experienced. She has worked in the corporate world and is very spontaneous, affectionate, and free. There is something very nice about her. But she is not at all reliable. There is no reason to expect her to be. She is beautiful the way she is – honest to herself. Stephen got fascinated by her and thought he ought to buy a Jaguar to impress her. Since he is only a student, why should he buy a Jaguar? Now he needs two jobs to pay for the car and the insurance.

If you or I tried to tell him, he wouldn't listen because when you are impulsive and insecure, the issue is not that you need a car, it is that you need to impress. That is the controlling factor. Today it is a Jaguar, tomorrow it will be a better home, then financial advantage, then political power. In the end, he is not going to be true to anything – least of all himself. Vanity is the only gratification left for him. In order to support itself, vanity must become ambitious. It is inevitable that he will find the wrong companions.

As a mother, you should know that this tendency is going to shape his life and bring him sorrow. If you saw this, you would find a way to respond.

A beautiful meeting is related in Mr. J. Krishnamurti's book, *Commentaries On Living*, in which an elderly woman comes to talk with him:

> "She was a small, elderly lady, with white hair and a face that was heavily lined, for she had borne many children; but there was nothing weak or feeble about her, and her smile conveyed the depth of her feeling. Her hands were wrinkled but strong, and they had evidently prepared many vegetables, for the right thumb and forefinger were covered with tiny cuts, which had become darkened. But they were fine hands – hands that had worked hard and had wiped away many tears. She spoke quietly and hesitantly, with the voice of one who had suffered much; and she was very orthodox, for she belonged to an ancient caste that held itself high, and whose tradition it was to have no dealings with other groups, either through marriage or through commerce. They were people who were supposed to cultivate the intellect as a means to something other than the mere acquisition of things."

Look how much is conveyed in this one paragraph. The detail with which Mr. Krishnamurti describes her tells us that here is a woman who has served. She is alert and sensitive, and you wonder, what is she going to say? Her bearing, her caste, and family are related to other values which are fast disappearing. What would she say?

This is how to read. Stop the momentum and question yourself. Make some space within your own brain to receive the truth of what is going to be shared.

> "I am now seventy-five," she began, "and you could be my son. How proud I would be of such a son! It would be a blessing."

You begin to discover that this is a unique being. We could not say what she has just said. We are not that honest. We do not have that originality. And we are not that dignified.

> "But most of us have no such happiness. We produce children who grow up and become men of the world, trying to be great in their little work. Though they may occupy high positions, they have no greatness in them. One of my sons is in the capital, and he has a great deal of power, but I know his heart as only a mother can…. My sons will go their way, and I cannot hold them, though it saddens me to see what they are coming to. They are losing and not gaining, even though they have money and position. When their names appear in the papers, as often happens, they show me the papers proudly; but they will be like the common run of men, and the quality of our forefathers is fast disappearing. They are all becoming merchants, selling their talents, and I can't do anything to stem the tide." [11]

This is indeed a wise woman. That she would know, and be able to say that only a mother would know what her son is. Mothers today don't really want to know their children, but unless you do, you cannot guide them or help them deal with their issues. It is the mother's responsibility to find out, in truth, what their child is. That awareness must be in you because it is there all the time to be witnessed: selfishness, ambition, vanity. If you don't want to look at it, you are partly responsible for the way the child is.

Life is a great responsibility. And in this culture, the one thing we unanimously justify is irresponsibility. No one is a father, a mother; no one is a wife or a husband; no one is even a friend.

Mr. Krishnamurti emphasized the significance of education because first impressions have such a powerful impact on a life. Once certain conclusions are set into motion, they become fixed and it is almost impossible to undo them.

The brain, in fact, cannot undo them, for all it knows is external. It is not related with its own Source and it does not want to be. Any improvement at the verbal or horizontal level fails to alter the disconnectedness, for separation cannot be improved. If change is to take place, it should start in childhood.

*       *       *

PARENT: Is there any action that is consistent with...*receive only what You have given?* [12] Certainly, it is not a passive state.

It means to be aware. Only in awareness will you not react to the way things are. Awareness is at peace. Thought is not. Thought wants to change other people, which is the best way of evading inner correction. All through our life, this is the only thing we have done. That is where each one's ending would begin. Where there is awareness, all is perfect. You may have debts to pay. And you say, "I'm so glad. I am forever grateful to the person who made me aware."

Awareness transforms the relationship because you accepted the fact as it is. Irrespective of what the other person is, you want to go beyond appearances. Your mother may not like what you are doing, but the fact is she is your mother. Can you inspire the confidence in her that she has a son? Don't make petty matters the issue. Say to her, "Mother, on this issue we disagree, but it does not affect my love and respect for you."

Secondly, don't go to see her only when you want something. Do you have something you can give to your parents? Can you give them respect, space, not wanting to make them change? Then you have something of your own to give

Life had intimated to me that relationships within the family entail a responsibility of a different kind. We need to bring these relationships to love. That doesn't mean that there may not be a wide gap between you and the members of your family. You may not really be able to share with your parents. This doesn't matter. There is no need for you to do what they are doing or live as they want you to. The only thing you have to do is love them and make sure you are always there to help when they are in need.

In the end, you have to be before God without any family, without any attachment, without any involvement at all. The only way to come through all of it is through forgiveness. Once your heart is purified, all debts and obligations are completed.

*     *     *

Barbara said that she felt obligated to her aging parents. Because they provided for her, she has never had any difficulty with money. Now she asks, "What am I to do?" I said that it can't be a duty to take care of them; it must be a joy.

If we could learn to love our parents we would love everything that breathes. Taking the step of forgiveness of one's parents is one of the most crucial in a person's life because it frees us from the past.

The birth of a child is a blessing to the family because it can invoke a very strong bond between the father and the mother. We have difficulty letting go of our opinions of each other and consequently, the awakening of that truth seldom happens. When the child is born, another energy is available to the parents, but it just passes us by.

The child brings with him another energy to relate the parents to the miracle of the action of life. The birth of the child is an actual blessing. When parents do not make contact with that energy or awareness, or when they quickly paint their past over it, the child grows up isolated and cut off. These children cannot make any claim on their parents because there is not a really deep bond with them. They suffer all their lives from this sense of lack.

Barbara, you are lucky to have your parents. If you put away your opinions about them, they will start putting away theirs also. It is a fact. They need your help to take care of them now. If it gets too much, you have the money to get a nurse to help you.

Always be grateful that now you have the opportunity to serve your parents and bring these blood relationships to rightness and completion. Life would reward you, for rightness is the greatest jewel you could ever receive on this planet. To do one right thing totally transforms your values. You don't have to search for it. Just care for them with gentleness. I assure you if that transformation takes place within you, you will see another Presence working with you. Rightness is never alone.

*　　*　　*

It is important for parents to have more than one child. One child gets very lonely. He spends more time with the parents and other adults, and it affects him. If there are two children, there is more balance because they have their own world.

Also, when parents have more than one child, they are not as pressured. Some things you have to do more of because there are two children, but there are other things which they can take care of themselves. They also have the friction which is so necessary for growth. There is friction in the world, and life is preparing them. It's far more natural. I have seen that if there is a divorce in a family where there is only one child, the child is primarily with one parent. They don't get to know the other parent as well. We cannot blame the parents. I am sure they give all possible consideration to the situation, but there are forces within one that are so much stronger than reason. At some level we conclude that the marriage just won't work.

And from then on, the decision is made; the separation has already taken place.

Somewhere one of the partners sees that the other person is not quite "up to them." The seed of discontent is sown and they may not even be fully aware of it until five years later. They won't remember when that seed was planted.

How important it is to spend time alone in quiet morning and evening. We might then become aware of the impulses which always move toward separation and fragmentation. If we don't sit quiet, our children are going to be confused because we are confused.

I don't think a mother has ever been so happy as when her child first needs her and she has milk to give him from her breast. The givingness introduces her to a state she probably never knew before. It is real giving. Out of that gentleness, she extends happiness to the child. It strengthens the bond between mother and child.

When this bond gets established, you have to listen to your own internal wisdom and bring correction and balance in your relationship with your husband. When there is disharmony, the child senses it, even if you speak in a foreign language. When tension begins, the changes in your nervous system and the way you breathe begin to disturb him.

That is why it is so important for both parents to sit quiet morning and evening and to bring that harmony with each other. First you get married, and there is a great deal of joy in the togetherness of building a life. Once the child is born, reverence for each other is the greatest strength and blessing. As parents, we must mature to having that reverence for one another. Wisdom says, "Don't start with the child. Start with making changes within yourself." Always moving towards harmony will bless your family.

PARENT: If there is not complete harmony, should one have a second child?

No. If there is not complete harmony it is better not to have a child. The correction must start with oneself. You can't evade that. Having another child won't bring the harmony you are seeking. When we try to change the situation without changing ourselves, we are starting on the wrong footing.

> PARENT: My concern is that we may be giving our daughter too many ideas. Do you have any suggestions to slow down our brains enough to give her space?

You will have to slow it down for her because she will want to learn. She will have a lot of questions. The real work of the parents is to help the child retain his innocence as long as possible. Intellectuality corrupts innocence. Pleasing corrupts innocence, as does too much stimulation.

> PARENT: We don't have the wisdom of your background to share with our children. Are there ways that we can share what is of eternal value with them?

I think we have to make contact with the vibration and roots of this country. We must also see how it is changing. *A Course In Miracles* was not given to India. It came to America and there is nothing more lofty to begin to introduce to your children regardless of their ages. The prayers in the later lessons of the Workbook are so uplifting. It is essential for children to sit quiet and make contact with the Holy Spirit. That is the eternal wisdom you can impart to your children. Awaken it in yourself along with your children.

Start thinking in terms of self-reliance. That is what Emerson talked about. Lincoln talked about goodness and rightness. We don't really want to listen to these voices. How few teachers teach that in the schools. If Emerson was taught in school, there would be no litter in the streets. Every school could take on to impart non-waste. Children love to participate in that kind of wisdom. We are not teaching our children to be responsible. We teach our children they can die for a flag. That is quite primitive, isn't it?

If you love virtue, you will impart a different kind of strength to your children, a moral strength, without using too many words. Just your presence would transmit it if that is what you value. Moral strength is the only thing that will protect you or your children.

# CHAPTER ELEVEN

# 11

## INNER AWAKENING

It is natural for parents to love their children. But what is not understood is that in our present society it is not natural for parents to evolve to having something to give to their children that will awaken their inner strength.

Even without our trying, the child has become an extension of who we are and how we do things. We have gone out of the way to provide all kinds of things for the child's needs, but the child's real need is to have parents who can shorten his sojourn on the earth at the brain level. In other words, the child needs parents who will help him outgrow the world. Like Jesus said, "BE OF GOOD CHEER; I HAVE OVERCOME THE WORLD." [1] Much depends on the parents' capacity to change their values.

Children are led by interest. That is why we have to introduce them to noble men and women. Once you, as parents, start to read inspiring books, you will notice yourself undergoing a change. And you can transmit that change to your child without any effort. You will not communicate anything of yesterday. Because you are affected and it is alive in you, you will share in a totally different way – not necessarily imitating the story but transmitting the spirit of it.

259

You will convey its effect on you because now it is yours. The parents have to journey with the child in making every day you have together new.

Now that the child is born, we must take on the responsibility to prepare ourselves and to grow inwardly. And we must protect the child from the artificiality that is going to crowd in upon him. Our work is to awaken his awareness and introduce him to something more than mere thought. As the child grows, he will make contact with a strength within that is his own. Responsibility comes into being when you discover your own inner strength and cannot be false to yourself.

Somehow we choose to evade God in everything we do. And for this reason there is great sorrow in life. It is true that a good portion of the population has moved from poverty and illiteracy to affluence. But sorrow has increased in proportion to the alternatives we have projected to discovering our true nature.

The mechanisms of evasion have become so efficient and powerful. In a certain sense, it is the only efficiency – the efficiency of loneliness. Let us discover at which point we choose an alternative to God. And then we must discover that we do so because we are sad, lonely, isolated. We live in a state of lack and unfulfillment which we evade through seeking outlets.

*A Course In Miracles* says: *Behind every image I have made, the truth remains unchanged.* [2] That truth is not sorrow.

We need wisdom to bring loose ends to a head. How many unessential things we have that are born out of vanity! There is work to be done. It comes about very naturally with simplicity and space. I love to see what I can do without. Have a yard sale. Give things away. Probably most of the things in your homes are unessential. Make some space in your life.

Is it essential for you to know God? To whatever your mind gives its energy, that is what is essential to you. Start first with those things that are easy. But please don't make a goal or an ideal out of this because it will merely intensify conflict. Start simply and one day you will find out that insecurity itself is unessential in your life.

Man has been dependent for a long time on governments and institutions, on industrialization and technology. Now corporations have the money and governments are under the burden of deficit. How will man handle disillusionment in a world where violence has conditioned his thinking? The parent's disillusionment may well be the impetus to raise their children with noble values.

Today, parents are faced with challenges unprecedented in all history. But that is only if the parents rely on the externals.

The child comes to awaken the parents to their need to relate with their own God-given, inner potentials. Internally speaking, one is not subject to the externals. *A Course In Miracles* points out: *No one can fail who seeks to reach the truth.* [3] Since we are boundless in our capacity to receive, no one needs to limit himself to the notion of scarcity. The needs are met of those who live by Divine Laws. We are as God created us, [4] alive in a glorious world of great beauty. The Intelligence behind creation is compassionate.

Jesus asked the Seventy: "WHEN I SENT YOU WITHOUT PURSE, AND SCRIP, AND SHOES, LACKED YOU ANY THING? AND THEY SAID: NOTHING." [5]

Your child need never seek a job or live under the shadow of another's authority if you, the parent, make the child aware of his own inner potentials. The parent has to impart trust, confidence, and inner strength. He must transmit the love for God.

We need to change our perspective in order to welcome the child entrusted to us by God. We must make silence a part of our lives. In the physical world, nothing is comparable to the purity of silence that doesn't busy the brain. Simplicity is one of the most precious treasures of man. Parents need to change so that they have their own serene and stable atmosphere.

You may ask, "Where will the parents get the energy?" Parents will lack nothing if they work with life rather than resist it. Compassion and interest have vast resources. Attention undoes all personal sense of helplessness. What brings about inner transformation is independent of brain thought. We go wrong when we rely only on the brain and its ideas, which are external to Reality. They are personal, subject to struggle, skills, and ambition. The power of True Knowledge is unlimited. In reality, there is no lack, no effort. Awareness of this fact is energizing.

Insight transforms the environment in which the child is to grow, play, laugh, and be true to his eternal identity. We need to renew our damaged brains by being willing to let go of the past. Working with life will bring the parents to rebirth. It will transform the family and introduce new values. The body of the child is of the earth. But his spirit, which extends through the body, knows no problem, no helplessness, no limits. The child has his own God-given destiny. Do not impose your limited perspective on him. Let him be. He is part of, and the extension of, the Will of God.

One of the ways to restore higher values in society is through the awakening of intelligence in our children. Through the children, a new light shines upon this age. We must help them step out of half-truths and partial attention. Without *A Course In Miracles* it would be difficult to have the right perspective. The Course, with its daily lesson and step-by-step curriculum, is the first scripture given in English to awaken the New World to new consciousness. It is an eternal gift to humanity, but it does not preclude the True Knowledge of other scriptures. The Course introduces us to the true nature of our God-created Self which is forever protected from contamination. In God's eyes, we are still impeccable. If you cannot read the Course, prepare the way so that your children can. We must help them grow with dignity so that they will have the strength to stand for something.

Do not undermine yourself, or your children, being very impressionable, will imitate you and pick up your weaknesses, your negativity, your doubt, and confusion. God's Laws are absolute. Love is absolute. How are we to relate the child to the direct knowing of truth and trust? He is to be awakened to recognize who he is as God created him. Can we prevent him from denying his true nature through outlets and indulgences? For rebirth is the child born – not for identification with the limitations of the body.

Each infant is a messenger – the light of heaven on earth. His holiness is what we are to awaken. You have all the help you need. This you must know as a fact, for without conviction there is no integrity.

The world knows only to think and to react. We are all educated to live this way, and we teach our children conformity. Inner awakening has a totally different premise. The parents must awaken the child's attention and interest. These make the brain receptive to the stillness that precedes the involuntary action of insight. The silent brain is the birthplace of heaven upon the earth. But we stop short and limit ourselves to what the brain has accumulated.

Do not limit the child to the past. Truly the world is his. Not only the physical world of objects and ideas, but also the eternal world of creation. When he is young, he should be directed inward, slowly. Imbalance sets in when the internal world remains undiscovered. This is an error to be avoided in the early years. The humble start of heredity begins to sprout when the child is very young and how we deal with the early tendencies determines his character. How do we cope with the deep-rooted patterns that actually control a life?

Parents are the architects of their children. Mary knew how to bring up Jesus. Give space; offer peace. Challenge yourself, but do not conclude that you are helpless. Call for help and the Holy Spirit will answer and guide you. Stimulation is poison. Children must be protected from stimulation in early childhood or in adolescence it gets out of hand. Then only the external is sought and given meaning.

Childhood is the preparation for holy relationship and a life free of consequences. Introduce the child to the peace and satisfaction that is within – the love of simplicity and wisdom, not just behavior and etiquette. Reverence for life is the real purpose behind social graces.

People so often read to learn, not to awaken the potentials of application. It becomes just a brain activity. But application is transformation. That is the challenge of *Awakening A Child From Within*. Parents cannot be content to leave what they have read at the idea level. A child is beyond the body. He is spirit, part of the Mind of God. What is important to you has significance. How do you emit the wordless Reality? You can arm him with skills or you can awaken him by awakening yourself. This is the natural design of creation. Be yourself. Give yourself the space to grow, with less learning and more joy and play. Much depends on the parents' silent aspiration – who you are and what your values are. Your inner life is a sacred, private relationship between you and God.

We need to heed the values espoused by the forefathers of this country – Emerson, Thoreau, Lincoln, Whitman, Jefferson, and others.

Thoreau said:

"Truly our greatest blessings are very cheap. An early morning walk is a blessing for the whole day. For my panacea, let me have a draught of undiluted morning air." [6]

"Beware of all enterprises that require new clothes." [7]

Emerson was uncompromising in his love for truth.

"What lies behind us and before us are small matters, compared to what lies within us." [8]

Abraham Lincoln, probably the only true president America has ever had, embodied the spirit of detachment.

"If elected, I shall be thankful; if not, it will be all the same." [9]

"Let us have faith that right makes might, and in that faith, let us… dare to do our duty…" [10]

Jefferson's lofty words are a strength.

"The man who never looks into a newspaper is better informed than he who reads them, inasmuch as he who knows nothing is nearer the truth than he whose mind is filled with falsehoods and errors."

"Adore God. Revere and cherish your parents. Never trouble another for what you can do yourself. Never spend your money before you have it. Never buy what you do not want because it is cheap. Make your first object: Give up money, give up fame, give up the earth itself, rather than do an immoral act." [11]

Our responsibility to our children is to prepare them to be good human beings. We have all the resources we need – within us and in the lives of noble beings – to meet this charge.

# CHAPTER TWELVE

# 12

## ENCOUNTERS WITH MEN AND WOMEN AWAKENED FROM WITHIN
## Part I

### THE INTELLIGENCE OF
### THE CULTURE OF THE ILLITERATE
My Home, Family, and Village Life
in Punjab, India

B ecause I had little schooling, three years at best, something of significance was protected in me – a vulnerability. This quality drew unique people to me throughout my life and made it possible to learn and receive from them. There is a blessing in not being conditioned. It encourages the awakening of other values.

In our family, I had over thirty close relatives. Two of my uncles and aunts lived with us in our three-story house. All of the others and their children lived in their own two-story homes surrounding ours. All of the homes were thoughtfully designed with courtyards.

We had the space to be ourselves and yet we had the voice of one family. My grandfather was everyone's grandfather. And all the children who were close in age had an intimate bond. This shared togetherness was a joy, a haven for children who naturally love festivities.

Ours was a prominent family of the prosperous, agricultural village of Birak, in Punjab, the northwest province of India. The family owned a large parcel of farm land. We had half a dozen wells for irrigation. I was fascinated by how the crops would grow right before your eyes. First there was just the plowed field; then, little green sprouts appeared. It does something to a child's impressionable mind to see acres and acres of brown earth suddenly turn green, fresh, and bursting with life.

All of our food grew right there in the village – seemingly endless melons, mango trees, and sugar cane. So much wonder. The children knew when a colt had just been born and were eager to go and give him something special. Who was aware of a need for toys? It was a very different environment. The only thing we knew was that there is God.

The preparation of each meal began with a prayer. A small portion of kneaded flour was taken and put aside to be offered to Mother Earth. When the beggars came, the children ran to the kitchens to get food for them. Daily life taught us the joy of giving. We looked forward to our birthdays at which time the child whose birthday it was gave gifts to others. I recall being weighed every year on my birthday and an equal amount of sugar, wheat, and flour being given to families in the village on my behalf. That was relationship.

Not everyone in our family worked. There was the freedom to do what we liked. Leisure was natural and there was little pressure. When relatives from other villages visited, we feasted for days.

At dawn, everyone observed the calm beginning of the day. Here and there, people could be heard chanting prayers or holy verses from the Sikh scripture, the *Guru Granth Sahib*. The holy ones sat in meditation in their own spacious aloneness. In the early morning, no one in the family spoke loudly, much less harshly, nor did they gossip about the neighbors. The hour was too auspicious. Only the purity of silence was in place. Then at twilight, when stillness spread its sacredness upon the land, we began to quiet our body senses and bring the mind to peace. Many of us would go for an evening walk. The atmosphere was also conducive to peace and harmony.

Hardly anyone in my family was educated but in all my experience throughout the world, I have found very few who could match the wisdom and compassion of some of my uncles, or the eternal principles of goodness and virtue imparted by my aunts. There is often great humanism amongst the uneducated.

One of the characteristics of the East is the reverence that exists for men and women of true words. When I left India many years ago, there were five hundred fifty thousand villages and not a single policeman in any of them. When a conflict arose, the wise of the village would facilitate harmony. They would ask each party to rise above their differences, saying, "It does not become you to be ignoble."

In those times, there were fewer clergy than wise people. The priest had his function and he was often a good man, but worldly issues were settled by the elders. If one person was hot-headed and refused to listen, then only a few persons would go to his son's wedding. He had to listen.

Correction was brought about without authority. The rightness of society was not always centered around self-interest or "me and mine." There was some other force that said you can't afford to isolate yourself. It encouraged people to correct their ways and value rightness. When you have a lawyer, there is no contact with the character of the other person – the primary objective becomes to discover how you can manipulate the situation.

My father was one of the few people in our village who was educated but he had gone abroad to Panama when I was less than a year old. With the exception of a distant uncle, no one else in our large family could read or write. Although they were illiterate, our family had a deeply religious atmosphere.

What was far more important to them was that I was given an education of ethics and morality. The code I was to live by was not curiosity but interest. Interest focuses one's energy and attention and brings one to awareness.

Sometimes singers came to our village. They were part of this ancient culture of India in which men and women could come to peace and silence their mind through the breath that breathes prana, the source of creation. Chanting and the breath are one and the same in that both have stepped beyond the thought process and made contact with another energy.

On occasion, a troupe of Sufi Qawali singers would come to the village and sing of the glory of Allah. They lifted people to another state of mind with their love for the sacredness of the *Koran*.

> "When this world was not,
> nor the world of men,
> nor the moon or the sun,
> nor even the sky –
> then there was no authority of one over the other,
> nothing was there except You, only You, Allah.
> Allah Hu, Allah Hu, Allah Hu – God Is.
> Tu He Tu, Tu He Tu – Only You Are."

Then a story was narrated and the chorus would again sing:

> "Allah Hu, Allah Hu, Allah Hu – God Is.
> Allah, You are the light of the eye,
> the voice of the heart."

These songs would intoxicate us with joy. As children, we climbed the trees to listen. The elders were so inspired they could hardly contain their generosity and gave money abundantly.

How did illiterates impart a life of ethics or value for virtue? How did they awaken the inspiration of God, or the love for honesty and courtesy? How did they introduce the source of joy, etiquette, gracious manners, and polite behavior?

My family was affluent yet I had not seen a coin until nine years of age. I was taught to be charitable and to give to others in need because it pleased God. I was schooled in the refinement of hospitality – how to give rather than to want. This appealed to me more than learning to spell. "Goodness," we were told, "will awaken sensitivity; and sensitivity purifies the mind to heed the voice within." One could not, and would not, live without integrity.

As a family we were called *macadam* – which means family of judges. We were respected for our honesty and reliability. Service was sacred. Over and over again, in many different ways, it was brought to my attention that I should be dignified, never casual; that I would find strength in rightness, and happiness in charity.

I recall my different aunts teaching me the virtue of obedience and humility. They would say, "It is crude and common to be arrogant. Only vanity is soiled with pride." Or, "Don't project desires or a sense of lack in yourself. Don't pollute yourself with greed or make yourself inferior by wanting. Wanting makes one a beggar. When you outgrow desire, you are strong within yourself. God will provide for you. God alone gives." They would caution me to beware of habits and not to let tendencies strangle me. They instilled in me an awareness that, beyond gratification, there is happiness.

As a child, I was caressed by the elders and the warmth of their kindness inspired me to listen to their calm, pure voices, which were like a whisper that opens the heart. Gentleness taught me to be gentle. We respected the elders and therefore spoke politely to them.

We were also taught by way of stories having eternal value. "Sarvan" was the story of the pure-hearted boy; "Beeba" was well behaved; "Balah" was kindness to all; and

"Naki" was the noble one. Whenever I was particularly well-behaved, my mother would call me "Beeba," or if there was purity in my heart, I was her son, "Sarvan." I had so many names. And the names lifted me to a new dimension. Our learning was an awakening, and our stories were the tales of men and women of strong character, living examples of principles. We were taught Divine Laws, not manmade rules and customs. However, it was not until I was in my twenties that I actually read a book.

My alphabet was not made up of letters, but the lives of Lord Rama, Sita, Lord Buddha, Guru Gobind Singh, Hanuman, Radha, Lord Krishna, and countless stories of other saints and prophets, sacred rivers, cities, mountains, stars. All of these transmitted the knowledge that God is ever with you.

Being part of the Sikh culture of brotherhood, as children we would often hear stories of Guru Nanak, the holy prophet and founder of the Sikh religion.

> "At the age of nine, Nanak was taken to school. The teacher taught Nanak the alphabet which he quickly learned, as if he knew it already. Nanak asked the teacher, 'What are these letters for?' The teacher explained, 'Letters put together make words, and words make sentences that transmit knowledge.'
>
> "Nanak sat quietly to make words with the letters. Some time later on, the teacher came and asked, 'What words have you formed?' 'I have formed a word – Him.' 'Who is Him?' asked the teacher. 'Him Who is the one Creator of the universe,' said Nanak, 'the God of us all.'
>
> "The amazed teacher asked, 'What else are you thinking of?' Nanak said, 'All learning is futile except to know Him and to be with His Divine Will.'
>
> "'Pundit,' the teacher asked, 'where is God you

speak of?' Nanak answered, 'He is everywhere. He is the Creator. His love is in everything. Only he who knows Him is learned.'" [1]

Nanak, the illiterate, lived and breathed the holy songs of God. He questioned and dissolved every belief, every concept and superstition of conventional religion. Meharban Janamsakhi, a Mohammedan, says of Nanak:

"A Hindu chancing to pass by would involuntarily exclaim, 'Great is Gobind, the Lord! Such a small child and yet he speaks so auspiciously. His words are as immaculate as he is handsome. He is the image of God Himself.' And if a Turk saw him, he would remark with equal enthusiasm, 'Wonderful is Thy creation, merciful master! How good looking is the child and how polite his speech! Talking to him brings one such satisfaction. He is a noble one, blessed of the Almighty Allah.'" [2]

\* \* \*

I lived in India for the first nine years of my life, but I didn't go to school until I was eight. My whole family, with the exception of my father who was away, supported my not going to school because, to them, education was not so important. It usually increased pretense and falsehood.

My father had gone to Panama when I was less than a year old because friends there needed an educated person to teach people and to write letters. He did not go with the intent of staying away. But because he held a patriotic view and had spoken against the tyranny of the British rule, he was not able to return to India lest he be placed in confinement as a rebel.

Imbued with the values of the Western world, my father did not want his son to be illiterate. He began writing frequent letters to the family, insisting that I go to school. After a period of time, the family reluctantly acquiesced and dragged me crying to school. I would run away from the school. They would buy me new clothes and give me good things to eat, but school just didn't interest me.

What interested me was the outdoors. I loved to go to the pond where the frogs were jumping and beautiful white cranes walked. The buffalo came to swim in the water and the shepherd would bring his whole flock there to drink. I loved to watch caravans of camels passing through the village and to be a part of the natural rhythm of rural life. Everything was alive.

Eventually, my father realized that he could not control my education from afar, and the only possibility was for the family to join him in Panama.

There are other forces at work in one's life. The village astrologer had predicted at the time of my birth: "This child has divine protection and he will bring good fortune and prosperity." He also foresaw that I would travel all over the world. Everyone wondered how this would ever happen. Most of us didn't even know the world was round. Had my father returned to India, we would never have gone abroad. Had I not refused to go to school, we would have remained in the village. Life has its own plan which is at work behind the scenes of one's existence.

No sooner did we arrive in Panama than my father said to me, "So, you didn't want to go to school? You're going to go to school now." Well, if Life ordained that I not be educated, what could he do? I stayed in Panama nine years and, despite my father's determination to send me to school, I attended for a total of two and a half years. The rest of the time I'd go swimming in the streams and rivers, or go to the beach or to movies.

I suffered at the hands of the other children at school because I was so different. But I learned about a whole new culture from them and was introduced to electric trains, candies, skates – a whole cache of new things to want. Because my parents didn't know about these sorts of things, I had to get them on my own.

My mother was my best friend. I shared all my secrets with her. I would also tell her about my skates and going to movies instead of school, and how afraid I was that I would get a scolding for not going to school. She would say, "Don't worry. Just call on God and everything will be all right." Because I was doing so many wrong things, I was actually praying to God most of the day.

My mother's advice never had blame in it. In fact, it was more like we were the same age. The quality of her voice filled the house with its peace. It was the kind of advice that goes beyond words. One could never forget it, as if it really took root in one's being.

If I told her that I had gone swimming in the stream instead of going to school, she would make sure I knew how to swim and was not careless, but she would never put fear into me.

When I first went to the movies and saw the cowboy rider get shot, I wondered who would unsaddle the horse and feed it. It took me awhile to understand what was happening. Cowboy and Tarzan movies were my favorites. My mother didn't know what movies were because she had never been to one. I would tell her about the horses running and she'd say, "Watch out for the horses." When I explained that it was only a picture, she'd become confused and say, "If it's a picture then it can't be running around, so why bother worrying about the saddle?" There was no way I could explain it to her. Somehow I would become like the mother and she the child. We would interchange roles that way.

When I told her about the shooting and fighting, she would ask, "Where are the elders to stop the fighting?" In India, if any two people started to fight, or even became abusive with one another, there was always someone to pacify the situation and bring things back to harmony. They helped put out the fires of anger.

I remember vividly the joy of sharing during spacious hours together, never rushed or pressured. There was always joy in the sharing and expressing the things I did for the day. Every one of us is looking for that love that allows us to share our deeper feelings. No matter what I did, she would always say, "It doesn't matter if you go swimming or bicycling or to the movies as long as it makes you happy. You can do all these things that make you happy because God loves happy children. But don't ever take advantage or be unkind to anyone."

I would say, "But Bibiji, I'm afraid that when I've been away for two or three hours, Phaiaji* will ask where I've been, and he'll find out." She would lovingly say, "Call on the Name of God. It will work as long as you are not doing anything that will hurt another."

I would ask her, "What if it doesn't work?" "Never doubt God," she would say. "The Name of God will keep you strong. But if you've done wrong things you will lose confidence in yourself and become weak. To have this protection of God, you have to be kind to others even when you're afraid."

Although she supported me in being happy, she would also wisely advise me never to get into habits. "Why?" I would ask. "Because habit will control you and make you weak. You will lose that strength inside of you."

My mother introduced me to thinking of God whenever I did anything wrong, whenever I would not conform. She related me to faith and a confidence within and never gave me guilt. She was at peace with herself, for her goodness was alive and she had space to give and to listen.

I was a child of two cultures – the East and the West. Now I see that one culture related me with eternal values and an inner relationship with God. The other related me to the external world. What I learned from my illiterate family and friends was a greater strength than what I learned from the

---

* Bibiji is an endearing name for mother; Phaiaji, for father. (Editor)

educated. The stability and values that were imparted in my youth provided a foundation of strength whenever challenged by any situation. But the atmosphere of the culture of the illiterate is rapidly disappearing in India.

I can unequivocally say that education does not necessarily open the heart. Abstract learning limits us to preoccupation with ourselves. True education should introduce faith in something larger than personal improvement. Perhaps then our children would not be schooled by borrowed thoughts. Now they are mere echoes of other people. The degeneration of the human brain, with its violence and selfishness, is frightening to behold. When I see this, I value the contact with those who were not lettered but had a different quality of mind. Whitman, Rilke, Valery, Emerson, Thoreau, and Lincoln are examples of this.

The culture of the illiterate is the culture of wisdom. Saint Joan never went to school. Sri Ramakrishna saw it as a breadwinning education, devoid of contact with one's own holiness. Rabi'a, the slave girl of Baghdad who became enlightened, never went to school.*

Then there was Lincoln who hardly went to school. In times of crisis he sought answers from outside the realm of thought and made contact with Divine Forces.

We have example after example of unschooled men and women who touched upon another reality, who knew that strength is inherent in rightness. Their value for the eternal brought them closer to wholeness.

Education does not liberate us from selfishness, nor does it free us from loneliness, guilt, and fear. What good is education if it does not introduce man to the holiness within himself?

\* \* \*

---

\* For a complete accounting of the life of Rabi'a, see *Women Saints: East And West* (Vedanta Press, 1979), page 260-271. (Editor)

My real education began when I was twenty-seven. I was in New York and utterly lonely. I didn't know what to do. This internal loneliness compelled me to educate myself by reading books of noble beings: Sir Thomas More, Socrates, and Lao Tzu, among others. These people virtually shaped my awakening. Every night, from eight to two in the morning, I had six hours for pure thoughts of a sanctified atmosphere. I did this regularly for almost five years. It was not an effort, but the greatest joy. This love of noble lives strengthens and enriches one. It didn't matter who the person was. It could have been Hui Neng; the Sufi mystic, Rumi; or Saint John of the Cross. I was touched by the fact that something else was awakened within them.

\* \* \*

## THE FACE OF A SAINT

In the culture of the illiterate, the presence of a saint is a refuge to humanity. His radiant face is a blessing upon the earth and unborn generations benefit from the light of his true words. He is still of mind. His is the countenance of contentment, for his seeking has ended. His divine light produces a glow that attracts and draws to itself those who are sensitive to values of the spirit. Being fulfilled, he does not commercialize his existence. His innocence is superior to the knowings of human experience.

Like the light surrounding a temple, a glow embraces the saint. The saint is not usually given to the activity of "doing." He is with "being." Through his stillness, the power of heaven comes to earth.

To be in the presence of a saint is called *darshan*. It is the vision of eternal light that surrounds the congregation in the presence of a saint. This auspicious gathering of *Sad Sangat*\* is much revered. Once you have seen the face of a saint, with its infinite tenderness and compassion, you have touched

---

\* "Sad" is the holy person and "Sangat" is the congregation about him. (Editor)

upon the compassion of your own Self. Everything external becomes trivial. Deep down, you realize the truth that God alone is real, and everything else is unreal.

When I first met such a being and entered the atmosphere of his holy presence, it purified me of the activity of unfulfillment. Then I knew what *darshan* meant. Later I met other men and women in the villages of India who were garbed in simplicity, for they were of the kingdom of heaven. They bore the serenity of dawn and the peace of twilight upon their faces. They were not educated, nor subject to the belief system of conventional religion. Anonymously, they kept the light alive. It is a great loss when such beings are not needed, or pass by unnoticed.

One wonders if the very planet could survive without their presence. We who limit ourselves to the world of appearances pass them by without even knowing. Man, the world over, is becoming less and less capable of having the eyes to see or the ears to hear. Progress has no fulfillment in it, and so preoccupation with the external continues.

The saint who wants nothing extends his gratefulness for all that is perfect and harmonious in creation. The wise know him by the quality of his voice, by the way he sits, and the way he walks. His expression is profound, his language mastered. He moves from insight, not opinion or point of view. His words carry the authority of his selfless life. They are an expression of Divine Laws. His is the knowledge of awareness. He represents the re-entry of love on the earth plane, extending the Life Force. He does not teach. The tranquility of the saint enters the heart and silences the brain. Jesus came two thousand years ago and the planet still vibrates with the words He spoke.

From the beginning of time there have been saints whose footsteps blessed the earth. Where life is Impersonal, Gratefulness is ever present. A woman saint, who insisted on remaining anonymous, awakened me to the miracle of Gratefulness that is ever present.

Children need to meet such holy beings who are free of conflict and whose voices are not horizontal. The touch of their light is worth more than years of education. What value has life without insight? I benefitted most throughout my life from the contact with men and women of direct knowledge. The purity of a saint's face reflects certainty.

> *The certain are perfectly calm, because they are not in doubt. They do not raise questions, because nothing questionable enters their minds. This holds them in perfect serenity, because this is what they share, knowing what they are.* [3]

\*　　\*　　\*

## ENCOUNTERS WITH MEN AND WOMEN OF DIRECT KNOWING, FREE OF PRETENSE, HAVING THEIR OWN CLARITY AND THE WILL TO SERVE.

### SANT HARI SINGH

While I was living in India as a young man, a saint resided not too far from my village. His name was Sant Hari Singh. Although he was a simple man and did not have a great following, he was well known in the region as a holy person.

For generations, people had talked about the need for a road to the Temple at Anand Pur, the Abode of Bliss, where hundreds of thousands of pilgrims go annually for a religious festival. Many streams flowed from the Himalayas and the dirt road was frequently flooded. In the winter the weather was especially unpredictable and conditions were hazardous for travelers on pilgrimage to the Temple. Although the Sikhs are known to be an enterprising people and the fellowship among them is renowned, no one could manage to implement the construction of the road to Anand Pur, a distance of approximately forty-five miles.

One day some of the leaders said, "Why don't we go and ask Sant Hari Singh. Let's urge him to inspire some action.

What he says will be respected." To preach scriptures and talk about holiness is easy, but a true saint is a rare phenomenon. It takes discrimination to recognize the person who lives the Word.

A committee of well-to-do, elite Sikhs went to Sant Hari Singh. They paid their respects and announced that they had come because he was an extension of their holy prophet, Guru Gobind Singh, the tenth Master of the Sikhs. After a few minutes they told him about the need for the road, that every year hundreds of thousands of people go on pilgrimage to the Temple at Anand Pur. They thought it a disgrace that the Sikhs could not build a road for their convenience. If the government would not do it, the people should get together and build it themselves.

Sant Hari Singh was almost illiterate and he knew very little of these things, but they thought he could probably persuade a few people. Implied in their words was the notion that if he took action, this committee would back him up. They needed someone like the saint to focus the energy behind the project. The saint himself had no needs, for he was outside of worldliness.

After Sant Hari Singh had listened very carefully to their plea, he asked, "Do you think it is really a need?" "Oh yes, sir. How long this deplorable condition has gone on!" "Very well," he said. Because he listened, he must respond to the need. Now we are going to discover how a man of awakened intelligence responds. How does that awakened intelligence, which is always self-reliant, work?

He sent one of his devotees to go and get a pen, paper, and an ink pot. Again he addressed each of the people who had assembled and asked, "Do you think that the road is necessary and that funds are needed?" They were all in agreement. Next he called the most vocal amongst them to come and sit beside him. Sant Hari Singh looked the man straight in the eye and asked, "How much are *you* going to donate?"

They never expected that this action was going to begin with them! The saint is not complicated. He doesn't know arithmetic. He doesn't know how roads are built. All he knows is that life has presented a problem that, for generations, the whole Sikh nation could not solve.

For the saint the action starts with what is at hand. He doesn't know lack. He sees everything is a gift of god. Everything. So he asked the first person, "If you believe in this, what would you donate?" That sent shivers amongst the group. The man said, "Oh, certainly, I would like to donate; I wouldn't have come here otherwise. I will give five hundred." The saint said, "Five hundred? How much do you own?"

What a challenge! You can't lie to a saint. When he told the saint how much he had, Sant Hari Singh said with a shock, "You are telling me how important this road is, how desperately it is needed, and you, who are so wealthy, are only going to give five hundred? Is this a joke?" The man was sorry he ever came. Now he had to donate a good deal more than he ever intended. The saint does not get taken over by the "idea" of the road, he wants to know the actuality of their commitment. A rule of thumb was then established about the right proportion between one's assets and one's contribution to the project. He turned to the next person, "Sir, what would you donate to get the road built?"

If you go to a saint with half-truths, you come away having learned what Truth is. Worldly people make causes. The saint doesn't make any cause. He sees something that our brains can never know. He sees the Will of God. He is with the Actual.

He went from one person to the other. They couldn't leave, nor could they lie. Their intellectual, abstract activity had no love in it. Each one was compelled to give honesty to his words. That is the great gift of the saint. When all was finished, he had quite a fund to start building the road.

There is a difference between having wealth and having capital. Wealth consists of a country's assets – its forests, minerals, metal ores, or rivers. That is wealth. But you need capital to use the wealth – to buy the ax to cut the trees, to use the river for irrigation, etc. Without capital, the wealth doesn't serve the country.

Sant Hari Singh's first action was to get the capital, the seed money. Observe how the awakening of new intelligence works. This inner awakening knows no calculation. It is simple, direct, uncomplicated. And it is extremely practical. It had nothing to start with and, in less than an hour, it has thousands.

Then the saint asked, "What is required to build a road?" It is good that he is innocent and doesn't know. He can find out. Implementation is easy once the resources are there. He found out that you need cement, gravel, mixed sand. And for the bridges, iron, steel, engineers, and surveyors were needed.

It occurred to the saint that in the villages there are huge kilns with the capacity to bake hundreds of thousands of bricks at a time from the native clay and so he asked, "Can't we use bricks to build the road?" The people said, "Oh yes, bricks are even better."

The saint traveled to the neighboring villages and told the elders there, "A committee came to tell me that a road is needed to Anand Pur. How do you feel about the need for a road to our holy place?" They said, "Yes, Santji, the road is definitely needed." He asked them, "Would you like to give your labor to bake the bricks for the road? You do not have money but could you give service?" They were delighted. Each village fired its kiln.

Sant Hari Singh made one important suggestion, however. He said that if two million bricks were needed for the road, they should bake twice as many. "Santji, why should we double the amount we need?" "Because we will sell the extra bricks and, with that money, buy the cement and steel that are necessary for the bridges."

This intelligence of self-reliance is not based on business or economy; it is born out of love and service. Sant Hari Singh was not only building a road, he was awakening the people with his own inner awakening. He was demonstrating the way to do things. Everybody was amazed and the villagers were singing songs of the Lord while they worked. Fifty thousand people had volunteered to build the road.

Everything Sant Hari Singh is going to do is simple. He introduces us to a state that has no lack. It is joyous because the power of givingness is in it. Nothing can stand before the power of love. Nothing. The saint teaches us that the currencies of this intelligence are the power of love and the joy of service. Because the modern world has lost this, we resort to buying and selling and exploitation.

Sant Hari Singh worked with what was at hand. "Should be" was not part of his world. He did not believe that what was at hand lacked anything. What was at hand began to multiply in the present. The road from Namaskar to Kirtanpur, now called the Nawashair Road, was built and there were still extra bricks left over, as well as all the original money. With that they built a high school and a much larger temple to serve the greater number of people coming there now that the road was safe. In Sikh temples, food is offered free to all who come, regardless of the number. Sometimes there were between ten and fifteen thousand people for lunch. There is a large kitchen and a large area for people to stay. There are no servants. People who come to the temple volunteer to serve.

How do we know Sant Hari Singh was a saint? He never touched the money. Through his action he imparted the strength of rightness. He demonstrated that he was related to Divine Laws because he spiritualized everything he did. In him we see a man who is content. He relates mankind to inner potentials. Only silence can contain thought; thought cannot contain silence. Sant Hari Singh silenced the words of others and quietly made the impossible possible. What a state of non-separation! It is known only to trust. *A Course In Miracles* phrases it this way:

*I need but call and You will answer me.* [4]

When I went to meet Sant Hari Singh, I didn't want to go empty-handed. I took a nice, woolen shawl which I put around him while he was sitting. The love of this saint transformed my life. I learned what it is to be yourself, what it is to be awakened from within, and how not to get lost in worldliness. The self-reliance he embodied sowed a seed in me.

I was honored when Sant Hari Singh, and his party of six or more, accepted my invitation to come and stay with me in Simla, an elite city in the Himalayas, seven thousand feet above sea level. They arrived with hardly any luggage, yet they were always very clean. Sant Hari Singh said, "It is your love and affection that brings me to the mountains. You will know service and holiness."

Entailed in this visit was not only serving the half-dozen or more people accompanying him but also the scores of other people coming daily to visit. All this introduced me to spontaneous hospitality which in turn awakened the joy of service and selfless devotion. Thoughtfulness came alive in me. Even though we had servants, as my sadhana or spiritual discipline, I would walk miles each day to get pure unadulterated milk, fresh from the valley. The "I" ceased to exist. The whole party got up early and we would prepare breakfast for them. There was no telling how many days or weeks we would have the privilege of their visit.

Sant Hari Singh did the service at vespers in the evening and hundreds of people came for *darshan*. It was like Jesus with His twelve apostles. Sant Hari Singh's peace and our reverence for his presence had a life-changing effect.

Since neither the saint nor anyone in his party touched money, when they were ready to leave we purchased the railroad tickets for them and provided the money they needed for the journey. There would be a crowd to meet them at the other end.

In the presence of a saint one learns the importance of self-mastery and witnesses the power of peace and humility. Nothing in the world is comparable to it. This is the education that affects one's life in a permanent way.

\*     \*     \*

## SWAMI RAMA TIRTHA

I never met Swami Rama Tirtha, my first Teacher.
It is he who unlocked the spirit in me.
So inspired was I,
frequently I mistook myself to be Rama Tirtha.
He had the same impact
on whoever came close to him.
His presence is still alive in each of us.
Having made the contact
we could never settle for things of the earth.
We owe our life to him, more than to our parents.
Such is the mystic touch
of this God-lit man in blossom.
Devotion seems so natural an expression
of man in the body.
And then when the "he" and "I" have ended,
one is not of the body, nor of time,
but an extension of God's Will,
without a cause or consequence.

As a young man, I was introduced to the life and writings of the extraordinary being, Swami Rama Tirtha, renowned in all of India. A sannyasi, he had renounced all worldly attachments. When he was young and very poor, he won the highest honors in school and college and eventually became a professor at the most prestigious university in Punjab. Even though at the age of twenty I could barely read, I read Swami Rama Tirtha's books.

Since he had very little money when he was a student, he would do his homework beneath the lamplight in the street. And yet he was so generous that he would give the few coins he had to buy food for someone in need. He hardly knew the difference between himself and another.

Eventually he outgrew the structure of the university and came to America in 1902-1903 to take part in the International Parliament of Religions in Chicago. When Swami Rama Tirtha got off the ship in America, the customs officer asked him, "Where is your luggage, sir?" Swamiji told him he had no luggage. "Where are you going to stay?" He told him he didn't know; that it never occurred to him for he knew perfection was in God. "But don't you have any friends here?" the customs officer asked. "Oh yes, sir, I have one friend." "Who?" "You."

When Swami Rama Tirtha says "you," it is similar to what the Oracle at Delphi said to Socrates when he inquired as to who was the wisest man in Athens. The Oracle proclaimed, "You." Swami Rama Tirtha's "you" cannot be evaded. Right there a relationship was established.

In the following years, Swami Rama Tirtha spent time on Mount Shasta in California. The people of San Francisco organized a procession honoring him as the "living Christ in America." Theodore Roosevelt was amongst those who paid homage to him. Swamiji's lectures were renowned in America and abroad. Seven or eight volumes of his lectures have been published.

When Swami Rama Tirtha returned to India he lived as an ascetic in the Himalayas, oblivious to the fact that he had been married at a very young age. His mind didn't have the past in it. The father of his young wife inquired all over as to the whereabouts of his daughter's husband. It is an uncanny thing how the villagers manage to find you in India. They talk to everyone. People here and there start helping as if you have the whole of humanity on your side. Finally Swami Rama Tirtha was found living in a cave in the Himalayas.

The father brought his daughter and deposited her outside his cave. "This is your wife," he said. "She is now your responsibility." And he left. The girl sat there for hours. Because she had no options, she had another strength. This is not just a story. She is an example of someone awakened from within. She did not complain; she did not want anything to be different from the way it was. This is another wisdom. He could not meditate as long as his wife was there. Every time he opened his eyes to look at her she was sitting just as she had been before. This is an unpredictable situation. Because it is not of the brain, it is new.

Swami Rama Tirtha thought to himself, "Now I have a wife." There was a force in her stillness. Her non-action was the force. She was a Brahmin girl who did not know deviations. She would not belittle herself for she was too noble for helplessness or demands.

Slowly the realization came that he was now a householder. They left the mountain cave and traveled by ferry to the city. On the way he saw that his wife was wearing several golden bangles on her arm. "You don't need those," he said. She gracefully took the bangles off her wrists and dropped them into the river. This woman had no dependence and no attachment. She was a wife, a wife that would make him a husband.

In the Preface to a collection of Swami Rama Tirtha's lectures, it is written:

> "Wherever he went, he was very highly respected and admired for his deep knowledge, learned oratory, loving nature, infectious smiles, and charming personality. The Christians called him the living Christ, the Buddhists saw in him the renunciation of Lord Buddha, the Mohammedans visualized in him the spark of prophet Mohammed, and the Hindus considered him to be the very incarnation of Adi Guru Shankaracharya…. Whenever he spoke, he spoke from the depth of his experienced conviction. He never uttered a single word which he had not

himself experienced to be true. He was all love, Love personified." [5]

Once when Swami Rama Tirtha was teaching, he suddenly got very shaken. The students asked him what was wrong. He said, "One of my students was just crushed under a train." It turned out to be so. He had a different connection. It was contact with Life, not personality.

Swami Rama Tirtha was seen digging with a fervor on the bank of the river. A man passing by asked him, "Sir, did you lose something?" With tears in his eyes, Swamiji said, "No. A snake the color of the complexion of Lord Krishna has gone in this hole. I want to hug him."

On the strength of the inspiration I received from this man, I left home and spent four years on the Himalayas. One time, in my wanderings, I slept in a place where mosquitoes were eating me all night long. I could not turn on my back for fear of killing them. I may have been a fool, perhaps I was inspired, but the only thing I knew was the fact that my body was of service. No fear touched me. I was in such a different state I could walk straight toward a bear. There were no consequences in it, no alternatives. There was no fanaticism. It was just a different state of being.

Swami Rama Tirtha took me out of domesticity and introduced me to the life of renunciation. He talked about Vedanta, the non-dual state in which we realize we are all one. Vedanta is the knowledge of truth, the knowledge of what God created. It is absolute knowledge. *A Course In Miracles* is the closest thing we know to Vedanta. It proclaims, *I am not a body, I am free. For I am still as God created me.* [6]

\*   \*   \*

## HIMALAYAN DISCOVERIES

When I was in my early twenties I spent four years in the Himalayas and became directly aware that the religion of belief, the religion of concepts and ideas, is limited. This awakening within started to undo. It didn't teach me. It helped me to question: Is this not borrowed? Is this not an idea? Are not idea and truth two separate things? I saw that the belief in Allah, belief in God, belief in Brahma were still dependent and therefore not Truth. A full inner awakening had not yet taken place in me but the undoing of all that was external had. It took me four years to go through this process. Mine was not a casual statement asserting, "I don't believe in this." I gave my whole life to making that direct discovery. Years later when I met Mr. J. Krishnamurti, I could say unequivocally to him, "This, I know, is not religious."

I did not see truth but dependence in the organized religion of belief. Admittedly, it may serve a purpose for a while but eventually it has to be outgrown for the inner awakening to take place. You can only be grateful for the religion that brought you to disillusionment for you have found something of who you are as God created you.

For four years I thought I was religious. Then I discovered that if you don't outgrow belief, you are not religious. This realization makes you compassionate towards others.

When you go to a religious elder to get your misperceptions corrected, you find that, for the most part, he is also caught in belief. Many religious people become disillusioned at one point but they may not have the moral strength to die to everything within. People start calling them gurus and they let it be. That is their reward. They allow others to take care of them but inwardly they no longer believe in it.

Most of the holy beings I went to seemed very honorable and had a following. But what they were saying was the same thing I would have said prior to becoming disillusioned. I was not yet awakened, but I knew that this was not it. I began to question my own thought, my own knowing. In this way humility begins, and the arrogance of finding God falls away.

This state of questioning can be almost unbearable. You are desperate to find the truth and you see that no one knows it. The majority of your acquaintances, however, think that *you* do. The temptation is there to open your own shop because wherever you go you are honored – your intent is pure and there is another radiance about you.

When you ask these "holy beings" for the truth, the same thing happens that happened to Socrates. They challenge, "Who do you think you are? To realize God takes generations, lifetimes." They become easily threatened even though you don't provoke an argument but only ask probing questions. I was only twenty-four and burning with fire.

I went from one guru to another. I nearly took my eyes out because I thought if I was blind my family wouldn't distract me from my love for God. But my love for God was still a belief. I used to get up at two a.m., take a bath in cold water, and sit quiet for hours. I would have gotten pneumonia twenty times over, but a fanatic will was activated in me. My mind had become so sharp, so clear, so persuasive, so self-convinced. I often spent ten hours a day in meditation. When I was home I put a big padlock on the front door so people would think I was gone. I would enter and leave by the back door. For weeks I would never leave home, so mesmerized was I by the scriptures and my own belief.

There is a well known experiment demonstrating that if someone believes he is going to be touched by a red-hot rod, he will get a blister even if he is only touched by a paper straw. The power of the mind can make you believe anything. You can become so convinced that other people think you have spiritual powers. But you have not stepped out of the known. Within the known it is possible to deceive the known world. Only the real saint knows that you yourself are deceived.

What you have accomplished becomes your bank account. You can impress the world. You become the "holy man" and play the role. That is the pension you can live on for the rest of your life. How seductive it is. Spirituality can be very ambitious. It can make one beastly. People have done such cruel things in the name of religion. There is the example of Saint John of the Cross:

> "St. John's unlit cell was actually a small cupboard, not high enough for him to stand erect. He was taken each day to the refectory, where he was given bread, water, and sardine scraps on the floor. Then he was subjected to the circular discipline: while he knelt on the ground, the monks walked around him, scouring his bare back with their leather whips. At first a daily occurrence, this was later restricted to Fridays, but he was tortured with such zeal that his shoulders remained crippled for the rest of his life." [7]

The world dislikes the one who shines away ignorance and vested interests.

The four years on the Himalayas gave me four hundred years of another vitality, another integrity. I had never thought I could dedicate myself so completely to anything. It educated me and awakened a new sensitivity. I was now able to reason. If you won't settle for becoming a saint and fooling people, you are a rare person in the world. If you can overcome that temptation, God's Grace is upon you.

\* \* \*

## PANDIT JAWAHARLAL NEHRU

When I left my retreat in the Himalayas, I was struck by the tremendous poverty in India. One has to do something with one's life. And, naturally, if you want to do anything you have to organize and you need capital. I became interested in the lives of those who were making a contribution, like Mahatma Gandhi. Gandhi thought that the enemy was not always wrong, that you cannot correct wrong with the overdoing of wrong. He came to simplicity and self-reliance.

Gandhi was a very successful lawyer when somebody gave him the book, *Unto This Last* by Ruskin. Ruskin wrote that because of widespread industrialization, the future problem would be the concentration of power in the hands of few. Gandhi was startled by this truth and recognized it immediately. He came to the conviction that he would not be a part of this concentration of power.

No consequences frighten such a person. Gandhi insisted that nothing in the non-violent movement would be done in hiding, out of fear. To his colleagues he imparted the courage to be forthright and open. Gandhi believed in awakening the goodness in man. He emphasized that one has no power over the results, one can only refuse to use wrong means. This deeply inspired me.

During this period of time I was blessed to develop a close relationship with the leader of the Sikh nation, Giani Kartar Singh,* a man of renunciation with the integrity of a saint. In me, he planted the seeds of serenity and the certainty of selflessness. We met with the leaders, the maharajahs, and the elders of the nation and were entrusted with six million dollars to start cottage industries to help India evolve from the plow and the spinning wheel to the use of electricity, mechanized farming, and sophisticated irrigation and reforestation projects.

This work brought me into contact with Pandit Jawaharlal Nehru, the first Prime Minister of India, a man of unparalleled greatness. "Impeccable and incorruptible" were the words used by Mr. J. Krishnamurti to describe Nehru. He was an advanced being, of the stature of an initiate, and he extended that incorruptible quality to his office. Where are you going to find a head of state who does not want to be the Prime Minister? He did not run for election. The people's love for him elected him to office. Nehru represented service in a world victimized by politics and nationalism.

---

* For further details of Mr. Singh's relationship with Giani Kartar Singh, see *How To Raise A Child Of God* (Life Action Press, 1987), pages 17-18, and *"Nothing Real Can Be Threatened"* (Life Action Press, 1989), pages 245-246. (Editor)

Born into an aristocratic family attuned to humanistic values, Nehru was not a politician. When I read that while in prison he shaved every single day, I remarked, "The days of the British Empire are coming to an end because such a being who cannot be affected by the externals is upon this planet."

Nehru was not reactive, he merely extended who he was. I became very inspired by his genius and his generosity. At the time of the partition of India and Pakistan in 1947, people felt free to go and see him about their loss or their circumstances. He would meet them on the lawn outside his residence and, with his secretary by his side, he would try to help every single person. He offered one-to-one contact. He had stacks of blankets for the poor. To know such a being makes a profound impact on one's life. Nehru completed the work of the day before he left his office and the bulk of it was done after midnight. He needed very little sleep. The order he established allowed him to make a new start each day.

Of Nehru's book, *Glimpses of World History*, the *New York Times* said in 1934:

> "It is one of the most remarkable books ever written.... Everything is more or less impromptu. Yet there is a coherence, a design, that must set Westerners gasping. Nehru makes even H. G. Wells seem singularly insular. One is awed by the breadth of Nehru's culture."

During World War II, more than forty-thousand leaders in India were made political prisoners due to India's policy of non-cooperation with the ways of violence. How could they support the brutality of any war? Besides, it would also mean strengthening the chains of India's slavery. A free India certainly would cooperate with the allies against any aggression but India at this point was not free.

While the Congress* leaders were in prison, the Communist leaders were released, or not even arrested, because Russia had

---

* The Indian National Congress was formed in 1885. (Editor)

become an ally of Britain. During these years, the Communist leaders gained significant ground because there was no one to oppose them. They took over the sentiment of the people and won their support. Communist flags were flying all over, even in remote, rural areas.

When Nehru was released, he was shocked to see what had happened while he was in prison. He started to bring to the attention of the Indian people that the Communists had betrayed India, that India with her own voice and ethics would not imitate anyone or be influenced by an alien doctrine based on expedience. His motiveless words which demanded conviction were like a sacred fire that spread instantly all over the country. Within a matter of weeks, people had uprooted, burned, and buried their Communist flags.

Nehru had dedicated his life to the awakening of an impeccable morality and virtue and had won the hearts of his people. It was his love and compassion that people honored, not his political party.

In 1946, when I was about twenty-six years of age, Nehru came to Lahore where I lived. The railroad station and the entire surrounding area was filled to capacity with college students, businessmen, and people from all walks of life. What magnetism!

I succeeded in getting an appointment to see him and went through four hours of agony not knowing what to communicate. I realized that I had nothing authentic to say except the vanity of having met him. I tried my utmost to come up with some plausible cause with which to impress him. It was so painful to go through the hours of falseness. By contrast, I felt that if I were to meet Gandhi, or Jinnah, the leader of the Moslem League, there would be no hesitation because they seemed predictable in their preferences and points of view.

But Nehru was a man who seemed to step out of time and even objectivity. What could I say to him that had any substance at all? It brought me face-to-face with my own pretense. Only after seeing your mediocrity will you either come to your own conviction or evade it with justifications.

What emerges out of humility is pure energy – for it has broken through the mirage of personality and made contact with its own spirituality. If I had seen Nehru and not been brought to this humility, I would never have had my own voice. Now that I knew what was needed, the compromise was over. Certainty, one discovers, is always the Given. It is not an achievement, nor is it learned.

The dignity in Nehru dispelled any falseness of intent in me. I was filled with wonder to realize that man indeed is created in the image of God when he is fully himself. In the end, I telephoned the secretary and cancelled my appointment. The secretary asked, "Why?" I said, "I have nothing to say to him now. But meet him I will when I have my own voice."

Years later, when I went to him to volunteer my services, he asked me where I came from and what problems were most pressing in my village. I told him that firewood is very expensive and sanitation neglected. He asked me what could be done. I said, "Every day, I would plant trees." He was stunned that here was a person who didn't champion a cause. "Panditji," I said, "the problem with our country is that we always think the uncle or the government is going to do it. My action would be one that is self-reliant. It is possible for a man to plant one tree today, five tomorrow, and thus learn of the joy of intrinsic work that makes life impersonal."

Nehru stood up and shook my hand. A different kind of relationship came into being. Only when you start with what you have do you find the unlimited potentials within yourself. The action towards inner awakening can occur all of a sudden, or it can be gradual. But whenever it happens, it is a contact with the living moment that knows no lack.

I met Nehru numerous times in the ensuing years to discuss questions pertaining to my concern for people in need. Once when we met, there was not the space to go into things. When I offered to come the next day, he said that he was going to the Commencement Ceremonies at Rabindranath Tagore's renowned school, Shantinekaten. He asked if I had ever been there. When I said, "No," he invited me to go along with him. He said, "Due to the commencement ceremony, there will be many people there. I hope you don't mind if the accommodations are somewhat crowded." Immediately, he called his secretary and asked him to telephone and ask Shantinekaten if they would mind if he brought a guest with him. Such thoughtfulness and humility. In everything he did, he was wholly present.

Since the plane was leaving early in the morning, he suggested that I come in the morning to have breakfast with him so that I wouldn't disturb my hosts at the early hour.

In Nehru's presence, one often felt the glow of his love for humanity. One sensed he had the space to heed your words and that his words emerged out of an unpressured space. It is a rare gift to witness what takes place at the internal level.

The order in his life was inspiring. He was very stately, meticulous. He was disciplined without ever imposing upon himself. This discipline emerged out of attention and spoke of his development. Nehru stood as an extension of a timeless law. Even in prison he had the same rhythm. The only other person I met with this sense of order was Mr. J. Krishnamurti, but then Mr. Krishnamurti was never a body but a state of being.

The light of faith was in Nehru, though not in a conventional sense. He was too real to fit into classifications. Knowing him personally one was able to discover the spiritual vastness of the inner man. His spiritual purity shines upon the moral force of humanity.

The post-war world was caught between the superpowers who sought success and prosperity and gave value to economy and defense. Nehru, on the other hand, represented not only the leadership of the Third World, but humanity at large.

Being wary of concentration of power in the hands of the few, he gave voice to the basic needs of man. To him, poverty, illiteracy, hunger, and disease were the issues upon which the human intelligence and the energy of nature were to be focused. He was humanism in action and his democracy was broad in scope. Not being a man of reaction, he would not become a party involved in the tension and struggle of the superpowers, whether capitalism or communism. Best of all, he was not a man limited to the past. He valued the inner potentials of the human being and was closely related to the Mind of the Age, far beyond the reach of "isms" or dogmas.

He was so objective that one could no longer be a Sikh, a Moslem, a Hindu, or a Communist in his presence. The fact, to Nehru, was that we were human beings first. Our secondary affiliations did not apply to the newness of the moment. Part of the wholeness of humanity, he seemed to act out of fulfillment. Nehru's life was dedicated to fact, not belief – a man of amazing consistency. And if one pointed out an inconsistency, he had the willingness and the capacity to correct it within himself instantly. I was surprised to see that he would not allow his body senses to take him over, separate him, or make him act out of isolation. Nehru reminds me of what Jesus said to his Apostles:

> "IF YOU CONTINUE IN MY WORD, THEN ARE YOU MY DISCIPLES INDEED; AND YOU SHALL KNOW THE TRUTH, AND THE TRUTH SHALL MAKE YOU FREE." [8]

\* \* \*

## INDIRA GANDHI

I met Indira Gandhi before she was Prime Minister. She was very simply dressed, gentle, but in total command of herself and the situation. Our eyes met and immediately there was a bond. Later, at a buffet luncheon, she came and sat with me and was greatly interested in who I was and was pleased as well to discover I was a friend of her father, Prime Minister Nehru. Following the meeting she wrote to me: "It was an unexpected pleasure to meet you during my brief halt at Kulu for I felt at once that there was something unusual about you."

Indira Gandhi had the makings of a Queen Victoria combined with the zest of Joan of Arc. She was a strong woman, reliable, direct, and confident, more decisive than her father, but very gentle also. Her compassion and statesmanship are almost unequalled in history. How little is known in the West of her greatness. Buckminster Fuller wrote this inscription to her:

> "To Indira, in whose integrity God is entrusting much of the evolutionary success of humanity and with utter safety...." [9]

Her will speaks of her intuition and her fearlessness, a rare example in all history:

> "I have never felt less like dying and that calm and peace of mind is what prompts me to write what is in the nature of a will. If I die a violent death as some fear and a few are plotting, I know the violence will be in the thought and action of the assassin, not in my dying – for no hate is dark enough to over-shadow my love for my people and my country; no force is strong enough to divert me from my purpose and my endeavor to take this country forward.

> "A poet has written of his 'love' – 'How can I feel humble with the wealth of you beside me!' I can say the same of India. I cannot understand how anyone

can be Indian and not be proud – the richness and infinite variety of our composite heritage, the magnificence of the people's spirit, equal to any disaster or burden, firm in their faith, gay spontaneously even in poverty and hardship." [10]

Indira Gandhi was clear on the basic issues of unrest in the Third World countries. They were not necessarily political or religious. She recognized the urgency of meeting man's primary needs first. The deterrence of communism, on which so many trillions of dollars were spent in the West, could be better used on improving roads, sanitation, education, and agriculture. In the absence of a response to the basic human needs, the threat of communism in Southeast Asia assumed an exaggerated importance.

Communism became a political issue, and later a military issue, only because of neglect in the economic development of the Third World countries bordering China. The West was interested in containing China. How much wiser it would have been to improve the conditions of the neighboring countries. The Third World countries – comprising over a hundred non-aligned nations – met a few years ago in Mexico and the meeting was given hardly any press coverage. It has always been the case in history that the extension of humanism in response to economic problems has rarely been in proportion to the needs; whereas, when the problem becomes a military issue, resources are seldom ever lacking.

For instance, America spent over 40 billion dollars and dropped more than six millions tons of bombs in Vietnam only to be defeated in the end. A fraction of that amount would have led mankind closer to sanity. It is amazing to observe the peril of industrialization and the abuse of human energy in our times. Now the future belongs to China because they developed a different kind of energy, one that is decisive. When they were not affected by world opinion, one realized that they had the strength. They were starting from their own core. It was action, not reaction.

I had written to Indira Gandhi in 1974 that the problems of affluence were no less threatening than the problems of poverty and illiteracy. There was a proportionate increase in tension and fragmentation and disharmony in families. There are no laws to contain the media nor is there any protection for the people. The commercialization which conditions the human brain is probably the most dangerous of all human folly. Distractions and indulgence, immorality and vulgarity are commercialized far beyond necessity. Violence is becoming a way of life. The whole world now wants to imitate America. It is a sign of progress. But what America has exported is the lowest standard of morality. People gravitate toward it because it doesn't demand anything.

While America may be militarily and economically strong, it is poor in virtue and ethics. There is always the good but with the modern media, it is difficult for the voice of goodness to be heard. Amusement, entertainment, and waste proliferate. What is India doing to protect the people from the vulgarity of Indian films and violence?

The life of Indira Gandhi was totally dedicated to the service of humanity; therefore, strictly objective. It was reported that she slept only one hour a day. She was ever so contained and dignified. It is refreshing to witness the moral superiority in the life of such a leader, having no pretense or the pride of status.

*   *   *

## JAYAPRAKASH NARAYAN

How does one introduce a man of the stature of JP, the revered Jayaprakash Narayan, one of India's foremost leaders? His position as prime minister after Pandit Jawaharlal Nehru was unquestionably assured by the people of India.

"JP spurned opportunities for occupying high office in government more than once and was inclined to give up the politics of power completely at a time when, in popularity amongst the people, as well as the elite, he stood second only to Nehru and was generally regarded as the most suitable person to succeed the latter as prime minister." [11]

When I first met JP in the early sixties, in a village near my home in Punjab, he had come to see Vinoba Bhave, the walking saint of India. Vinoba Bhave had gotten hundreds of thousands of acres of land from the rich to give to the poor. This was a charitable, Gandhian movement meant to revolutionize the villages of India.

The place was crowded but I was able to introduce myself. He freed himself from the others and we walked away from the crowd. He was interested to know that I knew Nehru and other eminent leaders of the country, and yet I was not in any way involved.

We discussed the fact that everyone in India was dependent – either on government, future technology, education, or holiness. To me, dependence was the basic problem, not agriculture or transportation. The need, as I saw it, was for an internal revolution where dependence on the outside was ended. "What do you mean?" he asked. I answered him with a totally different intensity, "JP, when one looks at Indian temples, shrines, or even forts, when one is exposed to the extraordinary Indian sculptures, dance, or music, one sees precision at its highest expression. There is an incomparable capacity to extend something more than just personality. This is where the awakening must begin. We need to introduce man to who he is, to what his potentials are. All this can be done without being dependent on the externals."

"But illiteracy is a major issue. Isn't education the means to bring about what you are suggesting?" JP asked. "Education is important of course," I said. "And it will be implemented because it is part of the trend. But the awakening I am speaking of has nothing to do with education. Mass education is irrelevant to awakening. The men and women who gave expression to ayurveda, astronomy, astrology, or yoga in its origin, extended Universal Laws because they were awakened, not because they were educated. The wisdom of the illiterate elders in the village surpasses, in its humanism, what educated people all over the world know."

JP was somewhat shocked. "I never thought about it this way. I see what you are saying – that what we call education merely trains the brain. It does not affect the character, the ethics, the morality."

"Yes, there is no insight in it. And without insight, there is no wisdom. India is the one country in the world that can give expression to something nobler than what we call *brain-training*. The uniqueness of Indianness, which survived two hundred years of foreign rule with its mental and materialistic values, still shines. That over forty-thousand people could go to prison without reaction to British colonialism, without wanting to correct wrong with the overdoing of wrong, honoring the ethics of non-violence, is a statement of what Indianness is. It is not founded on what Ramakrishna called the *breadwinning* education. Mass education, by and large, is for those who have earthly values."

JP asked if I was then opposed to education. "No. Its vitality is needed. What I am saying is that nothing can prevent education from flourishing. The external man will be shaped by it. But I am bringing up that man's internal life cannot be overlooked, especially in India where man's relationship with God or Divine Laws has always been esteemed. Mere external education is an expedience for the most part, for it usually isolates man. It does not necessarily relate him to his own integrity. The existence of education is justified partly because of the outlets and indulgences it provides. This may serve the industrial economy, but these can also be factors of degeneration in society."

"The sculptures and dances of the temples transcend time. They relate man to higher laws that silence the brain. Brain-training has its place, but will India preserve man's contact with the silence within himself? India looks to the man of the Spirit now. One day, this mass-education will stimulate and beguile man with frightening values of selfishness and ambition. The Western world is showing us what pleasure-seeking expedience will do."

Then JP said to me, "But you were educated at the university." "No, sir, in fact I went to school for less than three years." He was shocked and asked me how I ever managed to rise to the level where I was with no education. I said, "It is the power of attention that truly educates a man," and our hearts met. JP welcomed me to visit him in Delhi when he was next there.

When he was leaving from the railroad station at Phag-wara, near my village, thousands of people came to hear him and see him off. In his speech to them he said he was encouraged because he had met a young man that day who had inspired in him a confidence that a different energy was yet alive in India.

Some months later when I met him in Delhi, we had lunch and spent a good part of the day together. He wished to spend more time in discussion and asked, "Would you like to be our guest at our home in Bihar for two weeks? I am going to the remote, interior areas of India in connection with the Sarvodaya,* to get land from the rich for the poor. I think the trip would appeal to your mystic, poetic nature." He asked me if I had met Vinoba Bhave and I told him that we had met twice.

I accepted the invitation and went to visit with him in Patna, the capital of Bihar. From there JP, his wife Prabha, and I went by jeep to the rural country. It was beautiful to be near the forest. JP met with the village elders and Prabha cooked delicious meals for us in the wilderness.

---

* Social welfare movement in India involving volunteers who helped villages integrate community development programs, such as building roads, schools, etc. (Editor)

The relationship between JP and myself, as I observed, allowed an expression in which opinions sometimes differed, but the reverence for unity was not affected, nor loyalty or selflessness ever questioned. The wisdom of the ancient Indian sages was still intact and valued.

We seldom talked about politics, or even about what JP was doing. Our minds were not pressured with any set agenda. One day at lunch, JP said, "Since you have traveled extensively around the world, I am eager to know your outlook and your mind." JP asked questions in a unique way. And then he questioned my answers. It was a delight to probe past the realm of thought and come to an objective state in which both parties partook of the clarity. One could never forget the spaciousness of such an experience. JP communicated his joy, not in words, but in the enrichment of a friendship that offered newness. His eyes spoke the smile, the stillness of the moment. It felt like a blessing upon us both. We could share our innermost thoughts in an impersonal way.

He asked my views on the land reform movement. I said to him, "I question prosperity itself. At one level, it is beneficial. At another, it does not transform human life and values. Anything *about* something else is not of first importance to me. Inner integration and transformation are as important as external improvement. It is good for the rich to donate part of their land for the poor in their village, but the shift of ownership is incomplete, to me, because it does not increase food production."

JP asked what would increase food production. I said, "Water. Water for the land is the natural solution. Where there is one crop a year, now there would be two. This new wealth would transform poverty."

He was stunned. "But how does one do this? Wouldn't it require a polytechnical education?" he asked. "The technology and the capital required may not be as complicated as we may think. The farmer knows what to do with the water. It doesn't require a college education. Just as the land needs water, so the country needs strong bodies with good health. This new energy is of first importance, not ideologies," I answered.

Inspired, JP said, "Your perspective has the potential of revolutionizing the agricultural economy and the production of food." I said, "Money is never the issue. Neither Jesus nor Gandhi had any capital. Your integrity is established. Once you are clear, the money will flow. The farmer could repay the money from the income from the new crop." He said, "Yes, I see this is practical. It would work."

That evening when we met Prabha, JP said that since the death of Gandhi,* he had never heard anything like this. He also said that he had seldom been so happy in his life, nor had he ever remembered laughing so much with anyone since before Gandhi died.

JP felt that we should meet with Asoka Mehta, the head of the Five Year Plan, who was his close friend and colleague. I undertook to outline the plan for irrigation for the land, so that it could be presented to the Planning Commission and Prime Minister Nehru.

JP asked me if I would stay in India because he felt I was needed there. I said that I could be interested in discovering ways to protect India from political ideologies. He was shocked. The intensity of interest heightened. This is where real communication takes place. It brings one closer to the creative moment, into a newness that has its own presence. He asked, "What do you propose?"

I said, "JP, regardless of what you do, the present democracy will bring concentration of power in the hands of the few. I have seen that wisdom is on the wane in the West. The power of money and vested interest are in control. But affluence without wisdom is self-destructive. ** Thus, at some

---

* January 30, 1948.
** For further information on the lack of wisdom in society, see *The Future Of Mankind – Affluence Without Wisdom Is Self-Destructive* by Tara Singh (Life Action Press, 1992). (Editor)

point, democracy becomes anti-democratic. But the tradition of India is based on the simplicity of wisdom and the settlement of disputes between rival forces by rising to a higher level for reconciliation."

"Surely," I said, "India cannot avoid the modern-day progress of technology and commerce, but what it can introduce is the power of morality and virtue if vested interests allow its entry. The world requires India, with its humanism, to give another expression where human life is revered. Whatever is proposed would have to be consistent with what India truly is."

He inquired, "And what is that?" "India is a land of renunciation and detachment. Its highest goal has always been one of the spirit, or man's relationship with Eternal Laws. JP asked where we should begin. I said, "We begin with you. That is the only place the action begins, within one's own self, totally independent of the externals.

"We can see from time immemorial, ancient India honored the loftiness of selfless man. The kings bowed before a sage who wanted nothing because he had outgrown the world. People have always distrusted rulers with their pomp and show, and earthly powers, unless they were kings who extended divine will and were masters of themselves.

"Why do you think Gandhi refused to be head of state? Or Lord Buddha head of a kingdom? How many hundreds of kings in India renounced the status of kingship. We have a great example in Asoka, the Buddhist emperor of India. The legendary King Janaka and Harish Chandra who both gave up their kingdoms are unparalleled. The light of Yudhisthira and Bharat still shines in the minds of India. These beings provide not only an example, they also give faith in the capacity of man to outgrow the personal for the internal. For them, good was absolute because it did not know the bad. In India hundreds of thousands of people outgrow the personal world of the senses in their later life and walk free and pure.

The nation honors their sacredness and gains moral strength from their example."

JP listened carefully and said he agreed in principle. "It is not just a matter of principle," I said. "We must outgrow politics and come to eternal values. Even statesmen will not qualify for what we are talking about. It requires dealing with internal issues. And correction is made within oneself. Once that is done, only then will one be an extension of Eternal Laws. So we start with you, JP, and with Panditji* and Giani Kartar Singh, and a few others who have overcome the world of personality interests. This small group of five wise elders, a *panchayat*, would then guide both the nation and the government with higher values that still vibrate in the internal man. India still reveres those who outgrow power and position. Men whose values are pure and eternal are the real heroes of India. They have always been the liaison between the manmade world and the God-created world."

JP asked if Nehru would agree to resign from the Prime Ministership, or if Giani Kartar Singh would be able to let go. "We will find out," I said. "Mr. Krishnamurti has said that Nehru was incorruptible, so he is already out of it. And Gianiji is a selfless being. He will respond adequately to the challenge. Right now, I need to know: Will you challenge yourself?" "Am I worthy?" JP asked. "I would not have asked you if you were not." JP responded, "This is beyond choices. It demands a decision with the power of God behind it." I said, "Rightly so."

When JP expressed that he felt I was overrating him, I said, "We are not dealing with personality. Do you see that the Five would have a clearer and a stronger voice than the government, the political parties, or the religious sects? This transcends nationalism and affirms we are human beings, not nationalities." "Yes," JP said, "throughout history, humanism

---

* Jawaharlal Nehru.

has been consistent with the vibration and ideals of Indian-ness. It expresses that the highest man is the one who owns nothing, having found his peace within."

There was a long pause, a new opening. It was twilight and the forest, the earth, and the heavens were becoming one. Shortly thereafter I wrote a letter to Prime Minister Nehru suggesting that a grateful nation was shyly questioning whether he should continue in office because Nehru was needed outside the government to guide both the people and the leaders. I felt that this third party of wise heads could take place only in India. They would provide the example and leadership to help mankind out of its lower nature in times of crisis and confusion.

Without this voice, India, faced with gigantic problems of underdevelopment, would lose its ancient bearing and resort to imitating the West, thus degenerating into a non-entity with no light of its own.

I was to meet with Jawaharlal Nehru in New Delhi shortly thereafter, and JP had planned to come a few weeks later, but on May 27, 1964, Nehru had a stroke and passed away.

On the day Nehru died, I had just returned from Nepal. At the airport in Benares, the pilot said to me, "Panditji has passed away." My attitude towards death had always been that it was a natural part of life. But when I was told that Panditji had passed away, I noticed the effect his death had on nature. Upon our arrival in Delhi, the sky was so dramatic. Although it was a summer day, a cool wind blew. I wondered if this was the way it had been when Jesus was crucified. In silence the nation mourned, as if everything had come to an end. The shops and cinemas were closed and the taxis did not toot their horns. The Sikh at the wheel of the taxi I took said, "Panditji was for all." One could hardly speak.

After Panditji's death, I met with JP again. He was unable to rise to meet the challenge, and one could see the decline had begun.

\*　\*　\*

One could meet with Jawaharlal Nehru, Indira Gandhi, or Jayaprakash Narayan to explore what one thought was truth, knowing fully that each of our lives was dedicated to the discovery of the same impersonal truth. Whenever one of us saw that what he thought to be true was questionable, there was no resistance to making the internal change.

Obviously, correction within oneself is required for the transformation of values to take place. To overcome unwillingness and vested interest is one of the most difficult things in life. Personalities become so committed to their own ideas and beliefs. Intellectuality seldom leads man to reality.

The fact is: Without one's own conviction, one will not make contact with the truth of the moment, nor with men or women of excellence. Such meetings are an enriching and life-changing experience. Huston Smith writes in *The Religions Of Man:*

> "Around the middle of this century, Arnold Toynbee predicted that at its close the world would still be dominated by the West, but that in the twenty-first century, India will conquer her conquerors (culturally and politically). India's spiritual tradition Toynbee saw as destined to figure prominently in the long-range human future."

After the Second World War, India regained her own freedom from the British through non-violence. An independent voice emerged offering peace as an objective in itself, instead of the violence of "might is right." It provided an opportunity to mankind to consider issues without correcting wrong with the overdoing of wrong. Gandhi's approach of non-violence succeeded in overcoming reaction with the perspective that the enemy is not always wrong.

Politicians rarely rise above nationalism. Our lack of humanism is apt to result in consequences. The two social evils of poverty and conformity increase in prosperity. As Aldous Huxley pointed out, "Evil, lacking the power to resist temptation, in the end destroys itself." The laws of cause and effect are inevitable.

Humanism is essential if peace is the aim of life.

# CHAPTER THIRTEEN

# 13

## ENCOUNTERS WITH MEN AND WOMEN AWAKENED FROM WITHIN
### Part II

$W$hen I first came to America in 1947, I met men and women who led inspired lives, well-rooted in integrity, justice, and humanistic values, people who were broad-minded and objective. It was a joy and an enriching experience to hear authentic voices expressing the spirit of the New World.

Having a background of knowing ambassadors and prime ministers, I came to America in my twenties with a broad outlook on world affairs. Meeting great men and women in America helped me evolve a deeper conviction, a maturity, and then an awakening. I was a man of both worlds – the East and the West. But the seeds of the values of my Eastern culture became stronger rather than getting diffused and dispersed in the West. I was enriched by the noble lives of America's prominent voices, but I was not taken over by its more worldly values.

I was a newcomer from another part of the world. I was young, while the people I met were older. Although I had different values, the perspective I brought gathered attention and facilitated a real meeting of heart and mind. Despite the fact that I had less than three years of schooling, my

317

appreciation and gratefulness were my education. The friendship with men and women of integrity enriched my life. One is never alone in growth. So much is given and assimilated. In the end, it all leads to the values of impersonal life.

I had suffered a lot from not having much education, not wanting to work for another, and not having a skill. I volunteered my services to C.A.R.E. but refused to accept the ample salary offered to executives. What I stood for was something bigger than me and each step led me to the discovery of self-honesty, as if it was an independent entity within that prevented me from compromising in the face of great challenges.

Conviction invites challenges and confrontations. Non-compromise is never easy, but not having your own voice is degrading. This awakening of inner potentials and the strength of Rightness leads to a lifestyle free of consequences.

The one thing in common with all of the people of wisdom whom I met is that they never worked things in their own favor. They had something to give, a willingness to share it, and a keen sense of who had the capacity to receive. Their life shone through their words and the work they did.

Although I was young and impressionable and was inspired by the lives of these eminent people, contact with eternal beings of realized words made the greatest impact on me. These were the seers of the New World: Emerson, Thoreau, Lincoln, and Whitman. Whitman expressed it so well when he said: "I am as if disembodied of materiality." [1] These beings represented the humanistic quality in their own lives as well as a vision of eternal life. They held a different moral standard, outside the realm of thought, for they were in touch with timeless Reality.

Contact with these eternal beings made a lasting impression on me. For months, my heart sang with the joy of the wisdom they imparted. It is this that introduced me to yet another energy, an energy not of their words, but of discovery.

This discovery is the place within oneself where the flame of inner awakening is lit. The strange thing is that this discovery continues for years and one realizes the eternal value of contact with men and women of realized words. Mr. J. Krishnamurti and Dr. Helen Schucman are part of Infinity. They are the Light of the world, as Buddha and Jesus are the Light. What Mr. Krishnamurti said to me is still unfolding. What Dr. Helen Schucman, the scribe of *A Course In Miracles*, said to me will live within me for as long as the sun and the moon are there. Blessed is a student awakened to the love of True Knowledge.

\*   \*   \*

## ELEANOR ROOSEVELT

Eleanor Roosevelt was a woman of unassuming kindness. One could count on her simplicity which gave her space for thoughtfulness. She was a dependable friend. She often invited me to Hyde Park, to the United Nations Assembly where she served on the Human Rights Committee, and I took her to the movies. During the war, Mrs. Roosevelt kept the White House on the same ration of food and electricity as the nation was following. She felt that she and the President could not ask the people to do something that they themselves were not doing. Although she had an elite background, she never separated herself from the average person.

After our meals at Hyde Park, she would sit by the fire and knit a sweater, socks, or a scarf. When I asked her what she would have liked to have done had she not been the First Lady, she said that she would have liked to be a nurse. Mrs. Roosevelt had an abounding goodness and self-givingness that gave her space and peace. She never seemed pressured, yet was ever productive. Through witnessing a unique person's life – its rhythm, its leisure, its fortitude – one discovers those potentials within oneself. One-to-one relationship is invaluable.

*   *   *

## NORMAN THOMAS

Norman Thomas, the American author and socialist leader who ran for president four times from 1928 to 1944, left me breathless with his integrity, objectivity, and dedication to his cause. He ran for president at least three times knowing full well that he would not win. His interest was in voicing something of value that America needed to hear. Whatever political or economic system America started with would have flourished irrespective because of her vast natural resources and small population. Everything was to her advantage.

Norman Thomas was highly intelligent and direct. Although he was inspired by the life of Gandhi and traveled with him in Europe, he had his own conviction about socialism. When he retired he was celebrated by people of distinction.

I was young when I met Mr. Thomas but he sensed something in me and kept his door open to welcome me whenever I visited. I owe a great deal to his dedication and simplicity.

*   *   *

## HELEN KELLER

I met Helen Keller, the famed lecturer and author who overcame blindness and deafness, at the Carnegie Endowment Center for International Peace. When Helen Keller went to the podium to speak, she said, "Work is worship." Her words totally silenced us all. They had a life behind them, a life completely given and unpretentious. When her compassionate hand touched my face, I came to the serenity of stillness. Her goodness flowered out of stillness. Even in her old age, she was energetic and hospitable.

\* \* \*

## PEARL BUCK

Pearl Buck's perspective would have saved America from slowly becoming anti-democratic. She and her husband, Mr. Walsh, were kind and friendly to me. They saw something of the ancient culture alive in me which prevented me from being influenced by the externalized Western values. Therefore, there was a meeting of the mind and heart. They were inspired by the wisdom and humanism of the East, particularly China and India. Their concern about China, strangely enough, did not center on Communism but on whether, in their revolution, the works of Chuang Tzu, Confucius, Lao Tzu, and the sayings of the sages would survive.

For Pearl Buck, the spirit of religion resided in her love for God and the Bible. Her husband was a friend of rightness. They were sad to see American politicians support the corrupt dictators of the underdeveloped countries for the sake of military bases rather than for helping people. They saw that this anti-democratic action was a betrayal both of the true American spirit and the countries which held America in esteem. These countries looked to America because it was the one Western nation that did not take advantage or colonize. Having been exploited by the colonial powers of Europe, smaller countries valued America's democracy and its composite nature, incorporating races and peoples from all over the world. Pearl Buck felt that America had a responsibility to be true to this trust and provide a noble example.

\* \* \*

## MARK VAN DOREN

Mark Van Doren's kindness is still alive in me. He was so self-giving and encouraging to me as a young, aspiring poet. Pearl Buck introduced us and recommended that I show my poetry to him for his comments, as he was a Pulitzer Prize winning author and critic. Mark Van Doren invited me to come to lunch at Columbia University where he was the Chairman of the Department of English.

What a gracious man. He could overlook the awkward inconsistencies in a newcomer like me; nothing affected his warmth. He invited me to his home on Bleeker Street and fed me sumptuously. But when I invited him and his wife, Dorothy, to dinner, they chose a restaurant that would not be too expensive for me.

When I asked him if he would read my poetry, he said, "I would like to help you in any way I can, but don't ask me to support a cause." These wise words of advice enriched my life and protected me from being misled innumerable times.

Even before he had made any comments on my poetry, I asked him to guide me for I did not want to get involved in anything unless it was my real calling. He would be able to prevent me from wasting years by lending me his discrimination. Since I did not want to be a second-rate writer, I wanted him to tell me if he saw some exceptional spark in my poetry.

Listen to his clear words: "Not yet. I have to see more of it. Feel free to send me the poems you write. But don't expect any answer from me until I discover something unique. Then I will write to you."

How much better this is than encouraging or discouraging words. Here was a man who could give the space and the interest. He would not quickly conclude but let openness formulate its own authenticity.

*   *   *

## ALDOUS HUXLEY

When I was a young man, lost in idealism, but burning with the conviction that man is One and whole, I met author Aldous Huxley. He extended an open hand and heart to me. Fragmentation had little meaning for me. He appreciated this integrity and showered me with attention and the accessibility of his friendship.

Aldous Huxley was most aware of the potential problems that lay ahead of our society, and what technology and irresponsible ambition could do. He had great hope that India would contribute something of eternal value that mankind desperately needed. How many discoveries he made about all walks of life!

Wise and perceptive, he knew human nature, as he did the nature of politics, of science, and of education. He knew what each of these was capable of doing. One could not conclude anything in his presence. He freed me from any set view and added a different dimension.

\* \* \*

## DR. DAGMAR LIECHTI

I was in Positano, Italy, during the winter of 1968. It was an ideal place to spend the winter – a seaside resort town south of Naples, with cliffs the color of dry rose petals. While there, I was told directly: "Get healthy and strong. You will be needed. The path is clear. The way will be shown, and there is service."

Since there had been no external direction most of my life, this boon of service delighted me. One merited service! Yet, "get healthy and strong" became a challenge because I had never really been sick. The obvious conclusion was to go to a doctor and have a thorough examination. But one could not be casual.

The question was: Who is qualified to rise to the divine standard? A direct message compels one to face the unknown and not attempt to fit it into the littleness of the known. Local doctors would not do. The challenge demanded the wisdom of insight. Wherever one inquired, whoever one talked to, no one had ever known certainty. "Doctors, doctors everywhere; not a doctor anywhere." The predicament continued.

Since I could not afford to betray the instruction, the only thing I could be certain of, and rely upon, was my not compromising. Then I was doing my part. Life would do its part. The situation demanded that I rise to a level of non-duality and avoid going through the long journey, the trial-and-error, of experience. It was clear to me that it required direct knowing rather than borrowed learning.

I was still in Positano when an intimation came that Mr. J. Krishnamurti had a doctor in Switzerland. I found out, upon inquiry, that it was Dr. Dagmar Liechti of the renowned Bircher-Benner Clinic. There was a sense of rightness about the intimation, so I drove to Zurich.

At the clinic, they asked if I had an appointment. I said, "I never make reservations." So the lady at the desk replied, "We can't accept you without one." That was their problem, not mine. I had my suitcases with me.

She began to look over the appointment schedule and found they had an expensive suite available. Later in the evening the nurse came and I asked her about Dr. Liechti. She said, "Dr. Liechti does not accept new patients. She is retired and comes to the clinic only to see her old patients, who come from all over the world." She said I would be assigned to one of the other doctors who was very good.

The next morning I went to Dr. Liechti's office. The secretary asked me if I had an appointment. I said, "No, I don't." She said, "You can't see Dr. Liechti without the appointment." It was the obvious answer. So I said to her, "I want to see her for a few minutes. She can take her time. I had a very big breakfast this morning and I won't be hungry for a year. So tell her not to hurry. I will wait."

The secretary had never heard words like this and felt that something was odd. This led her to give the startling news to Dr. Liechti who came and opened the door slightly to peek. She exclaimed, "What an aura!"

Dr. Liechti welcomed me into her office with utmost courtesy. She said, "You are the healthiest man who has ever been to this clinic." Dr. Liechti had the insight of a seer. Hers was the voice of certainty. She was the awakened one of direct knowing – a true doctor, extending her God-given abilities rather than relying upon what she had learned.

My problem remained unresolved, however. How could I get healthy and strong if I was already healthy?

I explained what brought me to her. She offered much space and we talked for a while. She said to me, with the same kind of finality, "You have so much vitality, even archangels would be envious of you. Don't ever listen to another."

It was the first time anyone confirmed something which I had often felt even though the world around me denied it. I had seen a great deal of others' unnecessary jealousy and undermining of me.

Within the moment I was clear. To my surprise, I said to Dr. Liechti, "Does your responsibility to Life end in your coming to the office in the morning, and leaving in the evening?" She was a little startled by these confronting words and said, "I beg your pardon. What do you mean?"

I explained, "I come from India where there is an ancient medical system based on the laws of how creation renews and maintains its health throughout time. It is known as Ayurveda and is disappearing because of the Westernized, expedient approach to life which has invaded India with its half-truths. Is it not your responsibility as a doctor to protect Ayurveda and give it life in Europe while India is under the spell of imitating artificiality?"

Despite the fact that I was bold and confronting, she was elated. She said that her uncle had started the vegetarian clinic, in spite of a great deal of opposition. He was a man of vision and had told her that Ayurveda was vertical and supreme. Ever since, she had been eager to meet someone from India who was knowledgeable about Ayurveda.

Then she said, "Since you are well, you don't have to stay at the clinic. If you have the time, I would like you to come and meet my husband and children and stay with us."

"I always have the time," I said. As I left her office she put her hand out to me, saying, "I am your older sister, Dagmar." I met her family and stayed for some days, and talked about the contradiction between the Voice saying, "Get healthy and strong," and her saying that I was healthy. We could come to no clarity.

One day I began to question whether the traditional medical definition of health itself was consistent with the "health" the Voice spoke of while I was in Positano. Slowly it began to unfold – an ambitious, self-centered man is not healthy according to Heaven. I began to see that I indeed needed to get healthy, but it was not physical. As *A Course In Miracles* points out, the body is neutral and purification is invariably of the mind.

Step by step one moved from fact to fact, rather than relying upon the duality of thought. An internal inquiry began. Somehow, the name *yoga* occurred to me. I discovered that only yoga's definition of health was consistent with that of the Voice, for it dealt with the Divine Forces within the body, the temple of God.

Yoga led me to India. But to find an authentic yoga teacher is like finding a needle in a haystack. Everything is commercialized, everywhere. It is just about impossible to discover the authentic without determination and discrimination.

Once I was settled in India, I invited Dr. Liechti and her daughter, Barbara, whom I had met in Zurich and had stayed with in Paris, to come and stay with me so that Dr. Liechti could explore what was being done with Ayurveda. There were many Ayurvedic Research Centers in different parts of India that were supported by the government. Dr. Liechti was the first foreigner allowed to share in their findings. We became more than good friends, more like a family.

There is so much I learned from this great, gifted lady of beautiful mind and spirit. And so can you, the reader, if you make the demand upon yourself not to settle for second best.

\*　　\*　　\*

## PHYLLIS CALLEY

The good action of one person could be something very small according to the world's values; however, because it emanates from an inner awakening, that person's life is a blessing to all humanity. Some of us are fortunate to meet many people like this in our lives. I knew an English lady named Phyllis Calley from whom I rented a small place in Carmel, California. Her husband had died and she lived alone. Everything she did had something of innocence and wisdom in it.

The charm of Carmel is unforgettable – more like Europe than America. I had been living in Ojai, about ninety miles north of Los Angeles, but discovered Carmel on a return trip from Yosemite. Instantly I fell in love with it and inquired of a friend regarding a rental for the summer months when Ojai is hot. She agreed to look for me. When I arrived home in Ojai there was a letter waiting saying the lady's friend, Phyllis Calley, would allow me to stay in her home while I was looking for a place of my own. That is thoughtfulness, real giving. It is a different intelligence which always meets a need. Unless we have discrimination, we will never see it and without that discovery, there is no joy.

In her sixties, Phyllis was somewhat aloof; very nice, but factual. There was little conversation. If you had a need, good. She was kind but nothing more. I could see that she had a glow within her though. She lived alone in a large house with a lovely little garden. Her garden was the kind she could handle alone. It was her own expression and it didn't take much time.

For lunch, she fixed herself a salad and sat in the back garden on a lawn chair to eat. I don't think that she drank anything other than tea. She was energetic – no dogs, no cats, no T.V. Nothing. I was also in my own music. I sat quiet in the garden outside my room for hours by myself. One of her neighbors suggested to Phyllis that I needed to meet people since I was all alone. Phyllis said, "I don't think he is that kind of person." I knew she was not that kind of person either.

One day she suggested that I stay in her home until I had to return to Ojai. Although she protested against my paying, she finally had to agree since she realized I wouldn't stay in a place where I did not pay rent. I was totally on my own then to walk on the beach, go to Point Lobos, and fix my meals. I managed everything in a very simple way.

Phyllis had a potter's wheel behind the house and occasionally she would work on her pottery. Once or twice a week, I noticed that she would take her little car and disappear. I wondered where she would go. She didn't have too many friends. The telephone seldom rang. She asked me if I had ever been to Nepenthe at Big Sur. Since she had to go the next day, she invited me to come along. On the way, she told me all about her husband. They used to live in the Palo Colorado hills above Carmel. They had their own honey bees and fruit trees and were very happy. From his photograph, I could see he was a unique being – very present. He had been a teacher at the high school.

Phyllis said that after her husband died she no longer wanted to live in the large house. Although it was beautiful, it was too far and too much for a person living alone. Since she sold the home she now had enough money to sustain herself, and once or twice a week she volunteered at the Braille Center for the Blind. She told me how she admired a friend of mine, folksinger, Joan Baez, and the young people of the sixties because there was hope in them. Slowly I began to see that everything she did was caring. One might say that she was busy like I am busy or you are busy, but it was not so. Hers was a different lifestyle.

When we arrived at Nepenthe we took cartons of her pottery from her car. Nepenthe is a very large store, one of a kind. The people greeted her and said they wanted so many more of this, and so many more of that. I thought, "How surprising! As a rule pottery doesn't sell."

Phyllis said, "I am sorry. I can only make so many of each of these." While driving home I said, "Phyllis, normally pottery doesn't sell and they want more of yours. You have the space and the time, why don't you make the things they would like?" This is where the inner awakening manifests itself. She said to me, "Tara, there are so many potters in this area and they have a difficult time making a living. If I supply all that the store wants, then the other potters' work will not sell. I could not do that." This is an awakened mind.

We became good friends. When I took her to meet Mr. Krishnamurti, although there were hundreds of people present, he went straight to her and said, "I don't believe we have met before." Just her eyes showed how unique she was – so clear and unworldly. In her spare time she would read to her older friends who could no longer see well.

Years later when she sold the house and was preparing to move back to England, she called and said there was something she wanted to ask me but was afraid. I said, "Phyllis, you are like my sister, my dearest friend. How can you be afraid to ask me something?" "All right," she said, "I never had much money. Now that I have sold the house I have more money than I need. I would like to give you half of it." "Phyllis," I said, "don't you realize that I have to know how the Will of God works? You will be putting hurdles in the way.

I want to know self-reliance and how Life takes care." She said, "I knew you wouldn't accept it but I couldn't leave without offering it to you."

There are many people like Phyllis who always have something to give but you have to have different eyes to see them. Such people do not make headlines, but they are a civilizing factor wherever they live.

*   *   *

## MONICA

While studying yoga in India, I met a young woman who was like a queen. Her name was Monica. She knew something beyond pleasure and society's laws. Most of us are regulated by motives; she was not. Instantly she discerned the motivations of anyone who tried to stimulate her externally. Since she was free of deception, she could not be deceived by another. She was not the kind of person who belonged to any dogma, cause, or belief.

To her the purpose of sex was to have children. If it was used as an indulgence of pleasure and sensation, it was an abuse. She would only have a relationship with a man who was true to himself, not someone who was living a borrowed life. She was drawn to persons who were reliable and in love with self-honesty because she was responsible for whatever she did or said.

Monica was about twenty-three years of age when I first met her at Mr. Krishnamurti's Talks in Bombay. She arrived wearing an inexpensive, rust colored sari. The dignity and poise of her walk alone showed that she was a unique being, almost a different species.

Everyone's attention was focused on her when she sat down. It awakens something within to see such an extraordinary person. Her face was striking; it lifted one almost beyond desire. From Monica, I learned what a young woman of incorruptible refinement can be. She told me once, "How good it is to live without needs."

*    *    *

## DR. WILLIAM KELLY

A person who plays an important part in my life and is a valued friend is Dr. William Kelly. As a doctor, his care for his patients is incomparable for he is fulfilling what he was born to do. Life protected him from becoming distracted by other pursuits and he has remained true to his given function.

A man of real insight, he is not concerned about what he gets; his only interest is in what he gives. Dr. Kelly could learn in a matter of weeks what would take years for another person to learn, whether it is homeopathy, ayurveda, acupuncture, or chiropractic. Talking with him is uplifting because he embodies non-selfishness, vulnerability, nobleness, and profound care for the human being.

The purity and warmth of what he says leaves one spellbound. Yet one would never recognize him as the wise person that he is because he is so fun-loving. He is well-hidden, like a fruit behind the leaves. He could fit into any strata of society for he always has something original and authentic to say. Vulnerability is difficult to afford. But in Bill Kelly's case, *In my defenselessness my safety lies,*[2] is at work.

He is often quiet, but when asked to comment, what he says lifts one to another level. His is a voice of certainty. Usually when we are together, we help each other see a thought through to the end. The sharing of this pure space, free from any sound of thought, is the only real sharing for in it there is the newness of impersonal life. The world seems a safe place where there is one such person who is a friend.

Since meeting in 1976, we have both evolved in our own different directions, but with the same internal values. Now life is bringing us closer and closer. There is nothing more precious than to have a friend whose values are eternal.

What Bill Kelly knows is beyond appearances for he relates with the Fact. This demands not knowledge, but insight. That is probably what a doctor should be. He looks at the patient and knows what needs correction; the patient doesn't need to tell him. This inner awakening is very pronounced in him. He has integrated many different systems and knows what health is. Health is not merely physical. He deals with the body but he is not limited to it. This insight sees in a flash the total condition of the patient. He is like the ancient ayurvedic or therapeutae physicians who could instantly see the auric, astral, thought, and pranic energy fields that surround the body because their life was related to wholeness and dedicated to their Oneness with God.

These seers knew that anger, hate, miserliness, insecurity, or fear have their origins in the impurities of thought and heredity. One's upbringing, wrong values, and non-virtue affect the liver, the kidney, the glands, and the basic organs of the body. They knew the ailment of the organ and the source of its malfunction and offered the correction at the level of the body, the mind, and the spirit, for they dealt with the whole person. Such a healer is in the service of God.

The pranic energy, which is non-physical, passes through the body and outside the body, in the form of the figure eight. Pranayama* is for the wise, for the pranic breath is only possible when the brain is still. It is an ethical way of life which renews the body. Its purpose is to remove the impurities that block the way and to relate man with God.

Bill Kelly may not know, nor does he need to know, the ancient names related to Yoga. His is a direct contact with the timeless Source of Life that transpires through man. When he first began his practice, he did not even send bills to his patients. Whatever they paid was adequate, for money was not his concern. His heart goes out to anyone in need. He

---

* Control of pranic breath. (Editor)

recently said to me that if he did not have something of his own to give, life would not be worth living.

\*   \*   \*

## ALAN CHADWICK

A clairvoyant once said of horticulturist, Alan Chadwick, that he could change the climate of the area, such was his affinity with the Archangels. Alan Chadwick was a man of the spirit.

It is true that when Alan spoke of the Archangels passing the Holy Grail from one to the other at the times of the solstice, it was not just words. There was a sanctified atmosphere of integrity in what he said.

Alan Chadwick was a scientist in the true sense of the word. Thoreau said, "What an admirable training is science! Science is always brave; for to know is to know good."[3]

Alan was once heard to say: "I do not know, but I do perceive."

One cannot know a great being without being transformed oneself. Everything one learns in his presence is related to eternal principles. This learning continues to unfold the truth by which creation is sustained. Once you have contact with that energy, it never leaves you; therefore, such an encounter is an occasion for reverence.

In 1975, at the end of a three-year period of silence after my study of Yoga, I came across the name of Alan Chadwick in an article on horticulture. The article stirred me deeply because it was fundamental. It dealt with the issues of humanity, with the food situation, and a totally different approach to gardening.

Here was a man who was not a professional in the sense of being a specialist. He was related to life itself. He talked about the Biodynamic French Intensive Gardening Technique which he developed after studying with Rudolf Steiner. Seldom has anyone ever explored the significance of the garden as he did.

He talked about the fact that there were food shortages all over the underdeveloped areas of the world. And in the highly industrialized West, food production was becoming so artificial that great consequences were staring humanity in the face. On the one side was deterioration; on the other, starvation. Food and seeds were losing their potency and so few people were aware.

The article made quite an impact on me. Although I was not much for going places, shortly thereafter I did visit the University of Santa Cruz where Alan Chadwick had begun a teaching garden. Alan was not there, but his footprints were visible in the work. I was amazed to see how, on a very small plot of land, his new approach to gardening had produced such abundance. His method had no hostility towards weeds or insects, for they too had a part in life and kept a balance.

Alan shared wisdom and humanism, respect and reverence. He made everything sacred. And what he seemed to be teaching was that if you understood the principles, the quality could not decline. It would be related to some spark of energy within you that never declines, for its Source is of creation.

I first met Alan Chadwick a few years later at a religious community in Virginia, in which we were both involved. He was on a bicycle coming down a hill and I happened to be near the pathway. We had arranged to get a very good English bicycle for him since he disliked automobiles. He got off his bicycle and approached me – a tall, strong-bodied man, an unusually classic and striking figure. His face was angular and handsome, his complexion ruddy and masculine. You knew immediately he was an extraordinary being.

We greeted one another and shook hands. How austere and direct he was. He told me he had heard of me from Craig, one of his assistants. I said, "Yes, I have a love relationship with Craig." Alan remarked, "Is there anyone in the world with whom you don't have a love relationship?" He not only silenced me, but every tree and bush nearby.

We had agreed to meet after dinner for the bell had already sounded and people were gathering in the dining room. Alan had little use for the masses. He was a man of action and clarity. Therefore, he was never seen at group meals or celebrations. I told him that I would be free in forty-five minutes and would be honored to visit with him at his home. He got on his bicycle and rode off.

In the dining room there was one long table and benches on which to sit. Meals were served buffet-style. I stood in line, got my plate, and sat down. Lo and behold, who should appear but Alan. It was some entry. His presence instantly changed the atmosphere.

Alan came and sat next to me. He was extremely polite. He said he could not wait forty-five minutes so he decided to join us. The table was covered with a gaudy plastic table cloth. Alan condescendingly lifted it up with one finger and let it go. "And they talk about nature and natural things," he said. He saw the contradiction and the insensitivity of which hardly anyone else was aware.

After the meal we walked back to the house where he was staying and visited for about an hour. An hour with such a being is more meaningful than twenty years of one's life. One grows a century. There was a purity to our discussion and the warm feeling of having met each other.

In dialogue with Alan, he brought everything into relationship with everything else – nothing was fragmented, isolated, or seen out of context. Life was one and the glory of its relationship included all and everything. You felt another kind of gladness within.

I was living in Virginia Beach at the time and kept contact with Alan to make sure he had whatever he wanted. His needs were much too simple but whenever there was a need, it was effortlessly and miraculously provided. Simplicity is very discriminate – no one can intrude upon it.

When I next visited the community, some of Alan's student gardeners had arrived from Covelo, California, with an enormous truckload of tools, seeds, and plants. Alan taught through the garden. He was a teacher of life. A teacher of life is one of the great benedictions of heaven, for he brings the kingdom of God to earth. The impact of this man and the energy he embodied was visible in his students. It manifested itself in the external as they prepared the land and made raised beds for the planting. Everything was orderly, respectful, artistic, joyous. It was something to see – a symphony of vital men and women working, so exact and precise. Everything was related to universal principles.

Alan Chadwick himself lived in a dilapidated cabin. There were many other buildings on the property but for some reason this was the one given to him. It spoke of the lack of discrimination and reverence in the minds of the leaders of the community.

An unusually dignified and cultured person, Alan knew music, art, literature, and astronomy. He was a gourmet cook, a painter, a gold medal skier and skater, a violinist, as well as having been a Shakespearean actor for thirty-two years. He had known great beings such as Annie Besant, George Bernard Shaw, and Sir Laurence Olivier, and as a young man had studied with Rudolf Steiner.

As part of the gardeners' training, he gave classes in architecture, voice, and deportment. Diction and the quality of voice were important to him for it indicated the person that you were. During one of my visits to the community, Alan invited me to attend one of the classes. He sat me in the front row and had someone give a recitation of a Shakespearean sonnet. Students were transformed under his tutelage. He awakened latent abilities and strengths they never knew they had. He brought correction to every part of his students' lives and imparted a new order and strength.

Alan was impatient with the nonsense of the unessential but he was uplifted if anyone of his students ever touched upon their own original voice. How few people have a voice of their own. His work was to cultivate it in his students just as he cultivated excellence in the garden. He emphasized that one went to the garden to learn, not to impose. The garden itself was the teacher.

Pretty soon vegetables and flowers were in abundance everywhere. The one thing that was alive in this community was the Garden Project. It was one of the rarest experiments and could have become one of the greatest examples in history, if the circumstances surrounding it had had the same authenticity and appreciation for the eternal and the virtuous in life.

To listen to Alan Chadwick lecture on bees and how they represented obedience was to be transformed. He related everything to the one life behind it all. If he spoke about a tree, the tree became part of the stars and the planets.

Alan's voice and manner were dynamic. Most people, regardless of their worldly stature, were dwarfed in his presence. Their lives were shaped by success, external prestige, and wealth. Here was a man who rarely touched money.

Alan Chadwick was independent of thought and the externals. When he talked about the miracle of the seed and its reality, he related you to the origin of things. He was outraged at the violation of the seed by expedient, profiteering methods and adamant about the significance of hybrid plants. Hybrid, he said, was derived from the Greek word "hybris" which means: defiance of the Will of God.

Through Alan's eyes, you saw the horror of the corruption of agriculture. He talked about how difficult it was to find

pure strains of chickens or geese or cows. How almost everything had been perverted. One didn't know where to turn, for
half-truths were everywhere. But one felt blessed that here
was a being who was a protector and preserver of Truth.

Alan was not just a gardener. He integrated all aspects of
life, taught how this planet is related to other planets, and how
the integration actually is the key to life. You walked in an
atmosphere of reverence after leaving Alan for he brought a
sense of holiness when he shared. It affected your sleep and
the quality of your blood.

Indeed Alan Chadwick was a gardener, a divine gardener,
who planted seeds of purity in you to blossom. It was a delight
to see the extraordinary work taking place every two weeks
or so when I came to visit – something so alive in the midst of
ideas.

In the summer of 1978, a large conference was held at the
community and speakers and attendants arrived from all over
the country – nearly six hundred in all. It was a grand affair.
The flowers swayed in the breeze and everything was green.
City dwellers felt it was a holy place and many speakers came
with their optimistic views. Beneath the surface, un-
beknownst to them, litigations were in process. Those who
knew the inner picture were already disillusioned. There were
jealousies and frictions. The pure energy of harmony was
absent. Alan Chadwick's garden was feeding everyone there
– four hundred heads of lettuce a day. And no one gave thanks
for the abundance, the sustenance.

The false is always afraid of the real. Greece was afraid of
Socrates, the Church of Joan of Arc, and Jerusalem of Jesus.
Fear has its own atmosphere, own values of success and
failure and illusions of the future. In the midst, Alan
Chadwick lived and breathed in the present.

Before Alan Chadwick was scheduled to speak at the
conference, we made space to be quiet in order to listen to
what he would say. Such men always have something to

impart. They are never part of the mortal fuss. They are never in the world of appearance. They represent "what is." The "what is" clashes with the assumed and the concluded. We were eager to see how he would handle this situation. How would he express disillusionment? How would he impart the truth?

Such men are unpredictable for they are real. Alan told a Swahili tale about a beautiful gazelle who completely loved and was then disregarded. It was more than a fable. If understood, it would continue to unfold its truth for the rest of your life. He planted this fable like a seed in our minds. Another vibration was awakened within for having heard it.

Alan Chadwick did not conclude, nor did he get involved. He just presented the fact as a fact. Whether you heard it or not depended on your own development, integrity, and clarity. These simple beings are very discriminate. They don't interfere.

Later on that day I spoke at the Conference and tried to bring to awareness the fact that Alan was the gazelle who bestowed upon this community the most valuable jewel. It was a jewel of heavenly potential, unending in its resources for it was related to the very source of life. I introduced Alan Chadwick as a vertical man related to Reality.

Alan was not much appreciated although his work was the one thing that was real and alive. It was quite a challenge to the abstract, psychic values on which the community was based.

Encounter with the psychic is inevitable in the evolutionary process of growth. Life, in its great wisdom, must provide this encounter in order for the highly evolved person to see the limitations of psychic gifts and outgrow that world of projected illusions too. The psychic realm merely poses to be spiritual while it actually strengthens the personality. Only Truth dispels illusions and deceptions. Alan Chadwick had the gift of insight, so much superior to clairvoyance.

*A Course In Miracles* says this about psychic gifts:

*There is, however, a particular appeal in unusual abilities that can be curiously tempting. Here are strengths which the Holy Spirit wants and needs. Yet the ego sees in these same strengths an opportunity to glorify itself. Strengths turned to weakness are tragedy indeed....*

*Even those who no longer value the material things of the world may still be deceived by "psychic powers." As investment has been withdrawn from the world's material gifts, the ego has been seriously threatened. It may still be strong enough to rally under this new temptation to win back strength by guile. Many have not seen through the ego's defenses here, although they are not particularly subtle. Yet, given a remaining wish to be deceived, deception is made easy. Now the "power" is no longer a genuine ability, and cannot be used dependably. It is almost inevitable that, unless the individual changes his mind about its purpose, he will bolster his "power's" uncertainties with increasing deception.* [4]

Sri Ramakrishna offered to transfer all the supernatural powers he had obtained from the practice of austerities to his disciple Naren, who was later called Swami Vivekananda.

"'Will they help me to realize God?' Naren asked. 'No,' said Ramakrishna, 'they won't help you to do that. But they might be very useful after you have realized God and start doing His work.' 'Then let me realize God first,' said Naren, 'after that, it will be time enough to decide if I need them or not.'" [5]

I understood Alan's dilemma and knew the power and efficiency of jealousy, threatened by whatever outshines it. I was able to share with Alan my discoveries. Discovery is a gift of the holy instant which frees one from reaction, for the world of thought-images, in reality, has no existence. What the situation demands is the integrity of internal correction. In truth, there is no other. This was the basis of our relationship.

We both were protected, but so much wiser for the experience. Nothing is more precious in life than disillusionment. When the false is seen as the false, you are most blessed. There is no material gain in it, but there is the freedom. It is a joy to share this with the reader. Somewhere in your own evolution, you may find it useful. "God is." Knowing this silences the mind.

One day I told Alan about a friend who had come to Virginia with me from California. She was a very timid and withdrawn girl. I asked if Alan could take her on as one of his gardening students since she had an affinity for plants, and that possibly she could help care for him as she was an excellent cook. He readily agreed. We were relieved that finally he would be taken care of in the right way since this friend had the skill and the care to be thorough but never to intrude.

Alan was a self-reliant, independent man. He had no vested interest. It is very difficult to relate with a man who is not dependent. Only honesty and sincerity succeed. One could say of Alan what a poet once wrote: "The heart of a king trembles before a man who wants nothing." He didn't like things done for him and he was brusque and temperamental at times, a law unto himself. He was not happy at the community – it was so far below his standard. There were lots of mice in his house and he would throw them on the front porch for all to see.

In the ensuing months, Alan was not well. He had difficulty walking and was in considerable pain. He went through very trying times with doctors and hospitals, something that was abhorrent to his nature. He despised the sight of any pretense. He placed a log across the road at the entrance to his home so that no one would drive automobiles onto that part of the land.

Because he was not well, and was confined to bed a good deal of the day, I was concerned how we could get him outside. Although anything mechanical was offensive to him, we found that a golf cart made no noise and created no pollution. He loved it. It was charged in the evening and, in the early morning, he would ride like an emperor around the flower and vegetable beds, in the fields, and on the road.

One day Alan invited me to come for a ride with him. He was thrilled that now he was not so confined. When we were driving in a solitary place, Alan confided in me that he was ready to leave the community because he saw it was a fiasco. He asked me what I thought. "So many eternal laws have been violated at the community," I said, "and the doors at subtler levels have been closed. It is just a matter of time before it manifests at the appearance level. Why do you have to make the decision to withdraw? Leave things in God's Hands. The community may continue for a while at the level of pretense, but it is likely that its link with higher forces is severed." Alan responded, "Be it so."

Within a few months, this is exactly what happened. It was as if an unseen force that nothing could resist swept over the land. One only knew its passage by the footprints of destruction it left behind. A feeling of utter desolation permeated the atmosphere. Shortly thereafter, only the carcass of the community was left. Alan asked me what I was going to do now that things had failed. I said that the divine forces that selected and brought me halfway around the world to be a part of this community would take care of me. The future was not my concern. Alan moved to the farm of a friend of ours for the interim.

I asked Alan what his need might be. He said that to have a gardening school did not take much land. He was at the end of his life and he felt that the original parent project to the gardening school had failed. I didn't think so and I tried to assure him that he had not failed but that the world had failed it. The seeds were sown and in times to come, the garden projects would continue. It depended on the wisdom of the world. At a certain level of crisis, they would begin to value some things more than others.

He had brought something to this planet, a gift of God. He had done the right thing; he had fulfilled his part. His life was a benediction and it would take root.

I offered to help in whatever way he would like. With a man like Alan Chadwick, one has to be responsible for what one says and does. To him, justifications are never valid. Responsibility means that one sees things through to the end. Through that responsibility one is enriched to discover the joy of not being subject to external circumstances.

The thought occurred that perhaps he would like to return to England, his own country; he might be more at home there. There was a community named Findhorn, in Scotland, which was dedicated to holistic living and which might interest Alan.

I wrote to Findhorn and asked if they could have a board meeting or a meeting of the elders regarding Alan Chadwick's coming there. I also asked them to write to tell me in clear terms what their decision constituted. The letter was thorough so as to avoid endless correspondence. Findhorn wrote that they would be honored if Alan would come to their community. They would greet him and care for him as a scholar in residence.

Because he became too weak to travel, and the weather at Findhorn might be somewhat harsh for him, he chose to move to the Zen Center at Green Gulch in Mill Valley, California, to which Abbot Baker Roshi had invited him. It was probably the first airplane ride he had taken in recent years. He preferred to travel by train.

Alan was received with reverence by Baker Roshi. When I visited it was a joy to see the honor, the accommodation, the courtesy, and respect afforded this great man.

\*   \*   \*

All the energies of the universe are entrusted to man for his blessing to be upon all that is. The lives of these men and women, free of pretense, made a timeless contribution in this direction. Today, there is no longer the space to value the expression of men and women of excellence. Wisdom is becoming obsolete.

Where the heavenly aspect of man is ignored, goodness recedes. How does one revive goodness? Goodness is inherent in each one of us. The fact is, man is spirit. As you give what is Given you, you are awakened to the secret within life – the consecrated force that acts involuntarily. The wisdom of insight is the non-physical light of the spirit within man. It remains uninvolved, though in the thick of responsibility. The energy of wholeness is eternal and blessed.

In the present culture, where is the uninvolved space for parents and children to share the inspiration of the beauty of nature under the open sky? Children are children of divine leisure. We need to give them the space for self-knowing to actualize their own resources.

# CHAPTER FOURTEEN

# 14

## ENCOUNTERS WITH ETERNITY

### MR. J. KRISHNAMURTI

I met Mr. J. Krishnamurti in New York in 1953. He invoked in me the dawn of True Knowledge. In relationship with him, the duality of relative thought began to be questioned. He remained, and remains, my Teacher for life and beyond. His teachings continue to unfold in all that I do, for relationship with him is not of time. Mr. Krishnamurti is a life-giver, comparable to Lord Buddha. In his presence, one grew a century in a moment.

Mr. Krishnamurti imparted the energy to move from fact to fact in those who had the capacity to receive. Once a fact was realized, its vitality silenced the verbal chatter of the brain. He insisted that if the fact was made into an idea, it was devoid of Truth. Mr. Krishnamurti also emphasized that there was but one decision in life – to end the bondage of limitation. This decision was not of choice. Mr. Krishnamurti, Jesus, and *A Course In Miracles* extend Absolute Knowledge, not relative knowledge which is always "about" Truth, and never Truth Itself.

In my early twenties, I had spent four years in the Himalayas practicing austerities in the pursuit of God. I gave myself completely to the religious practices prescribed by the religion of my birth, Sikhism. During this time, I had developed certain abilities of the mind but, in the end, became disillusioned with conventional religion and its claims to lead one to the Truth of God. For years, I shunned any notion of meeting so-called saints or holy people. I was skeptical that anyone who claimed to know the Truth actually did so.

So, years later, when different friends on separate occasions encouraged me to make contact with Mr. J. Krishnamurti, I was not inclined. When I finally did make the contact I was in New York. It was my first encounter with the Voice of Truth. I had never met anyone who gave pure space and attention to hear my story. There was a sacredness in his listening without interpretation.

When he asked the question, "What does the known consist of?" I was taken aback. Then he said, "Memory and experiences. Is not all that one knows of the past?" It was as if he severed the contact with internal activity. Since then, the intensity of silence of this one moment has not left me. The memories are there, but so is It to silence them. I sat in an unknown space for awhile. When I looked at him with gratefulness, he said,

"There are no problems apart from the mind."

The impact of his words still stirs within me decades later.

After leaving him, I practically floated through nearby Central Park. There is an energy of silence that is intoxicating. It contained me in a way that I did not want to go anywhere. The first thought that occurred to me was, "How fortunate to be born at a time when such a being is upon the planet." Years later, I discovered that, similarly, Plato himself esteemed it as the "highest of fortune's favors" that he should have been born in the lifetime of Socrates.

I would have died blind had I not met Mr. Krishnamurti. I knew him for over thirty years. His kindness was a compassion I had not known. We went for walks, to dinner, and he would invite me to breakfast.

Once while we were driving with friends from Ojai to Ventura, California, he was seated in the back seat, giving me exact directions to where he was to go. On my way back to Ojai, I was alone. Because he had touched me several times on the shoulder while giving directions earlier, I found myself, much to my surprise, in a different state of mind. It was a state of bliss which lasted for days. I was passing a particular grove of trees along the way when I first became aware of it. To this day, whenever I pass those trees, the state involuntarily returns with its blessing. It was so sacred that one hesitated for decades to speak of it.

At another time, he looked straight at me and said, "Don't ever waste a penny." This was because I travelled all over Europe and was familiar with most of the exclusive men's stores. Instantly, his instruction was in application in my life.

Years passed by. Then, while in Geneva, Switzerland, I saw a sweater in the window of an elite men's store, a sweater that was so exquisite I was tempted to buy it. But I did not want to contradict his instructions. There was a moment of conflict.

For some reason, to do with or without something has not been very difficult for me throughout my life. Usually my decision would override any choice or preference. So I was saying to myself, "Why this sweater?" Something transpired in me that made me purchase it – not for myself, but for him. And a new discovery took place within me that transcends thought's knowings.

When I left the package at his residence, I was warned that he did not accept gifts. The next day, a telephone call came from his secretary telling me I should come and take it back. I wondered how I could have been wrong, for I felt certain that it met his need. I had not acted out of enthusiasm; therefore, how could I question my certainty?

He met me in the living room and suggested we go for a walk. On the walk, he said, "I do not accept presents. It would be a problem for me to say no to some and yes to others. It would complicate things. So I have to return the sweater to you."

I was sad to hear that, which he noticed. And he asked me, "How much did you pay for it?" I told him, even though it was embarrassing to talk about money. And then he asked, "Could I pay for it?" That saddened me further. He noticed and, after a pause, asked, "Can you afford it?" I quickly said, "Yes." And he said, "I need this sort of thing."

This validated the gift of certainty and clarity I had received at the moment I purchased the sweater. Now, the contact with his need was made, so I started sending him all sorts of things, from medicated Ayurvedic oils, to musical recordings, to photographs and books from different parts of the world. Because they met the need, I came to know the wisdom of impersonal action to which Life had introduced me.

Not until one has outgrown impulses and enthusiasm will one merit the gift of certainty.

There is a communication between a teacher and a student that defies understanding at the level of appearance. Because the action is impersonal, God remains the only witness.

And then there were years I went through agony in my relationship with Mr. Krishnamurti. I had a mystical experience after forty days of silent retreat by myself in a solitary place in California. I flew directly to Bombay where Mr. Krishnamurti was at the time, stopping nowhere along the way. I knew where he was staying and so I went there. I was told that he would be returning home in the evening. It was of first importance to me that I see him, so I sat under a tree and waited all day.

When he came, I met him at the gate and said, "I have come to India only to see you." He heard the word "only." He was cordial but he never stopped walking towards the house. He asked where I was staying. I told him I was staying at the Taj Mahal Hotel and, before he entered the house, I gave him a small envelope with the hotel's phone number and my room number. He put it in his pocket. I had learned to make sure that nothing is left to chance. Had I given the information to anyone but him, even his secretary, I would have been uncertain whether or not he himself had it.

Every day I waited for his call, often having meals in the room, so as not to chance missing him. Week after week went by. The waiting continued for a month. There were others at the hotel who had come to attend his Bombay Talks. He would see some of them and they would come back happy.

The day of his departure, I went to the airport at dawn. There were many people in the V.I.P. lounge to see him off. He looked at me as if with disdain and said, "I'm sorry I didn't have any time to see you." And everyone heard it, interpreting it to mean: "Here is another one who is constantly demanding attention."

A few months later, while he was in Switzerland, I wrote a short note to him saying, "There must be some monster in me of which I am oblivious. I wish that you would point it out so that I can deal with it." I didn't receive any response from him. I remembered that prior to the expression of seriousness on my part – the "only" – he would respond to every letter I wrote.

Some weeks later, I received a letter from a mutual friend who said that Mr. Krishnamurti would be glad to see me if I came. Since the offer was not directly from him, hence indefinite, and I had learned from him to move from fact to fact, I did not go. But then came a telegram stating a date on which I should come. So I travelled from the Himalayas down to Delhi, where I boarded a plane for Gstaad, Switzerland.

Going to see him was a delight, and all my friends were happy for me. He came into the living room to meet me. As we sat down, I said, "I would like to go over some things in a serious way. I hope you have the time." "You said this before. Why should I?" was his response. I was a little puzzled. Then he said, "You are not serious. Go and paint the town red. You're not interested." And he got up and showed me to the door.

I stood outside, bewildered. It was raining. After awhile, he opened the door to see if I was still on my feet. He said, "You are still there." I said, "Yes. It is raining." He said, "It's just a drizzle," and closed the door again. I walked down the hill from Chalet Tannegg, Krishnamurti's residence while in Gstaad.

I gave myself the freedom to "paint the town red" mentally, but I could find nothing whatsoever that interested me – no safari in Africa, no good times with women, or anything of the world or ambition. Nothing attracted my interest. I could not doubt his words, "You are not serious." But neither could I doubt my willingness to consider whatever else I might be interested in. I found nothing.

For over three years, he never saw me. Then, while I was staying in Madras, someone came from Krishnamurti Writings with a message for me to come to the office. I went. To my great surprise, Mr. Krishnamurti came out to greet me. Instantly, his blessedness enveloped me. He was so affectionate. He embraced me, took me to his room, and we both sat down quietly on the floor. It was divine – such love and affection.

He said to me, "It took guts but you stayed with it. How did you do it? Now that you have it, how would you like to express it?" Time disappeared. It was a meeting of life-to-life that left one speechless, for it was an experience that was not of words. Ever since then, I sense he walks with me.

Now one sees how a true teacher will not allow one to become dependent on him. He sees the potential in the student, and helps the student to recognize it by himself. It is not an intellectual learning, but one's own direct contact with a state that is consistent at all levels of one's being.

Suffice it to say, teachers test. Read the story of Job in the Bible, or *Milarepa: The Tibetan Yogi* by Evans-Wentz and you will know what I mean.

\*    \*    \*

## DR. HELEN SCHUCMAN

Dr. Helen Schucman, was a Professor of Medical Psychology at Columbia University College of Physicians and Surgeons when, in 1965, she began recording *A Course In Miracles.* For the next seven years – with the encouragement of Dr. William Thetford, head of the Psychology Department – she wrote down what was dictated to her by an inner Voice that made no sound and could be interrupted at any time. After completing the three-volume Course, she set it aside.\*

When *A Course In Miracles* came to my attention I had just completed three years of silent retreat and two years in semi-seclusion. I was not drawn to anything external, but when I read in the Introduction to the Course:

*Nothing real can be threatened.*
*Nothing unreal exists.* [1]

the very authenticity of it shook me. Surely, these were some of the strongest words ever spoken upon the planet. In 1976, I met Judith Skutch who was instrumental in publishing the Course. Later I inquired whether it was possible to make contact with its Scribe. Mrs. Skutch said she had spoken to Dr. Schucman about me and that it may be possible.

On July 27, 1977, Mrs. Skutch invited me to stay the night with her and her husband, Robert, in New York, where the

---

\* For further information on the scribing of the Course, see *A Course In Miracles* (Foundation for Inner Peace, 1976), Preface. (Editor)

meeting with Dr. Schucman was arranged to take place. When I arrived at their Central Park West apartment and walked out of the elevator into their living room, Dr. Schucman was seated in an upholstered armchair.

Judy introduced us and Dr. Schucman looked at me and abruptly asked, "Are you a holy man?" This caught me off-guard and brought me to attention. This question demanded nothing less than self-honesty. I did not know what to say, but I was certain I could not be casual in her presence. Sentimentality and politeness vanished.

I said, "In times past, in ancient India, there was a sage who had a temper. When the students could not respond adequately, he would throw stones at them. There was one student who would gather the stones and place them in a pile before the teacher's place prior to the next lesson. I am that student."

My second meeting with Helen Schucman took place at her home in October, 1978, on Yom Kippur, the holiest of holy days. Since that time, it is as if we have never parted.

Dr. Helen Schucman is the miracle of my life.

*Miracles restore the mind to its fullness.*
*A miracle is a correction introduced into false thinking...* [2]

To communicate the impact which the presence of such a being has in one's life is difficult. Knowledge of the "about," with its misperceptions, cannot relate the direct knowing, for thought does not introduce one to reality. Direct knowing is the benediction that enriches and transforms your very life.

I had never known the compassion with which Dr. Helen Schucman surrounded me for years. What does it mean to meet someone who trusts you implicitly! Her trust in me lifted me to recognize the sacredness of the Course. The paradox was that she virtually distrusted everything I said or did, but that was consistent with the undoing of illusion which I cherished. Her trust was for the Impersonal space she recognized in me. And she even made me aware of it.

An entire book would have to be written to share the many encounters I had with her, and to tell of the misperceptions she removed. Knowing her love transformed me. Her tenderness is something I never knew existed at the level of duality. She had the capacity to relate one with Eternal Forces. I may never have known the purpose of my life .without her blessings.

There are stories in the Upanishads and Vedas, and other Indian scriptures, that talk about many great beings who disguised themselves. They only revealed their reality to those who had the eyes to see, and the ears to hear their word. They did not want to draw attention to themselves, but rather to the Power that worked through them. They remained nameless.

I discovered that Dr. Schucman, the Scribe of *A Course In Miracles* who extended the Thoughts of God, was not a personality. And yet, she had a body, and was a personality to the naked eye. St. Paul, in Second Corinthians 12:7-10, gives us a glimpse of what appears as inconsistency:

"AND LEST I SHOULD BE EXALTED ABOVE MEASURE THROUGH THE ABUNDANCE OF THE REVELATIONS, THERE WAS GIVEN TO ME A THORN IN THE FLESH, THE MESSENGER OF SATAN TO BUFFET ME, LEST I SHALL BE EXALTED ABOVE MEASURE. FOR THIS THING I BESOUGHT THE LORD THRICE, THAT IT MIGHT DEPART FROM ME. AND HE SAID UNTO ME, 'MY GRACE IS SUFFICIENT FOR THEE: FOR MY STRENGTH IS MADE PERFECT IN WEAKNESS.' MOST GLADLY THEREFORE WILL I RATHER GLORY IN MY INFIRMITIES, THAT THE POWER OF CHRIST MAY REST UPON ME. THEREFORE I TAKE PLEASURE IN INFIRMITIES, IN REPROACHES, IN NECESSITIES, IN PERSECUTIONS, IN DISTRESSES FOR CHRIST'S SAKE: FOR WHEN I AM WEAK, THEN AM I STRONG."

During the three years of silence, I had an experience in which a voice spoke to me. I inquired, "Is it appropriate for me to ask whose voice this is?" The voice answered, "You are greeted by 'I See You.'" He said he was once a young ascetic who had died of leprosy. Also, he had remained silent in the last phase of his life. He was a healer, and knew it was possible to heal with the mind by just looking. He could even heal leprosy. But he was not believed by others because he never cared to heal his own leprosy. The skeptics said, "If you have the power, why don't you heal yourself?" Invariably the self-centered person would come to this conclusion.

But he didn't care. He knew there are men who walk this earth who can, by mere glance, heal. "Christ," he said, "had the greatest development and spiritual gift of healing. Even passing by while carrying the cross, He liberated and healed others."

"You, too," he said to me, "could have that gift of healing. 'I See You' will help and guide."

What Dr. Helen Schucman shared is beyond the reach of time. She, too, healed and will continue to heal the misperceptions of the human mind. Nothing like *A Course In Miracles*, with its curriculum, exists in the English language. Dr. Schucman kept herself anonymous. When people turned to her for the truth, she said, "Read the Course. If you are interested, it is there." She even refused to put her name on the books. Therein lies an impersonal action.

This does not mean that Dr. Schucman didn't have a personality. But I did not relate with it. There is an impeccable space within himself when a man is not completely externalized. It is that space which relates with Life, and not with the personality. Such a being is not dependent on the images of thought, for he relates directly.

If one was interested in clarity, or in correction in one's life, Dr. Schucman was never a personality. The non-student is incapable of relating with the absolute thought system. When

I was with total attention, she was not external. Duality is the invention of partial attention.

If I were to see her as a personality, then I was not a student. That was the choice given to whomever was the so-called student, or the observer. The eyes through which the separated see lack the light that can:

> ...lift you above the thinking of the world, and free your vision from the body's eyes. [3]

If one didn't have any interest in what is of God, she could make you miserable.

Dr. Schucman was not a channel; she rose to the state of the Course and met it. Her seeming abrasiveness seldom touched me because of my different background and culture in which one did not contradict the teacher.

Herman Hesse's story of India's Siddhartha speaks of the power of reverence. Siddhartha sought his parents' permission to leave home and become a *sannyasin* and lead a life of holiness. When they refused, the young man stood before his father for hours. He was steadfast, surrounded by his own stillness. His obedience spoke louder than words. Even upon waking the following morning, the father saw that Siddhartha had not moved throughout the night, and still stood before him with folded hands. Siddhartha's determination and non-contradiction won his parents' heart and gave him the blessing he wanted to accompany him.

My experience with Dr. Schucman was that whenever I had something basic to ask, the miracle and the Light were always there. It is the nature of doubt to question the authenticity of the messengers of God, since they do not promote or abide by the inconsistencies of customs, beliefs, and dogmas.

It was natural for those who knew Dr. Schucman to question her non-conformity to what is of time. Jesus, too, was often asked to prove Himself and give a sign. When He was being crucified, they said, "Let Him save Himself, if He be

Christ, the chosen of God." A clue was given by St. Paul when he said,"I TAKE PLEASURE IN INFIRMITIES, IN REPROACHES..."[4] The fact is that True Power never opposes; it only extends.

Lacking certainty, the need for proof is inevitable at the relative level. Only miracles reveal the Truth. To me, Dr. Schucman and the Course and Jesus are inseparable. They share the same function of extending the Will of God. Dr. Kenneth Wapnick says in his commentary on Dr. Schucman's book of poetry, *The Gifts Of God:*

> "There are times when Jesus spoke to Helen about Mary, Jesus' mother. The basic idea was that she was like Mary. Just like Mary brought Him forth into the world 2,000 years ago, so is Helen bringing Him forth into the world now through *A Course In Miracles.* Helen is not Mary; nothing like that. They were talking about function, nothing else. But at the same time, Jesus also was intimating to Helen that she had the same kind of radiant light that Mary did, the same kind of purity. Implied in that, the same kind of intensity and intimacy of relationship that Jesus had with His mother, He had with Helen."[5]

In over 800 phone calls, Dr. Schucman gave me specific guidance. One of the instructions she gave was, "Don't ever act from anger." But we need to consider seriously what it would take to bring this into application. I discovered that as long as I am in a state of duality, anger is inevitable.

It is also important for each one of us to be fully aware of what constitutes an instruction, in order to deal with it as an objective in itself. This contact with Eternity is what we need to make.

We think it is enough for someone to tell us what to do. In essence the aspiration of America is the statement, "In God We Trust," because it is consistent with the vibration of the New World. All along our problems as a nation have been due to our lack of trust in God. Each instruction is an everlasting challenge because it demands self-mastery. What we do with it – ignore it, pretend to understand it – all of these are irrelevant.

For every instruction the opposite to the instruction is usually rampant in one's life. The instruction could be "Don't ever act from anger," or "Love thy neighbor," or "In God We Trust," but the actuality of one's life is in opposition to it. The true student is not interested in the idealism of the instruction but in the challenge of the actual application. This is how a student, having reverence for the truth, values and honors an instruction from his teacher. The non-student understands it but, without self-mastery, how is it possible to apply it?

Behold the demand that instruction places upon oneself. When a true teacher gives an instruction, with it is given, then and there, the power to realize the truth of it. When an instruction emerges out of an idea, it is false to begin with.

When I met Dr. Schucman, I thought everything with my family was settled. However, since I had opinions and knew the "wrong" and "right," it was not. She brought this to my attention and it became my joy to go back to my family and bring the relationships to harmony. In gladness there is no lack, nor opposing thought. There were loose ends of which I was yet to be freed that I may never have known, leave aside ever corrected, had she not made me aware.

If you asked Dr. Schucman about anything, she would say with confidence, "Pray and ask. Ask Jesus. Ask God. You will get an answer. The answer is in every lesson of the Course." She refused to draw attention to herself.

Another instruction given to me was, "Go to bed early; wake up fresh and happy." It is easy to agree with this, but mere learning maintains the unwillingness to change. What about the challenge of coping with the stimulation and pressures of a life subject to circumstances?

She imparted the truth that unless there is contact with the Real, one is incapable of holy relationship – that, if one has motives, holy relationship is impossible. And for the ego, everything has a motive beneath it. We are nothing without having something of our own to give to another. It is the pure energy of selflessness that affects another's life.

Dr. Schucman emphasized the need to purify myself with gratefulness. Gratefulness makes the false powerless, and lack of gratefulness makes one weak. Her very life was a statement to me.

Dr. Schucman did not quit her job, even though, for seven years, a good deal of time was spent almost every day taking down the Course. And she had a husband. She made the space in her life for the entry of the Course for millions of human beings and unborn generations to come. "The Course," she said, "is for the active person in the world." It stresses not seeking to change a situation, but helps to make corrections within oneself.

To me her life itself is a law and, when seen beyond one's own images, an example. She accomplished the miraculous as a service to mankind, seeking nothing for herself. And her life will remain an instruction as far as the true student of the Course is concerned. Just as she made space in her life to receive *A Course In Miracles*, the student has to make space for the practice of the daily lesson of the Course, in order to train the mind to receive miracles.

Dr. Schucman completed her function of bringing *A Course In Miracles*, the Thoughts of God, to this plane and made it accessible to the mind of the age. Beyond this, she did not get involved. It is easy to get entangled with implementation at the relative level, but she knew that *A Course In Miracles* is an extension of Divine Intelligence and has its own power and direction.

She handed the Course over to those whose given function was to publish and promote it.

In my relationship with Dr. Schucman, there was the fragrance of her love and compassion – the sound of words failed to affect the serenity. "Love alone has God's own Voice," said Dr. Schucman. And for the first time in my life I heard that Voice, for there was neither she nor I, just the Voice.

*   *   *

Mr. J. Krishnamurti and Dr. Helen Schucman are still alive in me, for they shaped and inspired my life and gave direction to it. The Truth of what they said continues to unfold. It is like the light of a star that never dies.*

---

* This chapter is an excerpt from Tara Singh's forthcoming book, *My Brief Encounters With Eternity: Relationship With Mr. J. Krishnamurti and Dr. Helen Schucman, Scribe Of A Course In Miracles.* (Editor)

# CHAPTER FIFTEEN

# 15

## A CHILD IS PART OF ONE LIFE

Inherent in every child is a non-physical, God-given faculty – a sensitivity. It always expresses itself in a spontaneous way. One could say it is the wisdom of the heart. This spontaneity is awakened, not learned. Only those who are totally attentive can recognize it as it expresses itself in us and in the child. This spontaneous expression is an internal contact with the energy of the one life. Life is One.

Each child has this contact; but will the parents provide the atmosphere to nurture it? Are they willing to protect their child from stimulation and external pressures? How difficult it has become for that spontaneity to flower in the present generation. Outer influences rush in to the child from the very outset.

Then we mislead him by directing him toward skills. We think we know the "real" world and give it an exaggerated importance; we divert the child's energy to ever more external values, suppressing his contact with his own being; we endow him with intellectuality and speculation which can never know love. The child hardly has a chance.

First, he wants attention and the parents limit him to gratification. Then he goes to school and the emphasis on abstract information takes the place of direct discovery. Then he gets a job and gradually becomes more and more cut off from who he is.

Whoever would give the child the space to awaken his own inner discoveries would also have to make contact with those intimations himself. The source of this insight is silence. In stillness, all is achieved; and when given the space, silence intensifies itself. This contact is important for parents to share with their children. We emphasize the external and almost completely neglect this internal life. Balance between the internal and the external is essential in growth.

The shared stillness between adult and child is like the sunshine of life. Superior to any teaching, it bypasses the brain and its knowing. Very few of us try to come to this sacred space that is absolute and free of words. In fact, we are afraid of it. When most people meet they want to learn, not silence their knowing.

Parents may feel that they are not aware of this state of being. It may well be true, but the birth of the child in the family requires that they make contact with it. Life will provide the guidance. The parents now have new potentials to work with. It only needs their willingness to receive and their insistence on being responsible.

The Law of Creation is the Law of Certainty. Certainty is a direct force; it does not intellectualize. The world of thought, in which most of us live our entire lives, makes everything mental: life, death, sex, war, science. It is the intellectuality of nothingness.

At the root of our anxiety and insecurity is the fact that we are lonely for this spontaneous contact with the silent Mind. We don't even know what we are missing, but we long for it. We try to appease the loneliness with all kinds of gratification. By so doing, our lives have become more and more externalized. Unaware of our own resources, we lose all sense of the Oneness of life.

"All that exists is One.
People call this One by different names."
*The Vedas*

We want our children to be free of negativity, of loneliness, of restlessness, while we remain in a world of alternatives. And the alternatives to truth and sanity pass for self-improvement.

There is a very strong belief in man that if he doesn't do anything, he cannot survive. Parents may ask: Is this approach practical? What is practical might also be a compromise. Can we question this and not settle for a conclusion? A true question does not accept any conclusion. When the internal, non-divided state extends itself into the external world, it extends order; it extends what is real. Therefore, there is no need for alternatives. The glory of a life related to Eternal Laws is that it is never touched by the externals because it is timeless. What is real is undivided, whole, and holy. No one who touches upon the Real can fail to see the peace of unity, the sacredness of everlasting contentment.

We may be able to understand this intellectually, but our brain will not allow us to venture into the Unknown. The brain has become the governor. Since we don't question this, we never go far enough to recognize the spontaneous action of life. Too much thinking and emotion brings anxiety and exhausts the mind. Only silence restores the dissipated mind.

We have a fear of stillness. This fear prevents us from contact with the creative action that we are to extend. Rest assured, your child is not going to vegetate if you provide him the space. The brain would be quiet but he would be a million times more alive.

Either there is activity, or there is action. Action is ever impersonal; it is creative. Activity is personal. There is an assumption that if you stop the activity you will stagnate. Very few people ever face this assumption. In the questioning of our assumptions is the awakening of awareness. But we seldom give this a chance.

What is the origin of skills? Question it. What do our motives consist of? Question them, too. In questioning, if we do not accept any external answer, we may awaken other resources. We are influenced by our answers. But there are no answers, only action. True questioning means that we accept nothing that is verbal. Then will we make contact with the spontaneous clarity. That is the only thing that is real.

The action of life is spontaneous. Conception takes place in an involuntary way. The personality and the flesh have nothing to do with this creative action. Once the child is born, that same divine intelligence relates the child effortlessly to the wisdom of the heart because that is his real nature. The parents' care for the child provides the opportunity for the involuntary contact with the Source of life to take place.

Today, many parents are not so connected with their children. The bottle is given instead of the breast and so much is artificial. He is put in a crib, usually in a room alone. My mother was unlettered. She could not count beyond twenty. But she had a wealth of love, tenderness, and joy in her heart. The atmosphere that surrounded her was imbued with the peace of God; and, in her presence, my anxieties would disappear. She would tell me stories of the impeccable lives of saints. Every night I was cleansed of the day's worry. The difference in modern society is that we put the child to bed in his own room, bless him, and then leave. In my family, I slept with my mother until I was nine years old. Something was transmitted when I fell asleep in her arms. Being held this way has its impact on one's whole life.

Since my father was abroad for the first part of my life, the other person I was closest to was my uncle. He was a compassionate man. Sometimes I would sleep with my uncle, sometimes with my mother. I felt safe knowing that they would keep me warm and covered, and have all my favorite foods to eat when I woke up. How could I not have known that I came first? I woke up when I wanted to wake up because I didn't have to go to school. My uncle lived on the farm and we were surrounded by natural sounds. No sense of lack ever touched me.

Parents and teachers may ask how to lead the child to this awakening. You don't have to lead the child to it. It would come by itself. The child cries spontaneously. The teeth come spontaneously. This awakening would also come effortlessly. The only thing for the parents or teachers to do is to give the child the space with its own divine potential.

You have to see that, in your own childhood, it is likely that you never had the opportunity for this contact, even though you are a child of wholeness. This recognition is not encouraged. We ignore what is valuable and put the emphasis on the fragmented, on the intellectual and the physical.

We believe in the teaching that leads to misperception and isolation. Like an oyster, we limit the child to the brain by teaching him the life of separation in which *we* live. All its knowledge is only "about" something – it doesn't connect with reality.

We must demand correction of ourselves because each human being has a divine function that he is to extend. The child comes to the time level as a messenger of eternity. Extension is his real function, for he is universal. The parents are responsible not to limit him to the thought world. Extension doesn't need skills because it is related to the creative energy of all life. The energy and the holiness of perfection doesn't have to go to school. It has so little to learn externally. It is this energy that blesses. It blesses nature; it blesses man; it blesses everything.

When the child becomes preoccupied with the body and its survival, its likes and dislikes, this psychological learning stays with him his whole life. All his attention is diverted, not to awakening and protecting the contact with his divinity, but to the insecurity of physicality. We have not related the child to the totality of the tree; we have related him with fragmentation. But it is still possible to awaken him to another intensity of awareness in which there is no distance. It is like seeing from within rather than merely with the eyes.

*A Course In Miracles* helps remove...*the blocks to the awareness of love's presence.* [1] It is also the function of the parents and the function of the teacher to help remove these blocks. When the child sees that he and the tree are part of one life, then there is not the conflict. This is a truth. There is only one life. No insecurity ever touches this highly attentive state.

The brain is the most sensitive organ of the physical body. It will learn what it needs to learn because of its own nature. Through experience, the child will learn. The problem begins when we try to teach the child more and more abstract things.

Can the parent or teacher put a greater emphasis on awakening than on teaching? I would never say that teaching the child physical skills is not necessary. The child would not know how to open the door unless you teach him. But unnecessary information merely makes the brain more and more busy. If you don't bring the child to the awareness of the sacredness of life, you abandon him to the world of jobs.

The parents should know that the child needs for them to discover the strength within themselves. When this discovery takes place, it is a joyous spiritual surprise that has its own order and heals conflict and confusion.

The minute you accept defeat in yourself, you undermine your potentials. Yet your awareness of this one fact, which is stronger than thought, would make you grateful. If you undermine yourself, you will also undermine your child. He will then not be surrounded by trust and faith which are his birthright. You will begin to put your child in the second place and what is spontaneous and natural will be ignored.

"Be not the destroyers of yourselves.
Arise to your true Being
and then you will have nothing to fear." [2]
*Lord Krishna*

Every challenge, when faced, introduces us to potentials we never knew before. But we want to change the situation and the circumstances. The fact is, inner correction is what is needed. If we are not responsible internally, then we are controlled by the externals.

Because we feel self-improvement is necessary, we enhance self-centeredness in the child. This is the status quo. To reverse this process we need to come to a higher intelligence that relates with the Universal Mind. All we need to know is the power of the Will of God we are given to extend. If we relate the child to the Universal Intelligence, he brings something of the light of the Kingdom to the earth. This light surrounds everything that lives.

Until we transcend the world of appearances, we will not see the sacredness of life that sustains the visible. Not until we have seen the perfection in creation will we be inspired by the power of our own stillness. Can you imagine a mind that is free of judgement and conflict? The holiness of creation would fill one with reverence and joy. It totally transforms one's relationship with all that is. Parents who want to free their child from conflict are not alone, nor is their child alone, for the light that sustains life surrounds them.

Beware of the tendency to undermine your own sense of responsibility. Correction begins in the parents. Their own inner correction will save the child a great deal of time and will automatically bring a change about in him. As he grows older, they will awaken him to making correction with another energy which is not intellectual.

Jesus was born in a barn. You can't say he wasn't taken care of. Some other force was always guiding the parents. That force said to Joseph: "Take the child to Egypt." How many people have read that story and yet they don't think that guidance is accessible to them. Since the child cannot hear the truth, the parents as the custodians receive it for him.

Mary was chosen as the mother of Jesus because she was the purest. She knew directly what was to be done. Mary received the intimations about how to care for Jesus. Joseph received the guidance about their external direction. Life always intimates. A mind accessible to intimations is a mind wholly attentive. These intimations are spontaneous, spiritual surprises. After Herod had died, Joseph was told that he and his family should leave Egypt. If Joseph went in the wrong direction, other forces would intimate the right road for him to take.

In this same way, mothers and fathers can be corrected if they are receptive to guidance. This means that they must not be dependent on their brain and their ideas which undermine them and tell them it's not practical to do the right thing. This guidance has no duality in it because it extends the one life.

We cannot discover a truth as long as the brain is active. When a spiritual discovery of truth takes place, it silences the brain. And because minds are joined, the discovery gets shared instantly with every mind. It does not just take place in your mind. Anyone who receives it, receives it only to share it. It must be expressed in a way that is natural. In the process of discovery, in the sharing, the holy instant takes place that enriches us all. Often, it is received only when it is shared. One person's awareness extends the fact to everyone else. And then, like Jesus said, "HE THAT HAS THE EARS TO HEAR, LET HIM HEAR." [3] It has been given. Within the one life it is shared. Always. Its intense awareness awakens the glory of the Given.

# ADDENDA

# THE FOUNDATION FOR LIFE ACTION

Life is too vast, timeless, and whole for the brain to grasp. Whenever one has some glimpse of its sacredness, attention intensifies and brings us to silence. We have to silence our brains to go beyond the world of appearances; thought has to cease in order to be with what is ever-present and unchangeable – the Christ that the human being is. Until we make that contact our real work has not begun and, in one way or another, the issue of survival consumes our energy.

But when, with the Grace of God, something else is awakened within, you begin to care for everyone and everything you see. One gets a glimpse that in moments of wholeness there is not the separation. As you begin to undo fragmentation in yourself – the way in which the brain separates – another action commences of which you may not be fully conscious. When this awakening starts to dawn, you begin to value miracles, the involuntary Action of Life. The learning phase is over and the unlearning of everything that blocks contact with truth begins.

A new action was born in me with the advent of *A Course In Miracles*. This is the experiment at the Foundation for Life Action in Los Angeles, California, a school to train students to bring *A Course In Miracles* into application. Through our work, eternal principles have been discovered to serve mankind in times ahead. This experiment belongs to all generations. To the degree it is impersonal, to the degree it is wise, it needs to be known.

The work of the Foundation for Life Action began as I was guided internally to give workshops and retreats. I was told,

377

"Put away your false modesty. You are a teacher in your own right."

When something is authentic, it is always one-to-one with the serious few. And it is non-commercial. The focus of attention is basic and an intimate atmosphere essential. Like the dialogues of the Upanishads or of Socrates and Plato, it allows for the sharing of something unknown.

Our action started in a small way. We insisted upon self-reliance and the commandment Mr. Krishnamurti gave to me: "Never take advantage of another." This eliminated dependence on the externals, for we refused to accept charity or ask for donations, and directed our energies toward finding the treasure within ourselves.

The small group that stayed on after the One Year Non-Commercialized Retreat: A Serious Study of *A Course In Miracles*, held during 1983-1984,[1] became part of the Foundation for Life Action and the nucleus of the school to train students to bring the Course into application.

A clairvoyant said of the One Year Retreat: "It is a process of inner selection, one of the golden opportunities on the planet. But who is ready? It has to be an inner calling, for that is the level at which the transformation will take place." Dr. Elisabeth Kubler-Ross, the physician known for her work on death and dying, said: "Those who emerge from the One Year Retreat will be self-reliant and dependable in crisis and catastrophe."

Self-reliance requires productive and intrinsic work. To come to self-reliance the students began transcribing tapes from the One Year Retreat. They felt that what had helped them could also help others; and so, they made the material available in books and audiotapes.

During a trip to England in 1988, I was directed internally to bring the hearts of all my blood relatives to gladness. I was being introduced to the action of completion in order to merit a motiveless life free of consequences. While in London, Joseph's Plan was intimated to me.

Joseph, a prophet of God in the Old Testament, [2] prepared the Pharaoh in Egypt for the seven lean years. The story is given in the Bible so that we may learn to be responsible because this pattern repeats itself throughout the centuries.

*Time* magazine reported: "In Biblical times, a famed Pharaoh once dreamed of seven fat years of plenty followed by seven lean years of want. With the United States economy in the seventh year of a record peace time expansion, signs are multiplying that for many Americans, the fat times are coming to an end. At the moment, no Joseph is available to persuade Washington to adopt frugal habits, even when the fat years are in danger of turning to lean ones."*

Joseph was a man who knew nothing of greed or fear. He extended who he was as God created him. In his wholeness, he intensified all men for all time. Such is Joseph, the prophet of God. This unseparated, eternal man inspired me with his pure abundance. In his stillness there was no opposite. Joseph was wholly himself. He always acted out of awareness. In truth, Joseph represents a state of celibacy, a life free of karma.

Spontaneously, his goodness and his sense of wholeness focused the rays of the Kingdom on earth. Yet in the world of time, this man of Divine Intelligence was falsely accused and cast into prison. Joseph had no revenge, no reaction. His honesty set him free to do God's Will. From Joseph we can learn that in the acceptance of Divine Will, man's life becomes selfless and impersonal.

The Pharaoh, whose dream Joseph interpreted, was a noble and farsighted king – one to whom the human being was important, not politics. The pharaohs, in their uninterrupted space, built the enduring and mysterious pyramids. It is likely that within the pyramid are held man's

---

* May 22, 1989 issue.

innermost vibrations which transcend the manifested world of appearances.

The Pharaoh had the discrimination of a true ruler and, in his heart, the kindness of a king for his people. His trust and courage made him an eternal king in the memory of men for all time. When the Pharaoh first met Joseph, there stood before him a man who had never told a lie. The Pharaoh, attentive yet serene, recognized Joseph from the strength of his certainty, which effortlessly extended the power of the Will. Stop for a moment and imagine: What must have Joseph's voice been like? Intensity of silence surrounded him. The Pharaoh saw that one who lives by Eternal Laws is a law unto himself.

Hearing Joseph's true words, the Pharaoh placed no conditions. He knew that a law does not compromise. Joseph had something to give and the wise Pharaoh responded with giving as well. That is the meeting ground of togetherness.

We need to know that true words leave their light behind for all generations to come. Thus what has once occurred need never victimize us again. Joseph's incorruptibility is now our strength. One's own attention is all-wise and ever resourceful. We can learn from Joseph and the Pharaoh how to prepare and how to relate with Universal Forces.

There is never lack in the wholeness of creation. Thus, the issue is always one of internal correction. Deprivation and scarcity are misperceptions; they are self-imposed.

Behold the example of the Pharaoh of generous heart and trust in goodness, who avoided the crisis by recognizing a man of awakened intelligence and impersonal life. The Pharaoh demonstrated that for both the state and the individual, transformation is possible.

On reading about Joseph, I was charged. It was not enthusiasm, nor anything necessarily mental. The direction was given. In my case it started in 1989 with the offering of a Forty Days Retreat in New Mexico. Over one hundred and ten participants attended. In addition, many other shorter retreats were subsequently offered around the country. The income from all of these retreats has been put aside for Joseph's Plan. It is entrusted to be used to meet the primary needs of mankind.

It is more than a joy to keep Joseph's Plan impeccable. What a blessing to know that ordinary people can be purified by the work they do when the Grace of God accompanies it. Nothing is as precious as selflessness that slowly purifies one's mind and spirit with the boon of service. I can truthfully say it is not I who is selfless. Selflessness is beyond the realm of words. But the Grace of God is miraculous. It can make the lame walk and the blind see. What is at work in all of this is the energy of Gratefulness.

Looking back, it is marvelous how Life prepared us with having our own intrinsic work; being detached and owning no property; and discovering the strength of rightness inherent in self-reliance. Until you have found your own voice, your own dignity, it is not possible to merit service. Now we are blessed with the sacredness of Joseph's Plan, which is the fulfillment of having something to give. When what you give is the Given, you are an extension of Joseph's Plan. [3]

Joseph, the servant of God, lives by faith for he knows that whatever anyone does externally is not of God. The external can put you in prison but it cannot disturb your peace.

As long as we live by thought, nothing we say is true. Everyone wants to do good but that good may not be sensitive. Good is absolute; it is not of personality. The goodness of God sensitizes you to another person's need and it is your joy to meet it. When you care, you heed another's words so intensely that your own interpretation and opinion are silenced. Then you qualify to be the blessed servant of God. Just by listening, you will know what to do and what to impart. To be the blessed servant is to know certainty. You receive what the other needs and bring light into confusion and darkness. In the world of insight there is the pure healing because you are not opposing the Will of God.

The blessed servant of God must live by Universal Laws. That is his preparation. Cleansed of relative knowledge, he purifies his speech and masters communication. He is ever aware of the divine action in his life. Order is needed to have the space and capacity to maintain the light that surrounds him.

Swami Brahmananda, one of Sri Ramakrishna's foremost disciples said that one becomes truly entitled to work only after God-realization. He shared that in the joy of samadhi, the world vanishes, and that peace comes by loving God and having true faith in Him. The one who is calculating would be lost.

> *Today we will receive instead of plan*
> *that we may give instead of organize.* [4]

Our experiment is not only to outgrow organization but also to bring fruit to the altar. [5] The servants of God need the energy of love in order to receive. They will go out in this chaotic world, having established this capacity to receive, and then it will be their own direct light and extension. The servants will be blessed with faith. They could be in the midst of earthquakes and fire and nothing could touch them.

Five or six years ago, I had an intimation that our work would one day become linked with that of Mother Teresa. It was a clear realization at a different level of being. It is interesting to see how long it takes for something to manifest and become implemented at this level. The more one leaves it alone, the more impersonal it is and, therefore, the more sacred. That is the way it is meant to be. This is easier said than done, however. In one way or another, we always interfere.

When Charles Johnson and I travelled to India in 1989, we visited Mother Teresa's Missionary Sisters of Charity in Calcutta. The words on the altar of their little chapel, "I THIRST," [6] silenced me through and through. Mother Teresa was not well, so we met with Sister Priscilla who was in charge. She said to us, "We don't want money. We need people with hearts to give and lives to serve." At the time I told Sister Priscilla that I believed there were those among us in Los Angeles who would be interested. She recommended that we contact Sister Sylvia who was responsible for the missions in the western part of the United States.

A letter was sent to Sister Sylvia upon our returning to California. Shortly thereafter, Sister Angelina, the Superior of the Lynwood Mission near Los Angeles, called and shared with us ways in which volunteers could help. She also made it clear that although active involvement was not necessary, prayers would be appreciated.

The Sisters provide a home for unwed mothers in Lynwood, about thirty-five minutes from the Foundation. We began sending two people for several hours every Saturday. There was gardening, sewing, carpentry, and other miscellaneous tasks to do. Sometimes we helped in preparing grocery bags of donated food items for the needy. One of the Sisters told us that they had been praying for someone to help with the work just before we came to offer our services. They were grateful and acknowledged the Hand of the Lord in answering this prayer. Our blessing was in making the commitment to come on a regular basis.

When our volunteers return from the Mission, they are always inspired by the atmosphere there. It is most refreshing to see that there is no judgment on the Sisters' part regarding the unwed mothers. What these Sisters must have imbibed from Mother Teresa that allowed them to totally respond to what she herself had seen – the Light of the Christ in the human being. It takes nine or more years to go through the training. But just that one would take nine years to come to inner awakening and this sharing of life speaks of the quality of the Sisters. It is not impulsive. Not many people would last nine years unless their calling were authentic.

Our students, on returning from the Lynwood Mission, have remarked that it is as if their hands are blessed in doing the work. What a remarkable discovery, the blessing of service. You exist for your brother and, out of that love, you work. Our volunteers were also affected by the uncomplicated and unsentimental approach of the Sisters. It is obvious that they are "about their Father's business." [7] There is warmth and joy, but they do not have the space for idle conversation or gossip.

When we discovered that they often do not have enough food to give to the poor, we committed ourselves to donating $50 a week for one year. We met as a group and discussed the value of being consistent in giving. We wanted to offer an amount that would allow others, too, to be a part of the program and receive the gift of being in contact with their work. The donation is used to purchase bulk food – hundred pound sacks of flour, beans, sugar, oats, powdered milk, etc. – to add to their limited food supply for weekly distribution to the poor.

We wrote to Mother Teresa in India thanking her for providing the inspiration and the means by which we could assist in the work of meeting basic needs of our brothers. Mother Teresa wrote:

"Thank you for your warm letter and the kind sentiments you have expressed in it. How beautiful it is to know that you all have allowed your lives to be touched by the presence of Jesus in the poor. He keeps using the poor to draw us all together. In allowing us to serve them and in accepting our service, the poor draw the best out of us, or rather, it is Jesus using the poor, Who makes us the sunshine of His love and compassion with them.

"In the measure we allow God to empty us of self and pride, we enable Him to fill us with His love so we may seek to give more than to receive, to serve rather than be served. Let us pray for all at the

Foundation for Life Action that they may make the prayer of St. Francis their own and live it in seeking to love rather than to be loved.

> "The Fruit of Silence is Prayer.
> The Fruit of Prayer is Faith.
> The Fruit of Faith is Love.
> The Fruit of Love is Service.
> The Fruit of Service is Peace."

Dr. Helen Schucman, the Scribe of *A Course In Miracles*, had said to me: "Send the world your love. It will come back to you." Mother Teresa's work best exemplifies this statement. When I asked Dr. Schucman if there was anyone who really lived *A Course In Miracles* in our time, she replied that Mother Teresa was one. Mother Teresa is not distracted by the abstract world of ideas. Hers is the energy of love and compassion which knows no lack. She is always present with what she is doing, for her life and God's Will are not in contradiction.

On my first visit to meet Sister Angelina, after our students had gone to volunteer for more than a year, she told me that her Sisters never knew such faces existed in the outside world as those of the young people at the Foundation. She also said that our presence at their Mission was a strength and an inspiration to the Sisters. When I asked Sister Angelina whether there were other projects which we could support, she thought for awhile and then said, "No, we have no needs." Now that is very simple.

Stop for a moment and consider what this means. They have no needs because they don't believe in the future. They know for certain that tomorrow will take care of itself and they have enough for today. It is a different language. When you really hear it, your conflict ends also. Their authenticity introduces you to a moment of wholeness.

We were blessed to become related with the Missionary Sisters of Charity in Lima, Peru, on my visit there in the Fall of 1990. We were told by the Sisters that on many days there was a shortage of bread. When we wrote to Mother Teresa inquiring whether we could establish bakery facilities in the Mission, she responded that she did not want her Sisters to get involved in a bakery.

In this statement one discovers the principles upon which her work is based. It is always related to an extension of the Will and compassion of God which provides. It is an action of faith and truth which only knows abundance. How inspiring this is. Mother Teresa and her Sisters have no sense of scarcity because they are the blessed servants of God. I wrote to Mother Teresa:

> "...We see such wisdom in your not getting the Sisters involved in the organization of a bakery. Your love for poverty and simplicity is a strength and a guidance to us.

> "We have been a witness to the work at the Mission here in Lynwood with which we have close contact. Our group goes and volunteers services once or twice a week regularly, and they come back beaming. We are also inspired by the work being done by the Sisters at Misioneras de la Caridad in Lima, Peru, and we are responding to some of the needs there with gladness in our heart.

> "We have what is called Joseph's Fund to meet the primary needs of man. It is to be kept impeccable, since it is entrusted by the Lord. We have dedicated two years to the service of Joseph Plan and now there are substantial funds.

> "What we would like to ask is that if any project in any of the Missions of Charity needs financial help, would you please let us know so that we may participate in it? We speak in an impersonal way; the funds are meant to meet the primary needs of man during the lean years.

"The Joseph Plan demands integrity and I pray daily, 'Lord, prevent me from making a mistake.' May your blessings and prayers be upon it."

Mother Teresa responded:

"I pray for you and for all at the Foundation for Life Action that you be God's Hands to serve the poor and His Heart to love the poorest of the Poor. Since God has already entrusted you with substantial funds set up a project yourselves so you may bring hope into the lives of those on the brink of despair through your service. Since you are interested in helping the poor, be fully involved in doing something concrete for them. I thank you for your kind interest in our works of love and for your thoughtful and generous offer."

God bless you, Mother Teresa.

Since receiving this letter, we have come to a unanimous decision. We see the rightness of disbanding the organization of the Foundation for Life Action by Easter, 1992, after having been together for nine years.

The Foundation has been a school to train students of *A Course In Miracles* to be productive and self-reliant, having something of their own to give. The Foundation was not to seek results, but to value what is intrinsic. Primarily, laws and principles have been shared with the students rather than concepts. Inner transformation is not possible at the level of mere teaching and learning of ideas and ideals.

Several years ago, we recognized that, ultimately, having one's own intrinsic work and not working for another were essential to be consistent with the lifestyle of *A Course In Miracles*. We have realized a life of service is intrinsic and free from the conflict of external thought pressures. The issue of self-survival limits one to the insecurity of personalized life.

Knowing that a motiveless life is free of consequences, the premise of the Foundation, from its very outset, has been not to be under obligation. People sent us money and offered us properties which we refused to accept because we did not feel a sense of lack. Our needs were always met. For us, the human being came first. We were determined never to expand the group beyond thirty students.

We have established a rapport with Mother Teresa's Missionary Sisters of Charity over the last two years. This has been most helpful. It is our dependability that has inspired closeness with the Sisters. They value our consistency.

The Foundation has provided years of one-to-one relationship, free of tuition, to prepare the students to realize that enthusiasm and sentimentality have little meaning in truth. Without dissolving the abstract and interpretations, it is not possible to be responsible for what you say or what you do.

The Sisters are a living example and their nine years of preparation directly with Mother Teresa herself have transformed their inner lives and related each one to values of eternal and selfless life. What the Sisters now extend is the natural goodness awakened within themselves. It is no longer work but an internal expression of their love for God.

The Foundation has taken many steps to integrate our group with Mother Teresa's work and values. Now we send students from the Foundation, two-by-two, to spend an extended period of a week or a month in active participation with the Sisters at their Tijuana Mission. By the time Easter comes everyone will have gone through the actual experience of what constitutes service, or what is entailed in loving a brother more than yourself. It is challenging – the work of cleaning, scrubbing, washing people who are ill, nursing the abandoned, the poorest of the poor.

But everyone at the Foundation is eager to go, and they come back inspired for having found some joy that was dormant within themselves. Each one is indebted to the

Foundation for the preparation that has introduced them to a different way of life. They are grateful, also, to close the Foundation and to stand on their own feet. Without detachment, man is a slave of the world.

Gratefulness is a power. Its spirit makes it possible for us to bring the external activity to an end without residue. We are all enriched for having witnessed the Hand of God in what we had undertaken to do and complete. During the nine years we never violated thoughtfulness; everyone has always been included in making decisions. Giving another the space for honesty is what made things work. This promoted a spirit of harmony and we have been blessed by it.

Our decision to disband the organization of the Foundation is an action similar to that of the Essenes of Jesus' time who, having completed their work, knew when to stop, and disappear. The Foundation for Life Action has succeeded in providing different values, virtue, and ethics in life. We feel blessed the heavens have opened the door to be of service through the work of the Missionaries of Charity. Because of this link, after the closing of the Foundation, the group will not feel lost.

My instruction to each one at the Foundation has been: Be true to yourself. If you stay together after the closing, the One Mind of the group will attract Universal Forces to you because of your dedication to service. Those who have given their lives to ...*removing the blocks to the awareness of Love's presence,* [8] will be energized and protected by Divine Laws.

> *God indeed can be reached directly, for there is no distance between Him and His Son. His awareness is in everyone's memory, and His Word is written on everyone's heart. Yet this awareness and this memory can arise across the threshold of recognition only where all barriers to truth have been removed....All the help you can accept will be provided, and not one need you have will not be met.* [9]

Our non-commercialized experiment to bring *A Course In Miracles* into application in each student's life is a statement to everyone that the Grace of God is the Source of life and that newness is accessible. What the group will do will be their own creative expression. It may have no resemblance to Mother Teresa's work or to that of the Foundation, for how can you limit the glory of life to the bondage of the known. The new must always be free of the projections of goals.

Parents, too, can make an impeccable space within themselves that nothing external can intrude upon. It is this parents are to pass on to their children – man's link with God – so they, too, may know the truth of holy relationship where the illusion of separation has ended and the fragrance of goodness and thoughtfulness expresses itself.

*A Course In Miracles* embodies a power independent of the externals. It has its own resources and Divine Intelligence. The Course was published without the help of a traditional publisher and 750,000 copies have been sold without any formal advertising or promotion. At our relative level, the action of *A Course In Miracles* will continue to extend itself.

From its inception, the Foundation for Life Action, rooted in the sharing of *A Course In Miracles,* has stayed with self-reliance. It endeavors to remain non-commercial, having something to give.

The Foundation's first expression was through weekend workshops, followed by ten-day retreats. These resulted in a forty-day residential retreat in 1981. *A Course In Miracles,* having 365 lessons, one for each day of the year, finally led the Foundation to offer the first One Year Non-Commercialized Retreat in the Course's history, as well as in the history of the New World. The One Year extended for nine years, and now the Foundation dissolves its organization.

The students present have discovered that the mania of personal wanting, with all its tribulation, can only be dissolved when one has realized the wisdom of giving. There is no peace in wanting. Joy is in the giving; and moral strength lies in meeting the needs of another. Freedom from wanting comes naturally when one realizes all needs are met by Life's Divine Intelligence.

Now everyone in the group is determined not to work for another or become a mercenary. It is this conviction that leads one to the life of service. The students must evolve to stand on their own feet and give expression to the awakened goodness in themselves. The Foundation school, having completed its work, closes.

All things are completed in detachment.

Life is Impersonal. Until one realizes the truth of this, the survival issue is not resolved. The personal cannot end anything; and its meaningless activity continues its involvement with the past. Ending is internal. It lets the joyous and the peaceful BE. The State of the Living Present reveals:

*My mind is part of God's. I am very holy.* [10]

The next action emerging is the Joseph Plan, which is Impersonal. It remains to be seen how it will unfold. The Joseph Plan is endowed with substantial funds, and there are twenty-two blessed servants of God who have taken a vow to give their lives to service and not be subject to anything external.

Each student could be a civilizing factor wherever he goes, and spontaneously respond in his own area to the need of another. The Joseph Plan will extend simultaneously in different places with the precept of *A Course In Miracles:*

*To have, give all to all.* [11]

*What is God's belongs to everyone,*
*and is his due.* [12]

# RECOMMENDED READING/LISTENING FOR PARENTS AND CHILDREN

| | |
|---|---|
| *Touch The Earth* | T. E. McLuhan |
| *Self-Reliance* | Ralph Waldo Emerson |
| *Walden & Civil Disobedience* | Henry David Thoreau |
| *Leaves Of Grass* | Walt Whitman |
| *Abraham Lincoln: Wit and Wisdom* | Peter Pauper Press |
| *Thomas Jefferson: His Life And Words* | Peter Pauper Press |
| *Helen Keller* | Stewart and Polly Ann Graff |
| *The Kingdom Of God Is Within You* | Leo Tolstoy |
| *The Secret Life Of Plants* | Tompkins & Bird |
| *Letters To A Young Poet* | Rainer Maria Rilke |
| *St. Joan* | George Bernard Shaw |
| *The Story of Opal* | Opal Whiteley |
| *Glimpses Of World History* | Jawaharlal Nehru |
| *Towards Freedom* | Jawaharlal Nehru |
| *A Saint Among Savages* | Rosemary Kingsland |
| *The Panchatantra* | Translated by Ryder |
| *Twenty Jataka Tales* | Noor Inayat Khan |
| *We Were There With Florence Nightingale In The Crimea* | Robert N. Webb |
| *Saints of India* | "Anna" |
| *Tears And Laughter* | Kahlil Gibran |
| *The Story Of My Boyhood And Youth* | John Muir |
| *In The Wilds Of Africa* | Halmi |
| *The Prince Who Gave Up A Throne: A Story Of The Buddha* | Nancy Serage |
| *The Man Who Killed The Deer* | Frank Waters |

This is a select list, but each book would introduce you to others of merit.

Also recommended:

Books on the lives of saints and unique beings like St. Francis, Eleanor Roosevelt, Madame Curie, etc.

# MUSIC

*(By no means exclusive; performers of exceptional merit are noted in some cases.)*

*Composers:*

### BEETHOVEN
Piano Concerto No. 5, "Emperor"  . . . . . Wilhelm Kempff
Violin Concerto . . . . . . . . . . . . . . . . . . . . . Heifetz
Piano Concerto No. 3

### BACH
English Suite No. 3
Concerto No. 1 (harpsichord/piano) . . . . Sviatoslav Richter
Violin Concerto No. 1  . . . . . . . . . . . . . . . Isaac Stern
Brandenburg Concerti . . . . . . . . . . Herbert Von Karajan
Tocata in C (organ)
Goldberg Variations . . . . . . . . . . . . . . . Glenn Gould
Magnificat
French Suite No. 5  . . . . . . . . . . . . . Wilhelm Kempff
Tocata & Fugue in D (organ)
Flute Sonatas  . . . . . . . . . . . . . . . Jean-Pierre Rampal

### BENJAMIN BRITTEN
Simple Symphony

### MENDELSSOHN
Italian Symphony

### MOZART
Piano Concerto No. 23
Piano Concerto No. 24 . . . . . . . . . . . . Wilhelm Kempff
Piano Concerto No. 20
Piano Concerto No. 25 . . . . . . . . . . . . Walter Gieseking
Concerto for 2 Pianos . . . . . . . . . . . Elena & Emil Gilels
Violin Concerto No. 2  . . . . . . . . . . . . . David Oistrakh
Violin Concerto No. 4  . . . . . . . . . . . . . Joseph Szigetti
Violin Concerto No. 5
Concertante for Violin & Viola  . . . David & Isaac Oistrakh
Symphony No. 40 "Jupiter"

TCHAIKOVSKY
 Violin Concerto . . . . . . . . . . . . . . . . David Oistrakh
 Piano Concerto No. 1 . . . . . . . . . . . . Sviatoslav Richter
 1812 Overture
 Hamlet, Fantasy Overture

BARTOK
 Piano Concerto No. 3 . . . . . . . . . . . . . . . . . . Sandor
 Piano Concerto No. 2 . . . . . . . . . . . Sviatoslav Richter
 Music for Celesta, Strings & Percussion

SIBELIUS
 Symphony No. 1
 Symphony No. 5


*Collections:*

JEAN-PIERRE RAMPAL
 Eighteenth Century Flute Sonatas

MARIAN ANDERSON
 Spiritual Songs

YO YO MA
 Cello

JULIAN BREAM
 Spanish Guitar

ALICIA DeLARROCHA
 Piano (Spanish Encores)

PEPE ROMERO
 Renaissance to Baroque Guitar

ALI AKBAR KHAN
 Rag Mala

HARIPRASAD CHAURASSIA
 Mystical Flute

TIBETAN BELLS
 A Bell is Ringing in the Empty Sky, Shinichi Yuize

MUSIC OF EGYPT

PARVACH OF IRAN

## PLAYS AND STORIES ON TAPE

*Les Miserables* . . . . . . . . . . by Victor Hugo
Read by Christopher Cazenova
*The Little Prince* . . . . . . . . by Antoine St. Exupery
Read by Richard Burton
*Mark Twain Stories: Huckleberry Finn*
Read by Hiram Sherman
*West With The Night* . . . . . . by Beryl Markham
Read by Julie Harris (on Africa)
*Alice In Wonderland* . . . . . . by Lewis Carroll
Read by Holloway & Greenwood
*Great American Indian Speeches*
*Ralph Waldo Emerson: Essays On Education And Self-Reliance*
*Thoreau's World*
*Rhinoceros* . . . . . . . . . . . by Eugene Ionesco
*Native Son* . . . . . . . . . . . by Richard Wright
*Carl Sandburg Reading: A Lincoln Album*

Also recommended:

Stories of the lives of great musicians and their music.

Many other excellent stories and plays are available through your public
library or Caedmon Recordings, New York.

# REFERENCES

DEDICATION

1. *A Course In Miracles, Text,* page 503. *A Course In Miracles* (ACIM), first published in 1976 by the Foundation for Inner Peace, Glen Ellen, California, is a contemporary scripture which deals with the psychological/spiritual issues facing man today. It consists of three volumes: *Text* (I), *Workbook For Students* (II), and *Manual For Teachers* (III). The *Text*, 622 pages, sets forth the concepts on which the thought system of the Course is based. The *Workbook For Students*, 478 pages, is designed to make possible the application of the concepts presented in the *Text* and consists of three hundred and sixty-five lessons, one for each day of the year. The *Manual For Teachers*, 88 pages, provides answers to some of the basic questions a student of the Course might ask and defines many of the terms used in the *Text*.(Editor)
2. *A Course In Miracles* (ACIM), *Workbook For Students* (II), page 89.

CHAPTER ONE: RESPONSIBILITY FOR THE ENERGY ENTRUSTED TO US

1. "Too Much Of A Good Thing," *Time*, Sept. 8, 1986, page 22.
2. See Isaiah 6:9-10; Matthew 11:15 and 13:13-23; Mark 4:9 and 4:23.
3. The one commandment given by Jesus, "Love ye one another," appears many times in the New Testament. See, for example: John 13:34-35, 15:12, 15:17; Romans 13:8.
4. For further discussion of the significance of *A Course In Miracles,* see Tara Singh's *A Course In Miracles – A Gift For All Mankind* (Life Action Press, 1986). See also his *How To Learn*

*From A Course In Miracles* (Harper San Francisco, 1990).(Editor)

5. ACIM, II, page 399.
6. ACIM, II, page 300-301.
7. I Samuel 1:10-11, 14-18, 24-28.
8. Refers to the prayer, *Let me remember I am one with God, At one with all my brothers and my Self, In everlasting holiness and peace.* This is Lesson 124 of *A Course In Miracles.* See ACIM, II, pages 218-219.(Editor)
9. ACIM, *Manual For Teachers* (III), page 8.
10. ACIM, II, pages 315-317.
11. *Love: A Fruit Always In Season; Daily Meditation* by Mother Teresa (Ignatius Press, 1987), page 228.
12. ACIM, II, page 119.

CHAPTER TWO: AWAKENING AWARENESS IN THE CHILD AND THE PARENTS

1. Refers to *I will not value what is valueless,* Lesson 133 of *A Course In Miracles.* See ACIM, II, pages 239-241.(Editor)
2. *Nothing real can be threatened. Nothing unreal exists.* These sentences appear in the Introduction to the *Text* (I) of *A Course In Miracles.* The complete Introduction reads:
   *This is a course in miracles. It is a required course. Only the time you take it is voluntary. Free will does not mean that you can establish the curriculum. It means only that you can elect what you want to take at a given time. The course does not aim at teaching the meaning of love, for that is beyond what can be taught. It does aim, however, at removing the blocks to the awareness of love's presence, which is your natural inheritance. The opposite of love is fear, but what is all-encompassing can have no opposite.*
   *This course can therefore be summed up very simply in this way:*
   *Nothing real can be threatened.*
   *Nothing unreal exists.*
   *Herein lies the peace of God.*(Editor)
3. Luke 23:34.
4. *Diamond Sutra And The Sutra Of Hui Neng,* translated by A.F. Price and Wong Mou-Lam (Shambala, 1969).
5. Isaiah 11:6.
6. ACIM, II, pages 162-163.
7. *You Are The World* by J. Krishnamurti (Harper & Row, 1972), page 1.
8. *The Gifts Of God* by Helen Schucman (Foundation for Inner Peace, 1982), page 59.

9. Refers to I Samuel 1:24-28.

CHAPTER THREE: IN LOVE THERE IS NO DESIRE

1. See ACIM, III, pages 6-7.
2. ACIM, II, pages 239-241.

CHAPTER FOUR: TALKS WITH PARENTS – Part I

1. See *Truth will correct all errors in my mind*, Lesson 107 of *A Course In Miracles*. ACIM, II, pages 189-190.(Editor)
2. See I Samuel 1:1-28.
3. Refers to Matthew 18:19-20.
4. Luke 6:29. See also Matthew 5:39-40.
5. Refers to *My mind is part of God's. I am very holy*. This is Lesson 35 of *A Course In Miracles*. See ACIM, II, pages 53-54.(Editor)
6. See ACIM, I, pages 354-356.
7. See Isaiah 6:9-10; Matthew 11:15 and 13:13-23; Mark 4:9 and 4:23.
8. Numbers 6:24-26.
9. ACIM, I, page 96.
10. Ibid.
11. ACIM, II, pages 284-286.
12. ACIM, II, pages 16-17.
13. Refers to *I walk with God in perfect holiness*. This is Lesson 156 of *A Course In Miracles*. See ACIM, II, pages 287-288.(Editor)
14. ACIM, II, pages 284-286.
15. ACIM, II, pages 239-241.

CHAPTER FIVE: EDUCATION – HAVING SOMETHING OF ONE'S OWN TO GIVE

1. 1 John 4:16.
2. ACIM, III, page 8.
3. Luke 6:29. See also Matthew 5:39-40.
4. Matthew 5:39.
5. Matthew 5:5.
6. *With A Silent Mind: J. Krishnamurti* (Videotape released by the Krishnamurti Foundation of America, 1988).
7. ACIM, I, page 96.
8. ACIM, III, page 62.
9. See *Gandhi* by Jeffrey Ashe (Stein & Day, 1968).

## CHAPTER SIX: DEGENERATION AND INTELLECTUALITY

1. *Krishnamurti To Himself: His Last Journal* by J. Krishnamurti (Harper & Row, 1987), page 47.
2. ACIM, II, pages 329-330.
3. ACIM, II, pages 360-361.
4. *Beginnings Of Learning* by J. Krishnamurti (Harper & Row, 1975), page 158-159.

## CHAPTER SEVEN: WORKING WITH CHILDREN – Part I

1. ACIM, II, page 291.
2. *Opal: The Journal Of An Understanding Heart* by Opal Whiteley, abridged by Jane Boulton (Tioga, 1976).
3. *Ishi: Last Of His Tribe* by Theodora Kroeber (Bantam Books, 1989).
4. ACIM, I, page 96.
5. Ibid.
6. An excerpt from a prayer in *A Course In Miracles*, I, page 326: *Forgive us our illusions, Father, and help us to accept our true relationship with You, in which there are no illusions, and where none can ever enter. Our holiness is Yours. What can there be in us that needs forgiveness when Yours is perfect? The sleep of forgetfulness is only the unwillingness to remember Your forgiveness and Your Love. Let us not wander into temptation, for the temptation of the Son of God is not Your Will. And let us receive only what You have given, and accept but this into the minds which You created and which You love. Amen.*
   This prayer has been referred to as *A Course In Miracles'* version of the Lord's Prayer. See: *Journey Without Distance: The Story Behind A Course In Miracles* by Robert Skutch (Celestial Arts, 1984), page 68. This prayer is discussed in great detail in *Dialogues On A Course In Miracles* by Tara Singh (Life Action Press, 1987), pages 35-167.(Editor)
7. ACIM, III, page 1.
8. *Dear Papa* by John Muir (Panorama West Publishing, 1985).
9. *Commentaries On Living* by J. Krishnamurti (Theosophical Publishing House, 1967).
10. *The Secret Life Of Plants* by Peter Tompkins (Harper & Row, 1989).
11. *Glimpses Of World History* by Jawaharlal Nehru (Oxford University Press, 1989).

CHAPTER EIGHT: WORKING WITH CHILDREN – Part II

1. ACIM, II, page 119.
2. ACIM, II, page 476.
3. See ACIM, I, page 96.

CHAPTER NINE: THE MIND OF THE AGE – TALKS WITH YOUNG ADULTS

1. ACIM, II, page 473.
2. ACIM, II, page 32.
3. ACIM, II, pages 239-241.
4. ACIM, II, page 235.
5. ACIM, I, Introduction.
6. ACIM, I, pages 32-33.
7. ACIM, I, page 12.
8. Refers to Luke 22:19.
9. Matthew 6:9-13.

CHAPTER TEN: TALKS WITH PARENTS – Part II

1. Refers to *I am not the victim of the world I see,* Lesson 31 of *A Course In Miracles.* See ACIM, II, page 48.
2. Refers to a prayer from *Let me remember I am one with God,* Lesson 124 of *A Course In Miracles.* See ACIM, II, page 219.
3. *Ramayana,* translated and edited by C. Rajagopalachari (Bharatiya Vidya Bhavan, Bombay, 1951), page 15.
4. Sri Ramakrishna was a God-lit being who lived in India from 1836 to 1886. He taught that all religions are true, having discovered the truth of each of them himself by practicing them with total devotion. He found that God can be known directly through all forms of spiritual practice. Sri Sarada Devi (1853-1920) was the wife of Ramakrishna. She is often referred to as the Holy Mother.(Editor)
5. *Stories Of God* by Ranier Maria Rilke (W.W. Norton & Company, 1963), page 97.
6. Refers to: *Nothing real can be threatened. Nothing unreal exists.* See ACIM, I, Introduction.
7. *On Man And Nature* by Henry David Thoreau (Peter Pauper Press, 1960).
8. *Touch The Earth* by T.C. McLuhan (Simon & Schuster, 1971).
9. Acts 3:6.
10. Acts 9:1-20.
11. *Commentaries On Living, Series III* by J. Krishnamurti (Theosophical Publishing House, 1967), pages 197-198.

12. ACIM, I, page 326.

CHAPTER ELEVEN: INNER AWAKENING

1. John 16:33.
2. ACIM, II, page 91.
3. ACIM, II, pages 233-235.
4. Refers to *I am as God created me*, Lesson 94 of *A Course In Miracles*. See ACIM, II, pages 162-163.
5. Luke 22:35.
6. *On Man And Nature* by Henry David Thoreau (Peter Pauper Press, 1960), page 47.
7. Op. cit., page 14.
8. *On Man And God* by Ralph Waldo Emerson (Peter Pauper Press, 1961), page 30.
9. *Wit And Wisdom* by Abraham Lincoln (Peter Pauper Press, 1962).
10. Excerpt from Lincoln's speech at the Cooper Institute, New York City, February 27, 1860.
11. *Writings Of Thomas Jefferson* (Viking, 1984).

CHAPTER TWELVE: ENCOUNTERS WITH MEN AND WOMEN AWAKENED FROM WITHIN – Part I

1. *The Life And Teachings Of Guru Nanak* by Kaur (Brotherhood Of Life Books, 1972).
2. *Guru Nanak And the Origins Of The Sikh Faith* by Harbans Singh (Asia Publishing House, 1969), pages 70-71.
3. ACIM, I, page 109.
4. ACIM, II, page 455.
5. *In The Woods Of God Realization: The Complete Works Of Swami Rama Tirtha* (Pratisthan Press, India, 1979), page vi.
6. ACIM, II, page 372.
7. From the Introduction to *Poems Of Saint John Of The Cross* by Willis Barnstone (New Directions Publishing, 1968).
8. John 8:30-31.
9. *Indira Gandhi: Letters To An American Friend* written to Dorothy Norman (Harcourt Brace Jovanovich, 1985), page 121.
10. Op. cit., pages 178-179.
11. *Gandhi, Nehru, And JP: Stories In Leadership* by Bismal Prasad (Chanakya Publications, 1985), page 169.

CHAPTER THIRTEEN: ENCOUNTERS WITH MEN AND WOMEN AWAKENED FROM WITHIN – Part II

1. *Leaves Of Grass* by Walt Whitman (Penguin Books, 1959).
2. ACIM, II, page 277.
3. *The Writings Of Henry David Thoreau* (Houghton Mifflin, 1906).
4. ACIM, III, page 59-60.
5. *Ramakrishna And His Disciples* by Christopher Isherwood (Vedanta Society Press, 1965), page 208.

CHAPTER FOURTEEN: ENCOUNTERS WITH ETERNITY

1. ACIM, I, Introduction.
2. ACIM, I, page 3.
3. ACIM, II, page 221.
4. II Corinthians 12:7-10.
5. *The Gifts Of God: The Poetry Of Helen Schucman, Personal Reminiscences* by Kenneth Wapnick, Audiotape Workshop, February 23, 1986 (Foundation for A Course In Miracles, 1986), tape 1.

CHAPTER FIFTEEN: A CHILD IS PART OF ONE LIFE

1. See ACIM, I, Introduction.
2. The *Mahabharata* is the famous Hindu epic which tells the "...tale of heroic men and women, some of whom were divine. It is a whole literature in itself, containing a code of life, a philosophy of social and ethical relations and speculative thought on human problems...He who knows it not, knows not the heights and depths of the soul..." From "Kulapati's Preface" to *Mahabharata* by C. Rajagopalachari (Bharatiya Vidya Bhavan, Bombay, 1951), page 2.(Editor)
3. See Isaiah 6:9-10; Matthew 11:15 and 13:13-23; Mark 4:9 and 4:23.

ADDENDA
THE FOUNDATION FOR LIFE ACTION

1. The One Year Non-Commercialized Retreat: A Serious Study of *A Course In Miracles* with Tara Singh took place in Los Angeles, California, from Easter Sunday, April 3, 1983 to Easter Sunday, April 22, 1984 with 50 participants from all over the United States. The years and events which led up to the One Year Retreat are documented in Tara Singh's *The*

*Voice That Precedes Thought* (Life Action Press, 1987).
Tara Singh's work with *A Course In Miracles* centers around his one-to-one relationship with a small number of serious students. This work is sponsored by the Foundation for Life Action. Mr. Singh has shared about his relationship with the Course and the Foundation for Life Action in each of his books. These excerpts provide a fascinating tapestry of the years from 1983-1989:
Preface to *A Course In Miracles – A Gift For All Mankind*, pages xiii-xvi.
Introduction to *Commentaries On A Course In Miracles*, pages xiv-xx.
Preface to *The Voice That Precedes Thought*, pages xvii-xviii.
Introduction to *Dialogues On A Course In Miracles*, pages 20-31.
*The School – "Having The Ears To Hear,"* published in *Dialogues On A Course In Miracles*, pages 339-365.
Introduction to *How To Raise A Child Of God*, pages 39-42.
Introduction To The Second Edition of *How To Learn From A Course In Miracles*, pages 15-27.
Introduction to *"Nothing Real Can Be Threatened,"* pages 11-27.
Autobiography in *"Nothing Real Can Be Threatened,"* pages 255-262.(Editor)
2. See Genesis 37 and following.
3. For further discussion of Joseph's Plan, see the Introduction to Tara Singh's *"Nothing Real Can Be Threatened,"* (Life Action Press, 1989), pages 24-27.(Editor)
4. ACIM, II, page 248.
5. John 15:16.
6. John 19:28.
7. Luke 2:49.
8. ACIM, I, Introduction.
9. ACIM, III, pages 61-62.
10. ACIM, II, page 53.
11. ACIM, I, page 96.
12. ACIM, I, page 503.

# OTHER MATERIALS BY TARA SINGH

## BOOKS

*How To Raise A Child Of God*
*"Nothing Real Can Be Threatened"*
*How To Learn From A Course In Miracles*
*Dialogues On A Course In Miracles*
*Commentaries On A Course In Miracles*
*"Love Holds No Grievances" – The Ending Of Attack*
*A Course In Miracles – A Gift For All Mankind*
*The Future Of Mankind – Affluence Without Wisdom*
     *Is Self-Destructive (New edition forthcoming)*
*Jesus And The Blind Man – Commentaries on St. John Chapter IX*
*Letters From Mexico*
*The Present Heals*

## AUDIO CASSETTE TAPES

*Keep The Bowl Empty*
*Awakening The Light Of The Mind*
*True Meditation – A Practical Approach*
*"In God We Trust"*
*Conflict Ends With Me*
*What Is A Course In Miracles?*
*A Course In Miracles Explorations*
*Bringing A Course In Miracles Into Application*
*Discussions On A Course In Miracles*
*"What Is The Christ?"*
*Raising A Child For The New Age*

*Freedom From Belief*
*Stories From India For Children*
*"Creation's Gentleness Is All I See"*
*Undoing Self-Deception*
*All Relationships Must End In Love*
*Is It Possible To Rest The Brain?*
*Discovering Your Own Holiness*
*Finding Peace Within*
*Discovering Your Life's Work*
*The Heart Of Forgiveness*
*Audiotape Collection from The One Year Non-Commercialized*
  *Retreat: A Serious Study of A Course In Miracles*
*Audiotape Collection from The Forty Days In The Wilderness*
  *Retreat, 1989 & 1990*


VIDEO CASSETTE TAPES

*A Meeting With Parents At The Forty Days Retreat*
*"Nothing Real Can Be Threatened" Workshop*
*Finding Your Inner Calling*
*How To Raise A Child Of God*
*"Do Only That" – A Course In Miracles & Working With Children*
*What Is A Course In Miracles?*
*God Does Not Judge & Healing Relationships*
*A Course In Miracles And The Destiny Of America*
*A Course In Miracles Is Not To Be Learned, But To Be Lived*
*The Dawn Of Impersonal Life*
*"There Must Be Another Way"*

Tara Singh may be heard on
A CALL TO WISDOM.
Dial 1/900/226-2629
*(Current number as of the printing of this edition.)*

A CALL TO WISDOM
relates one to a state
that nothing external can affect.

*Messages change weekly and are five minutes in length.*
*Cost is $.95 per minute charged to your phone.*

For a free audio cassette sampler of Tara Singh
and free book and tape catalogue call
LIFE ACTION PRESS
at
1/800/367-2246

Additional copies of *Awakening A Child From Within* by Tara Singh may be obtained by sending a check, money order, Mastercard or Visa number and expiration date to:

LIFE ACTION PRESS
PO Box 48932
Los Angeles, CA 90048
1/800/367-2246

Hardbound                                    $28.95
      (plus $4.00 shipping/handling)

Softcover                                    $16.95
      (plus $3.00 shipping/handling)

---

*A Course In Miracles* may be purchased from Life Action Press:

Three volume, hardbound edition          $40.00
      (plus $4.00 shipping/handling)

Combined, softcover edition              $25.00
      (plus $4.00 shipping/handling)

---

California residents please add 8.25% sales tax.

*Thank you.*

*Cover Design:* David Wise, Montpelier, Vermont
*Typesetting:* Raging Fingers, Los Angeles, California
*Printing/binding:* McNaughton & Gunn, Inc., Saline, Michigan
*Type:* Palatino
*Paper:* 55lb Glatfelter natural (acid free)